Flash® CS3 FOR DUMMIES®

by Ellen Finkelstein and Gurdy Leete

BICENTENNIAL
1807
WILEY
2007
BICENTENNIAL

Wiley Publishing, Inc.

Flash® CS3 For Dummies®

Published by
Wiley Publishing, Inc.
111 River Street
Hoboken, NJ 07030-5774
www.wiley.com

Copyright © 2007 by Wiley Publishing, Inc., Indianapolis, Indiana

Published by Wiley Publishing, Inc., Indianapolis, Indiana

Published simultaneously in Canada

For general information on our other products and services, please contact our Customer Care Department within the U.S. at 800-762-2974, outside the U.S. at 317-572-3993, or fax 317-572-4002.

For technical support, please visit www.wiley.com/techsupport.

Wiley also publishes its books in a variety of electronic formats. Some content that appears in print may not be available in electronic books.

Library of Congress Control Number: 2007924230

ISBN: 978-0-470-12100-9

Manufactured in the United States of America

10 9 8 7 6 5 4 3 2 1

About the Authors

Ellen Finkelstein has written numerous bestselling computer books on AutoCAD, PowerPoint, and Flash. She also writes articles on these programs for Web sites, e-zines, and magazines. The seven editions of her *AutoCAD Bible* have sold more than 80,000 copies in the United States and abroad. As an Adjunct Instructor of Management she teaches e-Business and Human Resource Management courses. She writes at home so that she can take the bread out of the oven on time.

Gurdy Leete has been working as a computer animator, computer animation software engineer, and teacher of computer animation since 1981. He has been teaching Flash and other computer animation programs for 15 years at Maharishi University of Management, where he is an Assistant Professor of Art. You can see his art on the Web at www.infinityeverywhere.net.

Dedication

To MMY, for explaining that life is meant to be lived in happiness and teaching us how to realize that reality in daily life.

Authors' Acknowledgments

This book was very much a group effort. First, I'd like to thank my co-author, Gurdy Leete, without whom I could not have completed this book nor even thought of writing it. Gurdy is always a pleasure to work with, always in a good mood and helpful. He's a brilliant artist and something of a programmer, too, while I am neither. I've been quite impressed.

At Wiley, I'd like to thank Steve Hayes, our acquisitions editor, for trusting us with this book. Great kudos go to Susan Pink, our project editor, for doing such a tremendous job.

Personally, I'd like to thank my husband, Evan, and my kids, Yeshayah and Eliyah, who helped out and managed without me as I wrote every day, evening, and weekend. I love you all.

Thanks to Adobe, for supporting Flash authors during the beta period while we were learning the new features of Flash CS3, testing Flash, and writing, all at the same time.

Finally, I'd like to thank the Flash community and specifically all the Flash designers who contributed Flash movies to make this book and its companion Web site more valuable. Most computer books use dummy files, and we made up a few of our own to illustrate the point, but the real-world files we received for this book will help open up new vistas for our readers. And now, a few comments from Gurdy:

I'd like to echo all of Ellen's words and thank her for being such a great collaborator. She has such a talent for explaining things with the simplicity, precision, and humor that are so characteristic of the deeper workings of the cosmos. I'd also like to thank my brilliant students Alek Lisefski (www.blue sheepstudios.com) and Benek Lisefski (www.benekdesign.com), and my intrepid research assistants — Nutthawut Chandhaketh, of Thailand; Radim Schreiber, of the Czech Republic; Burcu Cenberci, of Turkey; and Praveen Mishra, of Nepal — whose research activities on the Internet were so helpful in writing this book. Thanks to my omnitalented M.A. in Animation student Mike Zak, for the wonderful collection of clip art drawings he created in Flash for the companion Web site. And thanks to my adorable wife, Mary, and my children, Porter and Jacqueline, for being so supportive during the many hours I spent working on this book.

Publisher's Acknowledgments

We're proud of this book; please send us your comments through our online registration form located at www.dummies.com/register/.

Some of the people who helped bring this book to market include the following:

Acquisitions, Editorial, and Media Development

Project Editor: Susan Pink

(Previous Edition: Kim Darosett)

Acquisitions Editor: Steve Hayes

Copy Editor: Susan Pink

(Previous Edition: Virginia Sanders)

Technical Editor: Sally Cruikshank
(www.funonmars.com)

Editorial Manager: Jodi Jensen

Media Development and Quality Assurance:
Angela Denny, Kate Jenkins,
Steven Kudirka, Kit Malone

Media Development Coordinator:
Jenny Swisher

Media Project Supervisor: Laura Moss-Hollister

Editorial Assistant: Amanda Foxworth

Sr. Editorial Assistant: Cherie Case

Cartoons: Rich Tennant
(www.the5thwave.com)

Composition Services

Project Coordinator: Erin Smith

Layout and Graphics: Carl Byers,
Joyce Haughey, Stephanie D. Jumper,
Jennifer Mayberry, Barbara Moore,
Ronald Terry

Proofreaders: Aptara, Brian H. Walls

Indexer: Aptara

Anniversary Logo Design: Richard Pacifico

Publishing and Editorial for Technology Dummies

Richard Swadley, Vice President and Executive Group Publisher

Andy Cummings, Vice President and Publisher

Mary Bednarek, Executive Acquisitions Director

Mary C. Corder, Editorial Director

Publishing for Consumer Dummies

Diane Graves Steele, Vice President and Publisher

Joyce Pepple, Acquisitions Director

Composition Services

Gerry Fahey, Vice President of Production Services

Debbie Stailey, Director of Composition Services

Contents at a Glance

Table of Contents

Introduction

● ●

Welcome to *Flash CS3 For Dummies,* your friendly Web animation companion. In this book, we explain in plain English how to make the most of Flash to create stunning, animated Web sites. We aim to give you all the information you need to start using Flash right away — with no hassle.

About This Book

As though you hadn't guessed, *Adobe Flash CS3 For Dummies* covers the powerful animation product Flash CS3, from Adobe. (The preceding version was Macromedia Flash 8.) Flash CS3 is the latest version of the popular software used on some of the coolest Web sites on the Internet.

We comprehensively explain the Flash features, including

- Working with the Flash screen, toolbars, and menus
- Creating graphics and text in Flash
- Adding sound and video
- Using layers to organize your animation
- Creating *symbols,* which are objects that you save for repeated use and for animation
- Animating graphics (the key to Flash)
- Creating interactive Web sites
- Publishing Flash movies to your Web site

How to Use This Book

You don't have to read this book from cover to cover. We provide just the information you need, when you need it. Start with the first three chapters. Then play around with graphics until you create what you need for your Web site. You might want to check out Chapter 6, on layers, to help you organize it all, and Chapter 7, which covers symbols. Then feel free to jump right to Chapter 9, on animation, to create your first real Flash movie. Chapter 13 tells you how to get your movie on your Web site. Then fire up your browser, sit back, and marvel.

You'll want to check out other chapters when you need them so that you can create text and buttons, add sound and video, and build an interactive Web site. Chapter 12 provides some ideas for putting all the Flash features together for your best Web site ever.

Keep *Adobe Flash CS3 For Dummies* by your computer while you work. You'll find that it's a loyal helper.

Foolish Assumptions

We assume that you're not a master Flash developer. If you want to use Flash to create high-quality Web sites and you're not an expert animator, you'll find this book to be a great reference. *Adobe Flash CS3 For Dummies* is ideal for beginners who are just starting to use Flash or for current Flash users who want to further hone their skills.

Because people usually add Flash movies to Web sites, we also assume that you know some of the basics of Web site creation. You should know what HyperText Markup Language (HTML) is and understand the process of creating and structuring HTML pages as well as uploading them to a Web site.

If you want some help on the topic of Web sites, you might want to take a look at *Web Design For Dummies,* 2nd Edition, by Lisa Lopuck (published by Wiley Publishing, Inc.).

Conventions Used in This Book

Sometimes it helps to know why some text is bold and other text is italic so that you can figure out what we're talking about. (A typographic convention is *not* a convention of typographers meeting to discuss the latest typography techniques.)

New terms are in *italics* to let you know that they're new. When we suggest that you type something, we show you what we want you to type in **bold**. Messages and other text that come from Flash, including programming code, are in a `special typeface, like this.`

When we say something like "Choose File⇨Save As," it means to click the File menu at the top of your screen and then choose Save As from the menu that opens. When we want you to use a toolbar or toolbox button (or tool), we tell you to click it.

How This Book Is Organized

We start by presenting an overview of the Flash universe and then continue in the general order that you would use to create a Flash movie. More basic material is at the beginning of the book, and more advanced material (but not too advanced!) comes later.

To be more specific, this book is divided into seven parts (to represent the seven states of consciousness — okay, we don't have to get too cosmic here). Each part contains two or more chapters that relate to that part. Each chapter thoroughly covers one topic so that you don't have to go searching all over creation to get the information you need.

Part I: A Blast of Flash

Part I contains important introductory information about Flash. In Chapter 1, we tell you what Flash is all about, show you what the Flash screen looks like, and explain how to get help when you need it most. You also find instructions for starting a new movie and opening an existing movie, and we give you a list of steps for creating your first animation. Chapter 2 explains in more detail the steps for creating a Flash movie. We also explain some basic concepts that all Flash users need to know.

Part II: 1,000 Pictures and 1,000 Words

Part II explains all the tools available for creating graphics in Flash. Chapter 3 explains the unique drawing tools included in Flash. We also explain how to import graphics if you don't feel like creating your own. Chapter 4 shows you how to edit and manipulate graphic objects, and Chapter 5 is all about creating text. Chapter 6 explains *layers,* which help you organize your graphics so that they don't interfere with each other.

Part III: Getting Symbolic

Symbols are graphical objects that you save to use again and again. Whenever you want to place an object on a Web page more than once, you can save the object as a symbol. You can also group together many individual objects, making them useful when you want to manipulate, edit, or animate them all at one time. Chapter 7 explains creating and editing symbols. Chapter 8 describes how to create buttons — not the kind that you sew, but rather the kind that you click with your mouse.

Part IV: Total Flash-o-Rama

Part IV explains how to put all your graphics together and make them move. Chapter 9 covers animation in detail — from frame-by-frame animation to *tweening,* where Flash calculates the animation between your first and last frames. Tween movement to make your objects move or morph into new shapes. You can also tween color and transparency.

Chapter 10 shows how to create interactive Web sites that react to your viewers. For example, when a viewer clicks a button, Flash can jump to a different part of a movie or go to a different Web page entirely. To create interactivity, you use *ActionScript,* Flash's JavaScript-like programming language. We tell you how to put ActionScript to work.

Chapter 11 is about adding multimedia — sound, music, and video — to your Flash movies and buttons.

Part V: The Movie and the Web

This part helps you put all your animated graphics and cool buttons together and publish your work on the Web. Chapter 12 outlines the various techniques that you can use to create a great Web site by using only Flash.

Chapter 13 explains how to test your animation for speed and suitability for all browsers and systems. Then we cover the details of publishing movies as well as the other available formats, such as HTML and GIF. You can also create *projectors* — movies that play themselves.

Part VI: The Part of Tens

What's a *For Dummies* book without The Part of Tens? Chapter 14 answers some frequently asked questions about Flash and introduces some fun techniques, such as simulating 3-D effects and dynamically loading music from the Web. Chapter 15 provides you with the ten best resources for Flash (besides this book, of course). Chapter 16 points you to the work of ten fabulous Flash Web designers.

Part VII: Appendixes

Last but not least, we come to the appendixes. They add valuable information to the end of this book. Appendix A adds instructions on installing Flash and setting preferences and options. In Appendix B, we show you what's what in the Property inspector and on the various panels.

Appendix C tells you what's on the companion Web site (www.dummies.com/go/flashcs3). We provide Flash movies that we illustrate in the book and others that you can just play with to see how they work. We also add our own library of graphics that you can add to your own movies.

Icons Used in This Book

Icons help point out special information. For example, sometimes they tell you that you don't care about this information and can skip over it without fear.

This icon flags new features in Flash CS3. If you have been using Flash 8 or even an earlier version, you may want to skim through this book and look for this icon to help you quickly get up to speed in the new version.

Look for this icon to find all the goodies on the companion Web site, at www.dummies.com/go/flashcs3.

This icon alerts you to information that you need to keep in mind to avoid wasting time or falling on your face.

Flash has some advanced features you might want to know about — or skip entirely. This icon lets you know when we throw the heavier stuff at you.

Tips help you finish your work more easily, quickly, or effectively. Don't miss out on these.

Uh-oh! "Watch out here!" is what this icon is telling you. If you skip this icon, you never know what might happen.

Where to Go from Here

If you haven't already installed Flash, check out the complete instructions for installing Flash in Appendix A. Then open Flash, open this book, and plunge in.

We would love to hear your comments about this book. You can contact Gurdy Leete at `gleete@mum.edu` or Ellen Finkelstein at `ellenfinkl@bigfoot.com`. Please note that we can't provide technical support on Flash. (If you need technical support, check out the resources we list in Chapter 15.)

Enough of all this talk. It's time to move into the real part of this book and start creating cool Flash movies! Enjoy!

Part I
A Blast of Flash

In this part . . .

In this part, you discover what Flash can and can't do and start to make your way around the Flash world. In Chapter 1, we introduce you to Flash, show you what it looks like, and explain how to use its toolbars and menus. You find out about the Stage and the Timeline, two central Flash concepts. Play your way through your first animation to get firsthand experience in the power of Flash.

In Chapter 2, you get an overview of the entire process of creating a Flash animated movie, from developing your concept to publishing your movie in the format a browser can display. We explain how to set properties that affect your movie as a whole and how Flash works with various kinds of graphics. We close with the steps for printing your movie on paper. This part provides the foundation for future success.

Chapter 1

Getting Acquainted with Flash CS3

- -

- -

*O*nce upon a time in a galaxy that seems far, far away by now, there was the Internet, which contained only plain, unformatted text. Then came the Web, and we gained text formatting and graphics. Then the Web grew up a little, and Web page graphics got fancier with things such as small animations in banner ads. But people, being used to movies and TV, wanted an even more animated and interactive Web experience. Along came Flash.

Flash, once from Macromedia but now from Adobe Systems, is the software that runs some of the coolest Web sites around. When you surf the Web and see sites that contain animation across the entire page or buttons that do spectacular stunts when you click them, you're probably seeing some Flash magic. If you create a Web site, you can use Flash to rev up the basics and actively respond to users' choices so that your viewers will say, "Wow!"

In this chapter, you find out what Flash is all about, what the Flash screen looks like, and how to use Help. Then you create your first, simple animation so that all the rest of this book makes sense.

Discovering Flash

Flash offers a powerful system for creating animation for the Web. In a nutshell, here's an overview of how you use the system:

1. **Create a Flash movie by creating graphics and animating them over the duration of the movie.**

   Besides animated graphics, you can add navigational buttons, check boxes, and other user interface elements. You can add a few Flash components to a Web site or create an entire Web site.

2. **Use the Publish command in Flash to publish the movie into a Flash Player file that a browser can display.**

   At the same time, Flash creates the appropriate HyperText Markup Language (HTML) code that you need for your Web page.

3. **Insert HTML code into your HTML document that references the Flash Player file.**

   It's similar to adding a graphic to a Web page. Or you can use the HTML code alone as a new Web page for a fully Flashed page.

4. **Upload the new or edited HTML document and the Flash Player file to the location where you keep other files for your Web pages.**

5. **Open your browser, navigate to your Web page, and presto! — there's your cool animation, navigation, or other Flash element on your Web page.**

You need the Flash Player to see the effects that Flash creates. These days, the Flash Player comes installed with most computer systems and browsers, so most people can view Flash-driven Web sites immediately without any special download or preparation. When you display a Web site that contains Flash effects, your system uses the Flash Player to play the animation. Users who don't have a Flash Player can download it for free from Adobe at www.adobe.com.

Web sites are getting more and more sophisticated. By using animation, special effects, and interactive techniques, you can distinguish your Web site from the also-rans. Creating animation isn't hard, and you don't have to be a professional graphic artist, either. Anyone can create simple animations to enhance a Web site; it just takes a little time.

To find Web sites that have successfully used Flash, check out the Adobe site at www.adobe.com/products/flash/flashpro/productinfo/customers/ and look at some of the examples. Don't get discouraged by seeing some of the truly sophisticated results at these sites. You can start with a simple, animated site and go from there. (Chapter 16 lists ten great Flash designers and where you can find their work.)

Understanding What You Can Create with Flash CS3

You can use Flash CS3 to create simple animation to add to your Web page. Or you can create an entire Web page or site with Flash and incorporate text, graphics, interactive buttons, user interface components, and animation. You can even program applications in Flash.

This book helps you use Flash to create a simple or complex Web site. The following list describes some ways that you can manipulate text, graphics, and sound by using Flash CS3:

- **Create still or animated text on your Web page.** You can choose to stop the animation after a few seconds or repeat it while your viewers view the page.

- **Use Flash tools to create your own graphics for your Web page or to import graphics.** You can lay out an entire Web page graphically or add graphics to only a part of a Web page.

- **Animate graphics and make objects appear and disappear by using the transparency feature.** Objects can move, get bigger or smaller, or rotate. Flash also lets you *morph* — that is, transform — shapes into new shapes.

- **Fill shapes and text with *gradients*, which are colors that gradually change into new colors.** You can even fill shapes and text with bitmap images that you import into Flash. For example, you could fill the letters of your name with dozens of flowers. (You aren't a flower child any more?)

- **Create Web page buttons that not only lead your viewers wherever you want them to go but also change shape or color at the same time.** You can make buttons change when you pass your mouse over them. People who view your page can click a button to display a movie (animation) or start a small application.

- **Add sound or video to your movie.** It's easy to add sound effects in Flash. You can control how long the sound or music plays and whether it loops to play continuously. You can play video files as well.

- **Create menus that viewers can use to navigate your site.** You can create navigation tools as well as forms, check boxes, and other interface elements that look a lot more stylish than plain HTML ones.

As you can see, you can go far with Flash if you want. And why not? It's great fun!

Determining When Not to Use Flash CS3

If Flash CS3 is so wonderful, why doesn't every Web site designer use it? Why aren't most Web sites created completely with Flash?

Here's the other side of the story.

Although the vector graphics and animation of Flash load quickly, they don't load as quickly as plain text and simple graphics. Adding a movie to your Web page creates some overhead. There's no point in using Flash if you want simple pages consisting of mostly text and a few graphics that you want to stay put and not move.

You can create certain graphic effects more easily by using bitmap graphics. Painted brush stroke and textured effects are examples. Artists create these types of graphics by using graphics editing software, and the results are bitmaps. Similarly, to add photographs to your Web page, you need to scan the photographs as bitmaps. Flash creates *vector graphics* (defined mathematically), which are different from *bitmap graphics* (defined by lots of dots). However, you can import bitmap graphics into Flash. Find out more about bitmap and vector graphics in Chapter 2.

If you want simple animation, such as a few blinking dots or a marquee effect, animated *GIFs* (the animated bitmap graphics that you often see on the Web) might be smaller than Flash movies, so they load faster. You can create animated GIFs by using animated GIF editing software.

Some sites don't lend themselves to animation. Animation can distract from your content, and overdoing animation can make a serious site seem silly. Animation is great, but it has its place. Also, although Flash has some features that allow accessibility for people with disabilities, it still isn't as accessible as plain HTML. You need to determine whether animation is right for your Web site.

Flash provides little in the way of 3-D graphics or animation. For those, you need to use more sophisticated software, such as Poser or 3D Studio Max. (See Chapter 14 for some 3-D possibilities in Flash.)

Getting the Right Start

Well begun is half done, as the saying goes. The easiest way to begin using Flash CS3 is with a shortcut or alias right on your desktop. Double-click the

Flash icon, and you're on your way. (See Appendix A for information on installing Flash.)

Starting Flash on a PC

Whether you installed Flash from the CD or by downloading it from the Adobe Web site onto your PC, you might or might not have a shortcut on your desktop. To create one, choose Start➪All Programs ➪Adobe Flash CS3. Right-click the Adobe Flash CS3 item and choose Create Shortcut from the pop-up menu that appears. The new shortcut appears on the menu. Drag that shortcut to your desktop.

To rename the shortcut, click the shortcut on your desktop. Then click the text beneath the icon. Type **Flash CS3** (or whatever you want) and press Enter. Just double-click the icon to open Flash.

Starting Flash on a Mac

You might find it handy to add the Flash CS3 icon to your Dock for easy launching. To do this, click the Finder icon on the extreme left of the Dock to bring up a new Finder window. Navigate in the Finder window to the Applications folder, and in the Applications folder, double-click the Adobe Flash CS3 folder to open it. Click and drag the Flash CS3 application icon to the Dock. A copy of the Flash CS3 application icon appears on the Dock.

Creating a new movie

Files that you create by using Flash are commonly called *movies*. When you start Flash, the startup screen appears (by default). In the Create New section, click one of two options to immediately open a new movie file:

- **Flash File (ActionScript 3.0)** takes advantage of the latest version of ActionScript, Flash's programming language.

- **Flash File (ActionScript 2.0)** creates a Flash movie compatible with ActionScript from previous versions of Flash.

If you have already opened a movie and have the menus available, choose File➪New. In the New Document dialog box, select Flash File (ActionScript 3.0) or Flash File (ActionScript 2.0) on the General tab and then click OK. You usually start by creating or importing some graphics. (To find out more about working with graphics, see Chapter 3.)

Opening an existing movie

If you want to work on a movie you've already created, do the following. When you first open Flash, choose the movie in the Open a Recent Item section or click Open to find the file. If you've already opened a movie and have the menus available, press Ctrl+O (Windows) or ⌘+O (Mac) or choose File⇨Open; then double-click the movie to open it. The first frame appears on your screen, and you can edit the movie any way that you want.

When you open more than one movie, you see a tab at the top for each movie. You can click the tabs to move from movie to movie. The tabs appear in the order you created or opened the movies.

Taking a Look Around

The Flash screen is different from screens in other programs that you might be used to, so take the time to get to know it. You can also customize the Flash screen. Figure 1-1 shows one possible display.

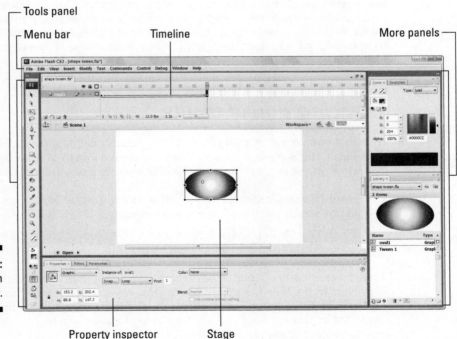

Tools panel

Menu bar   Timeline   More panels

Figure 1-1:
The Flash
screen.

Property inspector   Stage

If your screen opens with several rectangular panels strewn about or docked on various sides, don't worry about them now. We explain how to open and use these panels throughout this book, but you don't need them for this chapter. If they drive you crazy, right-click (Windows) or Control+click (Mac) each panel's title bar and choose Close Group in the menu that appears.

See Appendix B for a full layout of each panel and toolbar.

Tooling around the toolbars

Flash contains two toolbars in the Mac version: the Edit bar and the Controller. In Windows, Flash also offers the Main toolbar. To display or hide these toolbars, choose Window➪Toolbars and click the toolbar that you want to display or hide. Here is a description of the toolbars:

- **Main toolbar (Windows only):** Contains commonly used commands. Many of these are familiar from the Standard toolbar in other Windows programs. By default, Flash does *not* display the Main toolbar.

- **Controller:** Lets you control the playback of movies. For more information, see Chapter 9.

- **Edit bar:** Helps you work with the Timeline. The bar appears at the bottom of the Timeline. It includes a toggle to display and hide the Timeline, a button for editing scenes, a drop-down list to manage workspaces, and a zoom control. We discuss the workspaces and the Timeline later in the chapter. For detailed information about the Timeline and scenes, see Chapter 9.

Using panels

Panels give you access to the many Flash tools and settings. You access the panels from the Window menu. We discuss the specific panels throughout this book. In this section, we explain how to keep control over your panels.

Most panels are *dockable,* which means they can sit at the side or bottom of your Flash window without covering up your work and they fit together in a group with other panels. You can also stack undocked panels on top of each other. You control panels by doing the following:

- **To dock a panel:** Drag it by its title bar to the side or bottom of your screen. When you see a grey bar with a blue edge, release the mouse button.

- **To undock a panel:** Drag it by its title bar.

- ✔ **To open or close a panel:** Choose it from the Window menu.

- ✔ **To close an undocked panel:** Click its Close button.

- ✔ **To close a docked panel:** Right-click (Windows) or Control+click (Mac) its title bar and choose Close Panel.

- ✔ **To collapse a group of panels to icons:** Click the double right arrow at the top of the group of docked panels.

You can also stack panels. Drag a panel (by its title bar) to another panel to stack it below the first one. You can also collapse or expand panels: A *collapsed* panel displays only its title bar, so it doesn't take up much space. Just click its title bar. Repeat the process to expand the panel again.

The Tools panel contains all the tools you need to draw and edit objects. At the bottom of the Tools panel are options that modify how the tools function. (See Chapters 3 and 4 for a complete description of the Tools panel.)

The Property inspector is another important panel. This panel displays information about selected objects, such as size, name, and location. You can modify objects in the Property inspector as well. It is *context sensitive,* which means that its contents change according to what you're doing. For example, if you select a graphic object, the Property inspector provides settings relating to that object, and you can use the Property inspector to edit that object.

The Property inspector has several controls for changing its configuration:

- ✔ **Title bar:** Click the title bar to switch between collapsing the Property inspector completely (you just see the title bar) and displaying its previous state.

- ✔ **Tab button:** Click the tiny button to the left of the word *Properties* at the top of the Property inspector to switch between three states: fully expanded, half expanded, and collapsed (to the title bar).

- ✔ **Minimize/Maximize button:** Click the minus sign or box (depending on the current state) to switch between collapsing the Property inspector completely and displaying its previous state.

- ✔ **Resize grabber:** If the Property inspector is not docked, you can resize it by dragging the grabber at its lower-right corner.

Discovering the Flash menus

Most drawing functions are available only in the Tools panel. You often use the Timeline for creating animation, as we discuss in the "Following a timeline" section, later in this chapter. Almost every other function in Flash is on a menu somewhere. You just need to find it. In general, we discuss the specific menu functions where appropriate throughout this book. Table 1-1 offers an overview of the menus.

Table 1-1	Flash Menus
Menu	*What It Does*
Flash	(Mac only) Enables you to set preferences, create keyboard shortcuts, and quit Flash.
File	Enables you to open and close files; save files; import and export files; print; publish movies for the Web; revert to a previous version of the file; send a movie via e-mail, and quit Flash.
Edit	Provides commands that let you undo and redo actions; cut, copy, and paste to and from the Clipboard; delete, duplicate, select, and deselect objects; find and replace; copy and paste entire frames and motions on the Timeline; edit symbols (see Chapter 7 for the story on symbols); set preferences (Windows only); customize the Tools panel; and create keyboard shortcuts for commands (Windows only).
View	Helps you get a better view by letting you zoom in and out; show or hide the ruler, grid, and guides; and specify snapping preferences for objects for easy placement.
Insert	Enables you to insert symbols (Chapter 7 explains this topic); insert and delete Timeline features, such as frames and keyframes (see Chapter 9 for more); insert layers (check out Chapter 6); add Timeline effects (see Chapter 9); and add scenes (also in Chapter 9).
Modify	Helps you modify symbols, bitmaps, shapes, frames, Timeline features and effects, scenes, or the entire movie (called the *document*). Offers tools for transforming, aligning, grouping, and ungrouping objects, arranging and aligning objects, and breaking objects apart.
Text	Enables you to format text and check spelling.
Commands	Enables you to reuse and manage saved commands. A command is any action that you take in Flash, such as drawing or editing objects. You can save commands from the History panel. (See Chapter 4.)

(continued)

Table 1-1 *(continued)*

Menu	What It Does
Control	Provides options that let you control the playing of movies; test movies and scenes; engage certain interactive functions; and mute sounds.
Debug	Provides tools for debugging ActionScript code. (See Chapter 10 for more on ActionScript.)
Window	Enables you to open lots of things, including a duplicate window, panels that help you control objects, the Library (more on the Library in Chapter 2), windows for creating interactive controls (which we explain in Chapter 10), workspaces, and the Movie Explorer (to help manage your movie — see Chapter 12).
Help	Comes to the rescue when you need help. You can find a wide variety of resources in this new version, including Adobe online forums.

Many menu commands offer keyboard shortcuts. You can also create your own keyboard shortcuts. (See Appendix A for instructions.)

The shortcuts are displayed on the menus, next to the command name. Here are some of the most commonly used keyboard shortcuts (for more shortcuts, see the tear-out Cheat Sheet at the front of this book):

- ✔ **Ctrl+N (Windows) or ⌘+N (Mac):** Open the New Document dialog box so you can start a new movie.

- ✔ **Ctrl+O (Windows) or ⌘+O (Mac):** Open an existing movie.

- ✔ **Ctrl+S (Windows) or ⌘+S (Mac):** Save your movie. Use this shortcut often!

- ✔ **Ctrl+X (Windows) or ⌘+X (Mac):** Cut to the Clipboard. Chapter 4 explains more about using the Clipboard.

- ✔ **Ctrl+C (Windows) or ⌘+C (Mac):** Copy to the Clipboard.

- ✔ **Ctrl+V (Windows) or ⌘+V (Mac):** Paste from the Clipboard.

- ✔ **Ctrl+Z (Windows) or ⌘+Z (Mac):** Undo. Would you believe that by default Flash remembers your last 100 actions and can undo them? What a relief! And if you choose Window➪Other Panels➪History, the History panel lists each action so you know what the next Undo will undo. Think of it as a journey into the long-forgotten past. (See Chapter 4 for more on the History panel, and see Appendix A for details on customizing the number of Undos that Flash remembers.)

- ✔ **Ctrl+Y (Windows) or ⌘+Y (Mac):** Redo. This redoes actions that you undid by using the Undo button. (Got that?) This button remembers just as many actions as the Undo button. If you undo more actions than you want, click Redo (or press Ctrl+Y or ⌘+Y) until you're back where you want to be. Using the Undo and Redo buttons is like traveling through Flash time — and it gives you lots of slack while you're working.

✔ **Ctrl+Q (Windows) or ⌘+Q (Mac):** Exit Flash.

We mention other keyboard shortcuts throughout this book when we discuss their corresponding commands.

You should note, although it's not a shortcut, that you can find the Zoom Control box in the upper-right corner of the Stage — when the Edit bar is open (choose Window⇨Toolbars⇨Edit Bar if necessary). Click the arrow and choose a zoom factor to zoom in and out. Zooming doesn't change the actual size of objects — it just makes them look bigger or smaller.

You aren't limited to the choices on the Zoom drop-down list. Type a number in the Zoom Control box and press Enter (Windows) or Return (Mac) to set your own zoom factor. For example, type **85** to set the zoom factor to 85 percent.

Customizing the workspace

For the best in customization, you can save any layout of panels you like. Set up the panels and choose Window⇨Workspace ⇨Save Current. In the Save Workspace Layout dialog box that opens, give the layout a name and click OK. To restore that layout at any time, choose Window⇨Workspace Layout and choose your very own layout. Choose Window⇨Workspace ⇨Manage if you need to rename or delete a workspace.

You can access the same workspace features on the Edit bar. It's easy to choose a new workspace by just clicking the Workspace drop-down list.

Staging your movies

The white box in the center of your screen is the *Stage.* Think of the Stage as a movie screen where you place objects. You can place graphics and text there and then animate them. Flash also plays back movies on the Stage.

Around the edge of the Stage is a gray area called the *Pasteboard.* You can use the Pasteboard to store graphics that you plan to use soon but don't want on the Stage just yet. (For more permanent storage, use the Library, as we explain in Chapter 2.) You can also store data and other nongraphical content on the Pasteboard. Content that you put on the Pasteboard doesn't appear in your Flash movie.

Following a timeline

The Timeline window divides your movie into *frames.* Each frame represents a tiny stretch of time, such as ½2 of a second. Creating a movie is simply a matter of assembling frames, which are then quickly played in order.

Chapter 9 explains in detail how to make using the Timeline completely painless. For now, you should just understand the essentials. See Figure 1-2 for the basic Timeline.

Figure 1-2:
The Timeline is your key to managing animation.

On the left side of the Timeline is the layer list. When you open a new movie, you see only one layer, unimaginatively named Layer 1. A *layer* is like a sheet of transparent acetate on which you draw objects. Layers help you keep objects from running into each other, causing unfortunate, messy results. You organize your entire movie by using layers. For example, if you want to keep some text constant throughout the movie but animate a bouncing dot, you would give the dot its own layer and animate it on that layer. The layer list has room for more layers, and you can add as many layers as you want. (Chapter 6 gives you the lowdown on layers.)

You can lower the bottom edge of the Timeline to make room for more layers. Hover the mouse cursor over the bottom line until you see the two-headed arrow and drag downward.

To the right of Layer 1, you see a bunch of rectangles, each representing a frame. (Actually, before you start using the Timeline, they're just potential frames, like unexposed frames on a roll of film.) By default, each frame lasts ½2 of a second. Each layer has its own row of frames because you can have different animations or objects on each layer.

A *keyframe* is a frame that defines some change in your animation. In some animations, every frame is a keyframe. Other animations need keyframes for only the first and last frames.

You don't use the Timeline until you're ready to animate. While you work, however, you should organize your objects on separate layers. Don't worry — you can always move an object from one layer to another.

Getting Help in a Flash

This book is all that you need to start creating great animations, but we would be remiss if we didn't tell you about the Flash Help system. To use Flash Help, choose Help⇨Flash Help. You see a window like the one shown in Figure 1-3.

Figure 1-3: The Flash Help window.

Help's multiple manuals

Flash Help contains several sections:

- ✔ **Using Flash** is the main Help manual.

- ✔ **Programming ActionScript 3.0** is a manual on the latest version of ActionScript, Flash's programming language. (See Chapter 10 to find out more.)

  You don't need to program Flash to use it, if you are interested only in graphics and animation.

- ✔ **Learning ActionScript 2.0 in Flash** is a user's guide for ActionScript 2.0, Flash's previous programming language. You can still use this language. Several other Help sections offer more information on ActionScript 2.0.

- ✔ **Getting Started with Flash Lite 2.x** and related help content explains how to use Flash CS3 to develop Flash movies for mobile phones.

- ✔ **Getting Started with Flash Lite 1.x** and related content explains how to create Flash movies for the previous version of Flash Lite.

To search for a term, click the Search button. Then type the term and click Search. You can then choose from the list of topics.

Finding more help on the Web

Adobe offers support on its Web site. Choose Help➪Flash Support Center, which takes you to www.adobe.com/support/flash. There you can search the knowledge base and tutorials for answers to your questions.

Try It; You'll Like It

Perhaps by now you're getting impatient to try out Flash. Getting started is easy. You collect a few ideas, put together some art, add animation, save your movie, and publish it. Then you view it in a browser either online or offline. That's the gratifying part. In the following sections, you get to try out Flash by working through a basic animation. The rest of the book explains these concepts in more detail.

Conceiving your first animation

Suppose that you want to add an animated logo to a home page that you've already set up. You want the animation to run when the page loads and then stop. Figure 1-4 shows the Rainbow Resources company logo — unanimated, of course — that you can find on this book's Web site, at www.dummies. com/go/flashcs3.

Figure 1-4:
A company
logo that
could stand
some
animation.

Suppose that you want the word *Rainbow* to fly into your page from the right and the word *Resources* to fly in from the left. At the same time, you want the graphic to rotate 180 degrees. The following section shows you how to create this animation.

Creating flashy drawings

You can use Flash to create a company logo, but importing one from this book's Web site is simpler. Often, you import existing graphics (such as a company logo) from a file rather than create them from scratch. (Chapter 3 explains how to import and manipulate graphics.)

If you're going through the steps and make a mistake, choose Edit⇨Undo (or press Ctrl+Z or ⌘+Z) and try again. You can use Undo repeatedly to undo several steps, if necessary.

To import the Rainbow Resources logo into Flash, follow these steps. (The steps might vary if you're importing some other graphic in a different format.)

1. **Start Flash.**

   See the instructions in the section "Starting Flash on a PC" or "Starting Flash on a Mac," earlier in this chapter, if you need help.

2. **In the Create New section of the Startup screen, choose Flash File (ActionScript 3.0).**

   You see a spanking-new movie on your screen.

3. **Go to www.dummies.com/go/flashcs3 and download the rainbow. gif image file.**

   You'll need to unzip the file and extract the image file. Extract this image file to the location where you plan to save your Flash movie.

4. **Choose File⇨Import⇨Import to Stage.**

   The Import dialog box opens.

5. **Browse the dialog box until you find rainbow.gif in the location where you saved it, and then double-click the file to open it.**

   You see the logo on your screen. You need to break the logo into pieces and make it a vector graphic so that you can animate sections of it separately.

6. **Choose Modify⇨Bitmap⇨Trace Bitmap.**

   The Trace Bitmap dialog box appears.

7. **In the Trace Bitmap dialog box, set the color threshold to 100, the minimum area to 1, the curve fit to Pixels, and the corner threshold to Many Corners. Click OK.**

   In our example, we chose to use settings that reproduce the bitmap as faithfully as possible. Flash creates a vector graphic and breaks up the graphic into individual components. The entire graphic, however, is selected.

8. **Click anywhere outside the graphic to deselect it.**

You've got your logo! Now you need to set it up for animation.

Turning your objects into symbols

In the logo that you imported in the preceding section, each letter is a separate object, which can get pretty confusing. Each line in the logo's design is also separate. But you want your words — and the little design — to stay together. So you must combine each word and the logo into a symbol. A *symbol* helps keep objects together and is required for some kinds of animation. (See Chapter 7 for the scoop on symbols.)

To turn the words and the logo into symbols, follow these steps:

1. **To get a better view of your image, click the Zoom Control drop-down list (at the upper-right corner of the Stage area) and choose 400%.**

   If you don't see the Zoom Control drop-down list, choose Window⇨ Toolbars⇨Edit Bar to display it.

   Use the scroll bar to scroll the words of the logo into view, if necessary.

2. **Click the Selection tool on the Tools panel if it's not already selected.**

3. **Click the upper-right corner of the word *Rainbow* (just above and to the right of the *w*) and drag to the lower-left corner of the first letter, *R*.**

   Dragging from right to left makes it easier to avoid selecting the logo at the same time. The entire word should be selected. If it isn't, click outside the word and try again.

4. **Choose Modify⇨Convert to Symbol. In the Convert to Symbol dialog box, click Graphic for the Type and then click OK.**

   It's usually good practice to name the symbol, but doing so is not necessary for this exercise. When you click OK, Flash places a box around the word so you can see that it's one object.

5. **Repeat the procedure outlined in Steps 3 and 4 with the word *Resources*.**

   In this case, you might want to start clicking and dragging from the upper-left area of the word; then choose Modify⇨Convert to Symbol again and click OK. Now all the letters of the word *Resources* are a single object.

6. **Click the Zoom Control drop-down list and choose 100% so that you can see the entire logo.**

7. **Click above and to the left of the logo and drag to the lower right to select the entire logo.**

8. **Hold down the Shift key and click each word to remove both words from the selection.**

   Now the design portion of the logo is selected.

9. **Press F8 (the keyboard shortcut to create a symbol) and then click OK in the Convert to Symbol dialog box.**

   Flash creates a symbol from the lines of the logo's design.

See Chapter 7 to find out more about what symbols are and how to use them. Symbols are important building blocks in Flash movies.

Putting your graphics on layers

You need to place different pieces on different layers when you're animating. You use layers to organize your movie and keep shapes separate so that they don't interfere with each other. (See Chapter 6 for the complete story on layers.)

To split your three symbols onto three separate layers, you can use a convenient feature of Flash CS3: distribute to layers. Follow these steps:

1. **Click the Selection tool on the Tools panel if it's not already selected.**

2. **Drag diagonally across the entire logo, including the two words, to select it.**

   You should see two rectangles inside one bigger rectangle. All three objects in the logo are selected.

3. **Choose Modify⇨Timeline⇨Distribute to Layers.**

   You now have three new layers, named Symbol 1, Symbol 2, and Symbol 3. The three objects of the logo have been distributed to Symbol 1 through 3 and removed from Layer 1.

4. **Click outside the Stage to deselect any objects.**

You're now ready for the animation process.

Making graphics move

We explain earlier in this chapter that your goal is to have the word *Rainbow* fly in from the right and the word *Resources* fly in from the left. You also want the graphic to rotate 180 degrees at the same time. What you see now is how the animation will end — the last frame of the movie.

Follow these steps to create the last frame of the movie and save the file:

1. **For *each* of the three symbol layers, click frame 30 of the Timeline and choose Insert⇨Timeline⇨Keyframe.**

   You may have to scroll down to access frame 30 on the lowest layer. You can find out more about keyframes in Chapter 9.

2. **Choose File⇨Save and choose the same location you used for the rainbow.gif image file.**

   We don't recommend saving the file in the Flash CS3 program folder — it might get lost among your Flash program files.

3. **Give your movie a name, such as *Movie of the Year,* and click Save.**

   Flash creates a file named `Movie of the Year.fla`. Flash adds `.fla` for you because that's the filename extension for Flash movies.

Go back and create the beginning of your movie. Flash can fill in all the blanks in between. Follow these steps to create the beginning of the movie and the animation:

1. **If the Property inspector isn't already open, choose Window➪ Properties➪Properties to open it.**

   If the Property inspector is open but collapsed, click its title bar to expand the panel.

2. **Select the word *Rainbow.* Click the first frame of the Timeline in the highlighted row.**

   When you select the word *Rainbow,* you can tell which layer it is on by looking at the highlighted layer.

3. **Press and hold down the Shift key while you drag the word *Rainbow* to the right, just off the Stage into the gray area.**

   You might need to use the horizontal scroll bar or choose a lower zoom percentage in the Zoom drop-down list to see the gray area. Pressing Shift keeps the object from moving up or down while you drag to the right. By clicking the first frame and moving the word, you set its position at the beginning of the animation.

4. **Click the word *Rainbow*'s layer, anywhere between the 1st and the 30th frame.**

5. **On the Tween drop-down list of the Property inspector, choose Motion.**

   You now see a solid arrow on the Timeline between the 1st and 30th frames. Choosing Motion in the Tween drop-down list creates animation that moves the symbol from the position in the first frame to its position in the next keyframe, which is frame 30 in this movie.

6. **Repeat Steps 2 through 5 for the word *Resources.* However, in Step 3, drag the word *Resources* to the left, just off the Stage.**

7. **Select the logo design and click the first frame of the Timeline in the highlighted row.**

8. **Choose Modify➪Transform➪Rotate 90° CW to rotate the design 90 degrees clockwise.**

9. **Repeat the Modify➪Transform➪Rotate 90° CW command to rotate the design a total of 180 degrees.**

10. **Click the logo's highlighted layer, anywhere between the 1st and 30th frames, and choose Motion in the Tween drop-down list of the Property inspector.**

11. **If necessary, drag the horizontal scroll box until the Stage is in the center of your screen.**

    Otherwise, you won't be able to see the entire animation — and you don't want to miss this one!

12. **Click the first frame of any layer.**

    This takes you to the start of your movie. Your screen should look like the one shown in Figure 1-5.

13. **Press Enter (Return) and watch the animation. (Start writing your Academy Award acceptance speech.)**

14. **Save your movie again by choosing File⇨Save.**

Publishing your first animation for posterity

You can't watch the animation in a Web browser until you publish it and insert it into an HTML document. To do so, follow these steps:

1. **Click the Stage to change the display of the Property inspector.**

   You should see the Settings button next to the Publish label.

Figure 1-5:
Before you run the animation, *Rainbow* appears to the right and *Resources* to the left, and the line logo is rotated.

2. **Click the Settings button in the Property inspector.**

   The Publish Settings dialog box opens.

3. **Click the HTML tab.**

4. **Deselect the Loop check box in the Playback section.**

   We want the animation to play only once.

5. **Click the Publish button, and then click OK to close the dialog box.**

   With scarcely a blip, Flash publishes your movie and creates two files, named `Movie of the Year.swf` (assuming you used that name) and `Movie of the Year.html`. They're in the same folder as your `.fla` movie file. `Movie of the Year.swf` is the file your browser reads to play the animation. `Movie of the Year.html` contains the HTML code required to display your movie on a Web page.

6. **Open your Web browser.**

7. **Choose File⇨Open (or Open File) and find `Movie of the Year.html` (or whatever you named your movie file).**

   You might need to click Browse and navigate to the file.

8. **Double-click the file.**

   Your browser opens the HTML document and reads its instructions to play the Flash movie.

9. **Sit back and watch it roll.**

   Don't blink or you'll miss it. (If you do miss it, click the Refresh or Reload Current Page button in your browser.) You can see the movie in Figure 1-6.

10. **When you finish watching the movie, close your browser.**

You can find the Movie of the Year files (`.fla`, `.html`, and `.swf`) on this book's Web site, `www.dummies.com/go/flashcs3`.

Exiting Flash

When you finish creating something in Flash, choose File⇨Exit (Windows) or Flash⇨Quit (Mac).

Figure 1-6:
The Movie of the Year animation in detail.

Chapter 2

Your Basic Flash

In This Chapter

▶ Examining the big picture

▶ Setting movie properties

▶ Getting and managing graphics

▶ Using templates

▶ Printing your movie

This chapter starts with an overview of the process of creating animation in Flash. We then discuss some tools and features that are fundamental to using Flash efficiently.

As you find out in this chapter, you can set the screen size and color, frame rate, and measurement units for the Flash movie as a whole. We also discuss the Library and how it's a storehouse for images, symbols, and sound. Templates enable you to create great movies without much work. Finally, near the end of this chapter, we explain how you can print a Flash movie.

Looking at the Big Picture

When you use Flash to create animation for your Web site, you generally go through several steps of construction. The steps might vary in their order, depending on your situation. After you know the basics, you can start getting creative and make your Web site rock. Here's a typical path to add animation to an existing Web page:

1. **Think about it.** Noodle around, maybe make some doodles on a napkin, collect a few ideas, and choose one or all of them.

2. **Set up your movie.** Flash lets you choose the size and color of the Stage, the speed of animation (number of frames per second), and other general

parameters that affect the entire Flash movie. See the next section of this chapter for details.

3. **Add some graphics.** You have to decide whether you want to create graphics in Flash, create them in another graphics software package, or import existing graphics. Your choice partly depends on how artistic you are, whether you have other software available to you, and whether you can find the right graphics elsewhere. You can also use a combination of sources, which is a common practice. (See Chapter 3 for some suggestions on great places to get graphics.)

4. **Lay out your graphics the way you want your animation to start.** Here's where you might want to scale, rotate, or otherwise fiddle with your graphics. (Chapter 4 has more on transforming your graphics.)

5. **Add some text.** Using Flash is a great way to get terrific text onto your Web site. Add text (also called *type*); then reshape it, make it transparent (if you don't want to be too obvious), add other effects, and move it where you want it. (Check out Chapter 5 for typography tips.)

6. **Organize your text and graphics by using layers.** Layers help you keep track of what each graphic and text object does while you organize everything into a powerful, coherent statement. Layers keep your animations from going bump in the night and getting entangled. Create as many layers as you need and transfer your existing graphics and text to those layers. (See Chapter 6 for further details on layers.)

7. **Turn a graphic into a symbol and multiply it all over the Stage.** Making objects into symbols is a way to keep them from merging with other objects while they merrily animate. You also use symbols to keep the file size down, to enable animation, and for interactivity. (Turn to Chapter 7 for more info on symbols.)

8. **Design some buttons.** You know those buttons you click on Web sites all the time? The coolest ones are made in Flash. You can even create animated buttons. (Chapter 8 has more on buttons.)

9. **Animate!** You can create your animation frame by frame or let Flash fill in the animation between your first and last frames, which is called *tweening.* Flash can tween motion, shapes, colors, and transparency, which means that you can create some real magic. (See Chapter 9 for more on animation and the section in Chapter 1 where we step you through your first animation.)

10. **Get interactive.** You want to start a relationship with your Web viewers, so you can create buttons, frames, and symbols that respond to your viewers' actions. This is probably the most complex functionality of Flash, but we make most of it seem easy. (Turn to Chapter 10 for additional info on interactivity.)

11. **Make it louder! Make it move!** Who wants a quiet Web site? Add sound to your movies or your buttons. You can also add a video file. (Check out Chapter 11 for more on sound and video.)

12. **Publish your magnum opus.** Flash makes getting your movie to your Web site easy by creating both the Flash Player (.swf) file and the HyperText Markup Language (HTML) code for your Web page. Flash has other options, too, so you can publish to other formats if you want. (Chapter 12 explains how to put all the elements together, and Chapter 13 shows you how to publish your animation.)

Congratulations! You've completed your first Flash Web animation — in fantasy, at least. The following sections cover some details about how to get started.

Setting the Stage

Before you create graphics and animate them — all that fun stuff — you need to make some decisions about the structure of your entire movie. You should make these decisions before you start because changing midway can create problems.

The first step is to decide on the size and color of your Stage and other fundamental settings. Make sure that the Property inspector is open (choose Window⇨Properties⇨Properties). When the Stage is active (just click the Stage), the Property inspector looks like Figure 2-1.

Figure 2-1:
You can change movie properties in the Property inspector.

Choosing the Stage color

You can set the color of the Stage to create a colored background for your entire movie. As with other settings, you need to consider the context of the Web page that will contain the Flash movie. For example, you might want to match the color of your Web page's background. If your Flash movie will constitute the entire Web page, set the Stage color to the color you want for the Web page background.

To set the Stage color, click the Background Color swatch in the Property inspector. Flash opens the Color palette. Click the color you want.

Specifying the frame rate

In the Frame Rate text box, specify how many frames that a Flash movie plays each second, and then press Enter (Windows) or Return (Mac). A faster rate allows for smoother animation but might present a performance problem on slower computers. Chapter 9 explains more about this setting. The Flash default is 12 fps (frames per second), which is a good starting point. Beware that changing the frame rate midstream in the creation process changes the rate of all the animation in your movie, which might not give you the results you want.

Setting the Stage size and adding metadata

The Size button displays the current size of the Stage. By default, Flash uses a Stage size of 550 pixels wide by 400 pixels high. To determine the proper setting, you need to know how your Flash movie will fit into your Web page or site. The default fits on almost everyone's browser screen. However, you might want to fit your movie into a small corner of a Web page — for example, into an animated logo in a top corner of a page. In that case, make the Stage smaller.

To change the Stage size, click the Size button to open the Document Properties dialog box, as shown in Figure 2-2. Type the dimensions that you want in the Width and Height text boxes.

Figure 2-2:
The
Document
Properties
dialog box
sets the
movie's
overall
parameters.

Flash offers two shortcuts for setting the Stage size in the Document Properties dialog box:

  ✔ **Match Printer:** Click this option to set the Stage size according to the paper size set in the Page Setup dialog box (choose File➪Page Setup). (For the Mac, the Print Margins dialog box, which you access by choosing

File⇨Print Margins, also affects the paper size.) Flash sets the size of the Stage to the maximum possible area of the paper minus the margins. Later in this chapter, in the section "Printing Your Movie," we cover this dialog box in more detail.

✔ **Match Contents:** Click this option to set the Stage size to the contents of the Stage. Of course, for this to work, you need some objects on the Stage. Flash creates a Stage size by placing equal space around all sides of the entire contents of the Stage. If you want to create the smallest possible Stage, place your objects in the upper-left corner and then click Match Contents.

To change the units used for measuring the screen and objects, choose a unit in the Ruler Units drop-down list.

You can add metadata to your movies. *Metadata* is information embedded in the movie that search engines can find. In the Title text field, you can include a title that describes your movie. In the Description text field, add keywords and descriptions of your movie's content that you would like to be available when people search in a browser. For more information, see the section on adding Web search information to your Flash movie in Chapter 12.

Click the Make Default button to make your settings the default for all your new Flash movies. However, the Title and Description fields don't become defaults; you need to specify them individually for each movie.

When you've finished setting document properties, click OK to close the dialog box.

Grabbing a Graphic

The first step when creating animation for your Web site is usually to create or import graphics. Before you do that, however, you should know a little about the different kinds of graphics you can use in a Flash movie.

Understanding vectors and bitmaps

If you know enough about graphics to understand the difference between bitmap and vector graphics, feel free to skip this section. (We hope you always feel free.)

Bitmaps are created with lots of dots. Put them all together, and you get a picture. On-screen, they're displayed as *pixels.* As you can imagine, it can take a large file to store the information about all the dots in a bitmap. Another problem with bitmaps is that they don't scale up well. If you try to enlarge a bitmap, it starts to look grainy because you see all those dots (as in the left example shown in Figure 2-3).

Figure 2-3:
Bitmaps
lose focus
when
enlarged
(left); vector
graphics
remain
sharp and
clear (right).

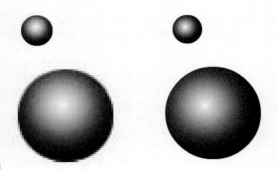

Vector graphics are defined with equations that specify lines, shapes, and locations. Blank space doesn't have to be recorded, and the equations are particularly efficient at storing information. As a result, file sizes are usually smaller than bitmap file sizes.

Vector graphics are infinitely scalable, either up or down. No matter how big you make your graphic, it always looks perfect, as shown in the right example in Figure 2-3. In fact, your graphic might even look better when it's larger because the curves are smoother.

Flash creates vector-based graphics. The small size of the files means that Flash Player files load and play super-fast on a Web page. As you undoubtedly know, fast file loading means that your Web page viewers don't have to wait a long time to see your effects. That's the advantage of Flash. Nevertheless, you can create great graphics with bitmaps that you can't duplicate with vector graphics; we explain how to import bitmaps in Chapter 3.

You can now retain more of the original features of Photoshop and Illustrator files when you import them.

Finding graphics

Okay, so you've doodled and played around with some ideas for your Flash animation and perhaps jotted down a few notes or maybe even made a few sketches. You're ready to start building your Flash animation. A logical place to start is to collect some of the graphics that will serve as building blocks in this process.

Where do you get them? You have several choices:

- ✔ Create your graphics from scratch (if you feel artistic) by using the Flash drawing tools that we describe in detail in Chapter 3.
- ✔ Create graphics in another graphics software package, such as Fireworks, FreeHand, Photoshop, or Illustrator.
- ✔ Import graphics from archives of art available on this book's Web site, from other places on the Web, or from digital (or scanned) photographs — perhaps your own.
- ✔ Combine any or all of these approaches.

You can also import video files. If you want to add video to your Flash movies, see Chapter 11 for detailed instructions.

Going to the Library

Every graphic that you create in Flash is precious and deserves to be archived in style. Each movie file that you create has a Library. The Library saves the following types of objects so that they never get lost:

- ✔ Graphic, movie clip, and button symbols
- ✔ Sounds
- ✔ Imported bitmap graphics (but not vector graphics that you create in Flash)
- ✔ Imported video files

You'll find yourself going to the Library often. Figure 2-4 shows a Library containing several types of symbols plus a sound and a bitmap.

To go to the Library of the current movie file, choose Window⇨Library. You can also press Ctrl+L (Windows) or ⌘+L (Mac). When you open the Library, Flash creates a new window or adds the Library panel to the set of panels that are already open.

To use any object in the Library, follow these steps:

1. **Select the layer on which you want to put the object or create a new layer for the object.**

2. **Click the point on the Timeline where you want the object to start or appear.**

   The point that you click on the Timeline must be a keyframe. Chapter 9 explains keyframes in detail.

Figure 2-4:
You can store graphics, animation, buttons, sounds, and video files in your current movie file's Library.

3. **Click and drag the object from its listing in the Library to the Stage.**

 You can also drag an object's image from the preview box.

 You can drag items to the Pasteboard, the gray area around the edge of the Stage, until you're ready to use them.

Using folders

A Flash movie can contain dozens or even hundreds of symbols, so you need to keep them organized. Flash provides several features to keep you from tearing out your hair.

If you have more than a few symbols, you should organize them into folders. To create a new folder, follow these steps:

1. **Click the New Folder button at the bottom of the Library panel.**

 Flash creates a new folder.

2. **Type a name that describes the type of symbols that you want to put into the folder.**

For example, you could create a folder named Intro and another one named Conclusion.

3. **Press Enter (Windows) or Return (Mac).**

To put symbols into a folder, drag them to the folder. You can also move symbols from one folder to another — just drag them. Note that folders exist just to help keep you organized. You can move symbols from one folder to another without affecting your movie.

To keep your symbol list from getting unwieldy, you can collapse folders. A collapsed folder doesn't display its contents. As soon as you need to see what's inside, you can expand the folder. Double-click a folder to either collapse or expand it.

To quickly see the structure of your folders, click the Library's Options menu. Choose Collapse All Folders. You can also choose Expand All Folders to see everything in the Library.

More Library housekeeping

By default, Flash alphabetizes items in the Library by name. However, you might have different ideas. You can sort from A to Z (ascending) or from Z to A (descending). You can also sort by any of the columns in the Library. To change the direction of sorting (for any column in the Library), click the Toggle Sorting Order button in the upper-right corner of the list (Windows only). To sort, click the heading of the column that you want to sort by. (On the Mac, you can click the column heading again to change the sort order.)

You can resize the Library panel by dragging its lower-right corner. Or you can click the Wide Library View or Narrow Library View button to grow or shrink its width, respectively (refer to Figure 2-4). You can resize any column by dragging the column heading's divider to the left or right.

To rename any Library item, double-click the item's name, type the new name, and press Enter or Return. Don't worry — the original filenames of imported files remain unchanged at their original location.

To duplicate an item, select the item. Then right-click (Windows) or Control+click (Mac) and choose Duplicate. To delete an item, select the item and click the Trash can.

If you want to find out which items in the Library you aren't using, look in the third column (Use Count) for items with a zero use count. To make sure that the use count is accurate, click the Library's Options menu and choose Keep Use Counts Updated or Update Use Counts Now. After you know which items you aren't using, you can delete them.

You can update imported bitmaps and sounds if the original files have changed. Select the file and choose Update in the Options menu of the Library panel.

Using the Libraries of other movies

After you place objects in a file's Library, you can use those objects in any other Flash movie that you create. Just open the movie and display its Library panel, and its Library's contents are available for you to use in your current movie.

Choose File⇨Import⇨Open External Library to open the Library of another Flash movie that isn't open.

You can switch among the Libraries of open movies by using a drop-down list at the top of the Library panel.

When you have libraries open from more than one Flash file, you can copy symbols or anything else in a Library from one movie to another by simply dragging them from one Library to another. Choose the Library that you want to use, select an item, and drag it into the other Library. Easy!

To create a new symbol that goes directly into the Library (rather than on the Stage), choose New Symbol in the Library Options menu in the upper-right corner (refer to Figure 2-4). You're transported to symbol-editing mode, where you can create your symbol as you normally would. To return to your main movie, choose Edit⇨Edit Document. For more information on creating and editing symbols, see Chapter 7.

Exploring the Flash stock Library

Flash comes with two Libraries that contain a basic assortment of button symbols. They are well made, so they're worth looking through. Choose Window⇨Common Libraries and choose Buttons.

Using a Template

To help you create Flash movies more easily, Flash CS3 comes with a few templates for common types of movies. Instructions are included on the templates. To create a Flash movie from a template, choose File⇨New and click the Templates tab. In the New from Template dialog box (see Figure 2-5), select a category, select one of the templates, and then click OK.

Figure 2-5:
Use the
New from
Template
dialog box
to create a
Flash movie
from a
template.

You can choose from the following template categories:

- ✔ **Advertising:** Contains a Stage of the ad size you choose.

- ✔ **BREW Handsets:** Creates movies for wireless handsets that use the BREW (Binary Runtime Environment for Wireless) software platform.

- ✔ **Consumer Devices:** Creates movies for Chumby and iRiver devices. For example, iRiver produces portable media players that can play suitable Flash movies.

- ✔ **Global Handsets:** Creates movies for Nokia, Sony Ericsson, and Windows Mobile 5 phones.

- ✔ **Japanese Handsets:** Creates movies for certain Japanese phones.

- ✔ **Photo Slideshows:** Creates a slide show of photos.

- ✔ **Quiz:** Creates a quiz, complete with several types of question formats and answer feedback. This template's instructions are fairly involved.

When you open a new movie from a template, you should save it as a movie. This way, the template is unchanged, and you are free to make any changes you want.

You can also save movies as templates. If you create a movie that you want to reuse in many variations, choose File➪Save as Template to open the Save as Template dialog box, as shown in Figure 2-6.

Type a name, choose a category, and enter a description for your template. Then click Save. From now on, you can open your template like any of the templates that come with Flash, just as we describe. Using templates can save you lots of work!

Figure 2-6:
The Save as
Template
dialog box
saves your
movies as
templates.

To create your own category for templates, type a category name in the Category list box instead of choosing one of the existing categories in the list.

Printing Your Movie

Usually, you don't print your movies — you publish them on the Web. But you might want to collaborate on a movie with others who don't have Flash. (How unenlightened of them!) Or you might just want to analyze a movie on paper, tack your animation frames on the wall, and rearrange their sequence. In this type of situation, you can print your animation frame by frame.

To print a movie, follow these steps:

1. **To set page margins, choose File⇨Page Setup (Windows) or File⇨Print Margins (Mac).**

   The Page Setup (Windows) or Print Margins (Mac) dialog box appears. See Figure 2-7.

Figure 2-7:
Use the
Page Setup
dialog box
to specify
how to print
your Flash
movie.

2. **In the Margins section, set the margins.**

   You can probably keep the default margin settings.

3. **Select the Center check boxes to center the printing horizontally and vertically on the page.**

4. **(Windows only) In the Paper section, select the size of the paper; define the paper source.**

   Usually you can leave this section as is because it's based on your printer's default settings.

5. **In the Layout section, click the Frames drop-down list and decide whether to print only the first frame or all frames.**

6. **In the Layout section, click the Layout drop-down list to choose from the following options:**

   - **Actual Size:** Lets you choose a scale. This option prints one frame to a page.

   - **Fit on One Page:** Fits one frame on a page, scaling it to fit the paper.

   - **Storyboard–Boxes:** Places several thumbnail sketches of your movie on a page. You can specify how many frames that you want in a row in the Frames Across text box. You might need to experiment to get the right result. In the Frame Margin text box, enter the space in pixels between the boxes. The Storyboard–Boxes option places each frame in a box.

   - **Storyboard–Grid:** Creates a grid of lines for your storyboard rather than individual boxes around the frames. This option is just a matter of aesthetics — don't get too hung up over these choices.

   - **Storyboard–Blank:** Leaves out the boxes or grid and just prints all your frames in the storyboard. You have the same Frames Across and Frame Margin settings as for the other storyboard options.

7. **(Windows only) If you chose a Storyboard option, select the Label Frames check box to give each frame a number.**

8. **(Mac only) When you finish setting your options, click OK; then choose File⇨Page Setup.**

   In Windows, you skip this step because you already opened the Page Setup dialog box in Step 1.

9. **In the Orientation section, select Portrait (taller rather than wider) or Landscape (wider rather than taller).**

10. **(Mac only) In the Format section, choose your printer in the drop-down list.**

11. **(Mac only) In the Paper Size section, select the size of the paper.**

12. **When you finish setting your options, click OK.**

13. **To print, choose File⇨Print.**

    Alternatively, you can press Ctrl+P (Windows) or ⌘+P (Mac). In Windows, you choose the printer in the Name drop-down list in the Print dialog box.

Figure 2-8 shows an example of the storyboard with the grid option. The storyboard shows four frames across with a portrait orientation. You can find out more about the Flash Player's special printing capabilities in Chapter 13.

Figure 2-8:
You can print a storyboard of your movie that displays a thumbnail sketch of each frame.

Part II
1,000 Pictures and 1,000 Words

The 5th Wave   By Rich Tennant

"You know, I've asked you a dozen times <u>not</u> to animate the torches on our Web page!"

In this part . . .

Graphics are the basis of animation. Before you can make anything move, you need to create the graphics that form the building blocks of your animation. Chapter 3 describes all the types of graphics that you can use, from basic shapes created in Flash to sophisticated imported bitmap graphics. The Flash tools are quite capable, and you can create exciting effects with gradient fills, softened edges, and transparency. The Flash editing features, as we describe in Chapter 4, offer more opportunities to create great-looking graphics — including skewing objects, using the Distort and Envelope options, and manipulating fills every which way.

In Chapter 5, you find ways to say great things with flexible text options and formatting. You can even break up text and animate it, letter by letter. To keep all the pieces of your animation from going completely out of control, in Chapter 6 you see how to use layers to organize your movie animation. You can use special layers to guide animation along a path and hide objects behind a mask. (Peekaboo!)

Chapter 3

Getting Graphic

In this chapter, you get down to the details of creating your own graphics in Flash. The Flash graphics tools (found on the Tools panel) offer you the capability to easily create interesting and professional looking shapes. You can also import graphics created in other programs.

After you master all the techniques for drawing and editing, you can create some very cool graphics. If you're new to Flash, take the time to try out all the tools and techniques until you feel comfortable with them.

For a handy reference to the Tools panel, which we refer to throughout this chapter, see the Cheat Sheet at the front of this book.

Sharpening Your Pencil

The Flash Pencil tool is designed to be used like a real pencil to create free-hand shapes. Whenever you want to create a shape not available from other Flash tools (such as the circle and square), you can use the Pencil. But the Pencil tool goes beyond a regular pencil's capabilities by incorporating cool features that smooth or straighten what you draw. In addition to those features, the Pencil also includes the *shape-recognition* feature (perfect for those who are less artistic). Draw something that approximates a triangle, and Flash forgivingly perfects it for you. In this section, we explain exactly how to use this tool.

 To start, click the Pencil tool on the Tools panel. To draw without changing the Pencil modifier, move the cursor onto the Stage, click, and draw. After you release the mouse button, Flash modifies the shape according to the active modifier setting, as we explain in the next section.

Setting the Pencil modifier

When you choose the Pencil tool, the Options area below the Tools panel changes to display the drawing mode modifier for the Pencil tool.

The Pencil modifier has three drawing modes:

- ✔ **Straighten:** Straightens lines and converts sloppy squares, rectangles, circles, ellipses, and triangles to perfect ones.
- ✔ **Smooth:** Smoothes out curved lines, eliminating unsightly bumps and lumps. You can specify the amount of smoothing.
- ✔ **Ink:** Slightly smoothes and straightens your curves and lines but leaves them mostly the way you drew them.

In Figure 3-1, you see a right-pointing arrow. Suppose that you have already drawn the horizontal line and now want to create the arrow's point. See how the point looks before and after Flash modified it by using the Straighten drawing mode to create perfectly straight lines.

Figure 3-1:
Use the
Straighten
mode to
draw
straight
lines.

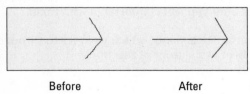

Suppose that you want to animate some waves on your Web site. You start to draw the outline of the waves. Figure 3-2 shows how the waves look before and after Flash smoothes them out by using Smooth mode. For more complex shapes, Ink mode helps you look good without taking away too much of your own authorship.

How to set smoothing and shape-recognition preferences

You can tell Flash just how much you want it to smooth or straighten curved lines when you draw with the Pencil tool. Choose Edit⇨ Preferences (Windows) or Flash ⇨Preferences (Mac) and click the Drawing category. In the Smooth Curves drop-down list, select one of the following options:

✔ **Off:** Flash doesn't smooth or straighten at all.

✔ **Rough:** Flash smoothes or straightens only slightly, honoring your own work as much as possible.

✔ **Normal:** Flash smoothes or straightens a medium amount. Normal is the default setting.

✔ **Smooth:** Flash smoothes and straightens more so that you get fewer bumps and jolts.

In the same way, you can tell Flash how picky you want it to be in recognizing lines, circles, ovals, squares, rectangles, and arcs (90 degrees and 180 degrees). For lines, select Off, Strict, Normal, or Tolerant in the Recognize Lines drop-down list. Normal is the default. Use Tolerant if you're a klutz; use Strict (or even Off) if you don't want Flash fiddling too much (or at all) with your work. For other shapes and arcs, select an option in the Recognize Shapes drop-down list. You have the same Off, Strict, Normal, and Tolerant options.

Figure 3-2:
Smooth mode makes you look like a real smoothie when it comes to drawing curves.

Before

After

Setting the stroke type

While drawing with the Pencil tool (and any of the other drawing tools), you can also control the type of *stroke* (line style), its *width* (also called *height* or *weight*), its cap (ending), and how it joins with other strokes. To modify stroke settings, follow these steps:

1. **Click the Pencil tool to make it active.**

2. **Open the Property inspector if it's not open by choosing Window⇨ Properties⇨Properties. Or if the inspector is open, make sure it's expanded to its full size.**

The Property inspector appears, as shown in Figure 3-3. As we explain in Chapter 1, the Property inspector changes depending on which tool is active and which part of the Flash window you're using.

Stroke height

Stroke color   Stroke style

Figure 3-3:
Use the
Property
inspector to
control line
type and
width.

3. **Click the Stroke Style drop-down list to display the available line styles and select a new line style.**

You can choose from seven line styles, including dashed and dotted.

4. **To change the line width, type a new value in the Stroke Height box and press Enter or Return, or drag the slider bar that appears when you click the down arrow to the value you want.**

The first available stroke width on the Stroke Style drop-down list is Hairline, which creates a hairline-width line. Flash measures *weights* (widths) of other line types in points. You can create a line up to 200 points wide. (A point equals $\frac{1}{72}$ of an inch.)

5. **To control the endings of lines, click the Cap drop-down list and select one of the styles:**

   • **None:** The end is square with no added ending.

   • **Round:** A rounded cap is added to the end of the line. The length of the cap is half the line's width.

   • **Square:** A squared cap is added to the end of the line. The length of the cap is half the line's width. See Figure 3-4.

6. **If you want, select the Stroke Hinting check box.**

Stroke hinting makes slight adjustments to avoid blurry horizontal or vertical lines. If your lines don't look as clear as you'd like, try selecting this option.

Figure 3-4:
These three lines were all drawn to be 100 pixels long, but the bottom two lines have round and square caps, so they're longer.

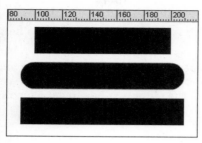

7. **Click the Join drop-down list and select one of the styles (see Figure 3-5) to control how lines look when they meet:**

   • **Miter:** A pointed corner

   • **Round:** A rounded corner

   • **Bevel:** A squared-off (beveled) corner

Miter   Round   Bevel

Figure 3-5:
You can choose how lines meet. How romantic!

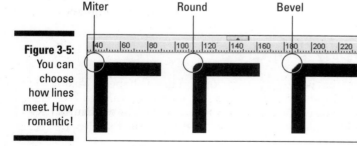

8. **In the Scale drop-down list, select an option to control how lines scale.**

   The Scale options specify how the thickness of strokes scale if you include them in a symbol and then scale the symbol. (We discuss symbols in Chapter 7.)

   • **Normal:** Thickness scales both horizontally and vertically.

   • **Horizontal:** Thickness scales horizontally only. This applies to vertical lines, so that they become thicker as you scale them.

- **Vertical:** Thickness scales vertically only. This applies to horizontal lines, so that they become thicker as you scale them.

- **None:** Lines don't become thicker as you scale them.

9. **(Optional) In the Miter text box, you can enter a limit to help prevent beveling a miter join.**

   When you draw two lines that meet at a sharp angle with a *miter join* (a sharp point), you might get a bevel instead. If you chose a miter join, you can increase the value in the Miter text box to get a nice sharp point where the two lines meet.

You can create custom line styles, as well. In the Property inspector, click the Custom button. In the Line Style dialog box that opens, you can create your own designer line styles.

Setting the color

 When using the Pencil tool, you can set the color of the stroke in the Property inspector or in the Colors section of the Tools panel. In either location, click the Stroke Color box to open the color palette and then select a color.

We explain more about using colors in the section "A Rainbow of Colors," later in this chapter.

Creating Shapely Shapes

In the preceding section, we explain that you can draw shapes by using the Pencil tool. You can also draw lines, rectangles, squares, ovals, and circles by using the shape tools. Use these tools when you want more control over your shapes — for example, when you want to draw perfect circles, perfect squares, and straight lines.

Line up

To draw a line, choose the Line tool in the Tools panel. Click the Stage at the desired starting point of the line and drag to the ending point. Then release the mouse button. To keep your lines at multiples of 45 degrees, press Shift while dragging. Flash creates the line at the 45-degree angle closest to your drag line.

When you use the Line tool, you can modify the line weight, style, and color in the same way as for the Pencil tool, as we discuss in the preceding section.

Be square

 To draw a rectangle, choose the Rectangle tool in the Tools panel. Click the Stage at one corner of the rectangle and drag to the opposite corner. Then release the mouse button. To create a square, press Shift as you drag.

 The Rectangle tool is on a flyout toolbar on the Tools panel. The flyout displays the last tool you used, so you may not see the Rectangle tool. Instead, you may see the Oval tool, the Polystar tool, the Rectangle Primitive tool, or the Oval Primitive tool. Click any one of these to display the flyout, where you can find the Rectangle tool.

When you click the Rectangle tool, you can modify the line weight, style, and color of the rectangle in the same way that you can modify a line when you use the Pencil tool. You can't see the effect of caps when you create a rectangle because it's a closed shape; however, if you later cut out part of the rectangle, the remaining lines take on the cap you specified.

Unlike lines, rectangles contain *two* objects: the *fill* (the area inside the stroke) and the *stroke* (the outline of the rectangle).

Flash provides the following tools for adjusting the settings for rectangles:

 ✔ **Fill Color:** Determines the color that fills the inside of the rectangle. You can click the Fill Color box — either in the Property inspector or in the Colors section of the Tools panel — and select one of the colors in the palette that opens. You can also select from the gradients displayed at the bottom of the palette. (See the section "A Rainbow of Colors," later in this chapter, for details about customizing colors and gradients.)

 ✔ **Stroke Color:** Determines the color of the stroke (the outline) of the rectangle. Click the Stroke Color box — either in the Property inspector or in the Colors section of the Tools panel — and select a color from the palette.

✔ **Black and White:** Sets the stroke color to black and the fill color to white. Click the Black and White button in the Colors section of the Tools panel.

 ✔ **No Color:** Sets either the stroke color or the fill color (whichever tool is pressed) to no color. You have to click either the Stroke Color box or the Fill Color box before you click the No Color box.

- ✔ **Swap Colors:** Switches the stroke and fill colors.

- ✔ **Rectangle Corner Radius:** Creates a rectangle with rounded corners. (It's located in the Property inspector.) Enter a new number in the Rectangle Corner Radius text box or use the slider to change the radius. The rectangle that you draw has nicely rounded corners. You can create cute cutout corners by using a negative number for the radius.

You can specify the dimensions of the rectangle in advance. Select the Rectangle tool, press Alt (Windows) or Option (Mac), and then click the Stage. The Rectangle Settings dialog box opens, with Width and Height text boxes that you can use to get exactly the size rectangle you want. You can also set the corner radius here. When you click OK, the rectangle appears immediately. You can then move it to the location you want.

If you want to create a rectangle with no fill, choose the Rectangle tool, open the Fill Color box, and click the box with the diagonal line in the upper-right corner of the color palette. To create a rectangle with a fill but no outline, choose the Rectangle tool, click the Stroke Color tool, and choose the box with the diagonal line at the top of the palette.

Be an egg

To draw an oval, choose the Oval tool in the Tools panel. Click the Stage at one corner of the oval and drag to the opposite corner. (Ovals don't really have corners, but you'll get the idea after you try one or two.) Then release the mouse button. To create a perfect circle, press and hold Shift while you drag.

The Oval tool is on a flyout toolbar on the Tools panel. The flyout displays the last tool you used, so you may not see the Oval tool. Instead, you may see the Rectangle tool, the Polystar tool, the Rectangle Primitive tool, or the Oval Primitive tool. Click any one of these to display the flyout, where you can find the Oval tool.

After you click the Oval tool, you can change the line color, type, and weight in the same way as we describe for the Pencil tool, in the "Setting the stroke type" section earlier in this chapter. You can set the colors as we describe in the preceding section on drawing rectangles.

You can specify the exact width and height of the oval. Select the Oval tool, press Alt (Windows) or Option (Mac), and then click the Stage. The Oval Settings dialog box opens. Use the Width and Height text boxes to specify the size you want, and then click OK to create the oval.

You can draw a donut by defining an inner radius and draw part of an oval by defining the start and end angles. For more information, see the instructions in the "Creating an oval primitive" section later in this chapter.

Go for the stars

The Polystar tool is on the same flyout as the Rectangle and Oval tools. This tool creates stars or polygons. Follow these steps:

1. **Display the Properties tab in the Property inspector.**

   Choose Window ⇨Properties⇨Properties to display the inspector if it's not already open. Or if it is open, expand the Property inspector to its full size if necessary.

2. **In the Tools palette's Rectangle tool flyout, choose the Polystar tool.**

3. **In the Property inspector, click the Options button to open the Tool Settings dialog box.**

4. **In the Style drop-down list, choose Polygon or Star.**

5. **In the Number of Sides text box, enter a number.**

   The maximum number is 32, which is probably plenty.

6. **In the Star Point Size text box, enter a value between 0 and 1 to indicate the depth of the points.**

   A lower value, such as 0.1, creates deeper points, making your star spiky looking. A higher value, such as 0.8, creates shorter points. This setting is irrelevant for polygons.

7. **Drag on the screen to create the star or polygon.**

Mixing and Matching Shapes

After you create shapes on the Stage, you need to understand what happens when two objects touch. It's a little weird, but you soon see how flexible the Flash drawing tools are. Two basic rules exist about objects that touch.

Cutting up shapes

The first rule is that when you use the Pencil or Line tool to draw a line that intersects any other shape or line, the line acts like a knife to cut the other shape or line. The line you draw is also cut into segments. You don't see the effect until you try to select or move one of the objects. Suppose that you want to draw a broken heart. You can draw the breaking line by using the Pencil tool. You now have several objects, and you can easily move apart the two halves of the heart. In the second heart (see Figure 3-6), we erased the line and separated the halves of the heart.

Figure 3-6:
Intersect
any shape
with a line,
and the line
splits the
shape and is
itself
segmented.

Placing objects on top of each other

The second rule about objects that touch is that when you place one shape
on top of another, the top shape replaces whatever is beneath it. Again, you
can see the results only when you try to select or move the shapes. But now
it gets a little complicated:

- ✔ If the two shapes are the same color, they merge into one combined shape.
- ✔ If the two shapes are different colors, they remain separate.

Figure 3-7 shows a circle and a triangle on the left. They are the same color.
On the right, you can see the result after moving the circle down over the triangle. Presto! It's an ice cream cone. If you try to select the shape, it's now
one object.

Figure 3-7:
Build
complex
shapes by
combining
basic
shapes of
the same
color.

When you combine shapes of different colors, you create cutouts. Rather
than adding the shapes together, the top shape just replaces the area beneath
it. Figure 3-8 shows how you can create a cutout. We display a grid on the
Stage (find more about that in Chapter 4) so that you can see that the image
on the right is a cutout.

Figure 3-8:
A cutout.
There's a
hole in the
bucket!

To create a cutout effect, follow these steps:

1. **Create two separate shapes of different colors.**

2. **Move one shape on top of another shape.**

3. **Deselect the shape that you moved by clicking anywhere off the shape.**

4. **Select the top shape again, and either drag it away from the bottom shape to create the cutout or delete it.**

See Chapter 4 for details on selecting and moving objects.

Keeping Objects Safe and Secure

What do you do if you want to put objects next to or on top of each other while maintaining their integrity? Two methods of drawing keep your objects safe from cutups, replacements, and cutouts. We discuss these in this section.

Using the object-drawing model

You can use the *object-drawing model* to keep your objects whole, no matter what else they touch. When you draw using this model, objects maintain their integrity — no dishonest objects here! Other objects on top of or beneath these objects do not cut up, cut out, or merge with them.

To draw any object with the object-drawing model, follow these steps:

1. **Choose any drawing tool in the Tools panel.**

2. **Click the Object Drawing modifier in the Options section so that the button has a white area around it (Windows) or the button darkens (Mac).**

   You click the modifier again to turn off the Object Drawing modifier.

   You can also press the J key to turn the object-drawing model on and off.

3. Draw your object.

Your object now has a blue rectangular bounding box around it. This bounding box is similar to the one you see when you turn objects into a symbol (as we explain in Chapter 7) or group objects (see Chapter 4 for more information).

If you change your mind and don't want your object to stay separate from touching objects, select the object and choose Modify➪Break Apart.

You can convert objects to object-drawing model shapes. Just select the shape, and choose Modify ➪Combine Objects ➪Union.

Getting primitive

A special type of shape, called a *primitive,* does not merge with other objects. These objects act like objects that you draw using the object-drawing model.

Primitives are new for Flash CS3. Two primitives are available: a rectangle and an oval. These primitives allow you to specify certain properties, called *parameters,* that define their shape.

Creating a rectangle primitive

When you draw a rectangle primitive, you can create a rounded rectangle by specifying a radius for the corners. Use the Rectangle Corner Radius text box or slider bar in the Properties palette to specify a value. But you can do the same with the regular Rectangle tool, as we describe earlier in this chapter, so what's the point? The difference is how you can edit the radius of the corners. When you select a rectangle primitive, you see markers at the corners. You can drag these markers to change the corner radii, as shown in Figure 3-9.

Figure 3-9:
You can change the radius of a rectangle primitive's corners by dragging the corner markers.

The other difference between a normal rectangle and a rectangle primitive is that the primitive acts like objects that you draw using the object-drawing model. You can't merge it or cut it out. Similarly, when you select it, you see a bounding box around the entire shape.

 To draw a rectangle primitive, select the Rectangle Primitive tool in the Tools panel. Display the Properties palette (choose Window ➪ Properties or click its title bar if it's collapsed) and specify a corner radius in the Rectangle Corner Radius text box. Then click the Stage at one corner of the rectangle and drag to the opposite corner. The rectangle is selected, so you can immediately drag the corners to adjust them if you want.

 The Rectangle Primitive tool is on a flyout toolbar on the Tools panel. The flyout displays the last tool you used, so you may not see the Rectangle Primitive tool. Instead, you may see the Rectangle tool, the Polystar tool, or the Oval Primitive tool. Click any one of these to display the flyout, where you can find the Rectangle Primitive tool.

Creating an oval primitive

To draw an Oval primitive, select the Oval Primitive tool in the Tools panel. Display the Properties palette (choose Window ➪ Properties or click its title bar if it's collapsed) and specify the Start Angle, End Angle, and Inner Radius, and whether or not the path should be closed, as explained next. Then click the Stage at one corner of the oval and drag to the opposite corner.

 The Oval Primitive tool is on a flyout toolbar on the Tools panel. The flyout displays the last tool you used, so you may not see the Oval Primitive tool. Instead, you may see the Rectangle tool, the Polystar tool, the Oval tool, or the Rectangle Primitive tool. Click any one of these to display the flyout, where you can find the Oval Primitive tool.

When you draw an oval primitive, you can specify the following parameters in the Properties palette:

- **Inner Radius:** By specifying a value from 1 to 99, you can indicate the percentage of the oval's fill that you want to remove, thereby creating a donut (yum)! See Figure 3-10 for an example. Enter a value in the Inner Radius text box in the Properties palette, or click the down arrow to display a slider that you can drag to change the value.

- **Start and End Angle:** By separately specifying a start angle and an end angle, you can create part of an oval (or circle), as shown in Figure 3-10. When specifying angles, note that 0 degrees is to the right and that degrees increase in a clockwise direction. Enter values in the Start Angle and End Angle text boxes in the Properties palette, or click the down arrow to display a circle with a small dot on it. Drag the dot around the circumference of the circle to specify the desired angle.

Figure 3-10:
I had a
donut. A
little crea-
ture came
and ate a
bite. Then it
went on to
eat the rest,
leaving only
the outline!

✔ **Close Path:** Select this check box to include a fill as well as an outline around the entire shape. (The Close Path check box is selected by default.) Deselect the Close Path check box to omit the fill and draw an outline only. If you used the Start Angle and End Angle controls to create part of an oval or a circle, you get an unclosed shape when you deselect the Close Path check box, as shown in Figure 3-10.

When you deselect the Close Path check box to create an open oval, you draw only the outline. What happens if you defined the oval without a fill? The entire object disappears! To get it back, choose Edit⇨Undo and add an outline. For detailed instructions, see the discussion of the Rectangle tool earlier in this chapter.

Figure 3-10 shows oval primitives with the following parameters from left to right: an inner radius; no inner radius, but start and end angles; a closed path with an inner radius and start and end angles; and finally, an open path with an inner radius and start and end angles. You can see that opening the path removes the fill.

When you select an Oval Primitive, you see two markers, one at the inner radius (or center, if the inner radius is 0) and one at the outer radius. You can drag the inner radius to change it.

Creating Curves with the Pen

The Pen tool lets you draw *Bezier* curves, also called splines. Bezier curves are named after the French mathematician Pierre Bézier, who first described them. By using the Pen tool, you can create smooth curves that flow into each other. You can also create straight lines.

You can set preferences for the Pen tool by choosing Edit⇨Preferences (Windows) or Flash⇨Preferences (Mac) and clicking the Drawing category. We suggest enabling the Show Pen Preview option to display a preview of the line or curve while you draw. This setting helps you get a better idea of what the result will be. Click OK when you finish setting your preferences.

 To create a line or curve, choose the Pen tool in the Tools panel. What you do next depends on whether you want to draw a straight line or a curve. The following sections show you how to draw both.

Drawing straight lines

To draw a straight line with the Pen tool, follow these steps:

1. **To create a line segment, click the start point and then click the end point.**

2. **Continue to add line segments by clicking additional points.**

3. **Double-click to complete the process.**

   You can also Ctrl+click (Windows) or ⌘+click (Mac) anywhere off the line. Flash previews segments in a color that depends on the layer you're working on — see the color of the square next to the current layer as shown on the Timeline. (Chapter 6 explains layers in full.) When you choose another tool, Flash displays Beziers in the current stroke color.

Close a figure by pointing near the start point. You see a small circle. Click the start point, and Flash closes the figure.

Drawing curves

Drawing curves with the Pen tool involves a couple of steps, depending on the complexity of the curve that you want to create. The main principle to understand is that you define the curve by specifying the location of anchor points. Each *anchor point* controls a bend in the curve. To draw a curve with the Pen tool, follow these steps:

1. **Click where you want to start and drag the mouse in the desired direction. About one-half of the way to the next anchor point (the end of the curve), release the mouse button, as shown in Figure 3-11(a).**

   You see *tangent lines* that define both the direction and length of each part of the curve, as shown in Figure 3-11(b).

Figure 3-11:
Drawing a
curve with
the Pen tool:
1, 2, 3, and
you have a
big nose!

(a)　　　　(b)　　　　(c)

2. **To create one curve, move the mouse cursor to the desired end of the curve; then double-click to end the curve, as shown in Figure 3-11(c).**

   If you set preferences to show a preview of the curve (as we explain earlier in the section "Creating Curves with the Pen"), you also see a stretchy line attached to your mouse cursor that previews the shape.

3. **To continue to draw curves, again click and drag in the desired direction, release the mouse button, and move the mouse cursor to wherever you want the end of the next curve to be. Double-click to end the curve.**

If you drag in an opposing direction to the first curve, you create a simple curve, sometimes called a *C curve*. If you drag in a similar direction to the first curve, the curve doubles back on itself, which is sometimes called an *S curve*.

For both lines and curves, you can press and hold Shift to constrain the lines or curves (the tangent lines) to 45-degree angles.

Drawing curves with the Pen tool takes practice, but you'll soon get the hang of it.

Getting Artistic with the Brush

The Brush tool lets you create artistic effects that look like painting. You can adjust the size and shape of the brush, and if you have a pressure-sensitive pen and tablet, you can adjust the width of the stroke by changing the pressure on the pen.

To paint with the Brush tool, select it on the Tools panel and then click and drag anywhere on the Stage. Press and hold Shift while you brush to keep your strokes either horizontal or vertical. The brush doesn't have a stroke (line) color. The brush creates only fills. Use the Fill Color drop-down list in the Property inspector or in the Colors section of the Tools panel to select a fill color.

When you choose the Brush tool, the Brush modifiers appear in the Options section of the Tools panel, as shown in Figure 3-12.

Figure 3-12:
The Brush
modifiers
control the
size and
shape of the
brush as
well as how
the brush
relates to
existing
images.

Brush Mode — / Lock Fill
Brush Size — / Brush Shape
Use Pressure — / Use Tilt

Brush mode modifier

The Brush mode modifier determines how the brush relates to existing objects on the Stage. Here are your choices for Brush mode. (Figure 3-13 shows some examples.)

- **Paint Normal:** You just paint away, oblivious to anything else. Use this setting when you don't need to worry about other objects.

- **Paint Fills:** You paint fills and empty areas of the Stage. The paint doesn't cover lines. Note that your lines seem to be covered while you paint, but they reappear when you release the mouse button.

- **Paint Behind:** You paint behind existing objects, but only in blank areas of the Stage. While you paint, the brush seems to cover everything, but your existing objects reappear when you release the mouse button. You can messily paint over your objects, knowing that they won't be affected.

- **Paint Selection:** You paint only a filled-in area that you previously selected. While you paint, your existing objects are covered, but they reappear when you release the mouse button. You don't need to worry about painting within the lines because Flash fills only the selected area.

- **Paint Inside:** You paint inside lines. Only the fill where you start brushing is painted. Paint Inside also paints an empty area on the Stage if that's where you start brushing. Again, at first the paint seems to cover up everything, but when you release the mouse button, Flash keeps your paint nice and neat, inside the lines — like every little kid discovers in kindergarten.

Original corn

Corn with worms
— Paint Normal

Corn with bad kernels
— Paint Fills

Corn with background
— Paint Behind

Sheath with gray gradient
— Paint Selection

Corn with bad kernels
— Paint Inside

Figure 3-13:
Set the
Brush mode
when using
the Brush
tool to get
the effect
you want.

Brush Size drop-down list

Click the Brush Size drop-down list and select a size in the list of circles. This list defines the width of the brush. If you use a Brush mode that helps you draw neatly, such as Paint Selection, you don't need to be too concerned with the size of the brush. On the other hand, if you're creating an artistic effect by using Paint Normal mode, the width of the brush is important.

Brush Shape drop-down list

Flash offers several brush shapes you can choose from. Click the Brush Shape drop-down list and select one of the shapes. Each shape produces a different effect, especially when you paint at an angle — you just need to try them out to see what works best. Figure 3-14 shows a honey jar drawn with various brush shapes.

Figure 3-14:
Each brush
shape
creates a
different
effect —
especially at
the ends of
the stroke.

Pressure and Tilt modifiers

If you have a pressure-sensitive pen and tablet, Flash also displays a Pressure modifier so that you can vary the width of your strokes according to the pressure you put on your pen while you draw. Click the Use Pressure tool (refer to Figure 3-12) to turn on this feature.

Flash fully supports pressure-sensitive pens and adds the ability to use the opposite end of the pen to erase — just like a real pencil. Figure 3-15 shows this type of pen and tablet.

A pressure-sensitive pen works together with a tablet to help you draw in Flash. The tablet tracks the movement and pressure of the pen while you draw. You can also use the pen as a mouse to choose menu and dialog box items. In other words, if you want, you can use the pen for all your Flash work. Alternatively, you can use the pen and tablet just for drawing and use the mouse when you want to work with menus and dialog boxes.

The Tilt modifier varies the angle of your brush stroke when you vary the angle of the stylus on the tablet. For example, holding the stylus straight up and down produces a different shape of brush stroke than the one you get if you hold the stylus at a 45-degree angle to the tablet.

Use the Tilt modifier for fine control over your brush strokes. Click the Use Tilt tool in the Options section of the Tools panel to turn on this feature. You see the effect most clearly with a large brush size and one of the narrow brush shapes. When you start to draw, change the angle of the stylus to the tablet. Watch the cursor shape turn, giving you a hint as to the shape of the brush stroke. Try brushing at a few angles to see how this works.

Figure 3-15:
This Wacom
pen and
tablet set is
easier to
draw with
than a
mouse and
enables you
to easily
vary the
brush width
as you
draw.

Photo courtesy of Douglas Little of Wacom

See the "A Rainbow of Colors" section, later in this chapter, for an explanation of the Lock Fill modifier, one of the brush tool's modifiers.

Brush smoothing

Smoothing brush strokes is similar to smoothing pencil strokes. You can finely adjust how much your brush strokes are smoothed after you finish drawing them. You can set smoothing anywhere from 0 to 100.

To set brush smoothing, follow these steps:

1. **Click the Brush tool.**

2. **Open the Property inspector if it's not open (choose Window⇨ Properties⇨Properties). Or if the inspector is open, expand it to its full size if necessary.**

3. **Use the Smoothing text box or slider to set a new value.**

   The lower values change your strokes less. Therefore, if you set Smoothing to 0, the brush stroke is closest to what you actually drew. Lower values create more vectors, resulting in a larger file size for your movie. The higher values smooth and simplify your strokes more.

Pouring on the Paint

The Paint Bucket creates fills that fill shapes with color. You might want to fill an enclosed area that you created with the Line or Pencil tool. You can also fill enclosed shapes created with the Pen or Brush tool, as we explain earlier in this chapter.

The Paint Bucket is also handy for changing existing fills. You can change the color as well as fiddle around with gradient and bitmap fills. (See Chapter 4 for more on editing fills.)

 To use the Paint Bucket, choose it in the Tools panel. Set the color by clicking the Fill Color tool and selecting a color. Alternatively, you can use the Fill Color drop-down list in the Property inspector.

 Flash can fill areas that aren't completely closed. The Gap Size modifier (in the Options section of the Tools panel) determines how large of a gap Flash will overlook to fill in an almost enclosed area. Choices range from Don't Close Gaps to Close Large Gaps. Because *small* and *large* are relative terms, you might have to experiment to get the result you want. After you choose an option from the Gap Size modifier, click any enclosed or almost enclosed area to fill it, as shown in Figure 3-16.

Figure 3-16:
Fill areas
that aren't
completely
closed by
using the
Gap Size
modifier.

 After you use the Paint Bucket to fill a shape created with another tool, you can delete the outline of the shape and keep just the fill.

Strokes, Ink

You use the Ink Bottle tool to create an outline on an existing shape. You can use the Ink Bottle tool also to change an existing line, or *stroke*.

To use the Ink Bottle tool, click it on the Tools panel. Click the Stroke Color tool to select a color. Use the Property inspector, as we explain earlier in this chapter (in the discussion of the Pencil tool) to select a line thickness and line style. Then click anywhere on the shape. If the shape has no existing line, Flash adds the line. If the shape has a line, Flash changes its color, width, or style to the settings you specified in the Property inspector.

A Rainbow of Colors

Flash offers you lots of color options. By default, Flash uses a palette of 216 colors that are Web safe, which means they look good on all Web browsers and monitors. Or, in these days when most computers can displays millions of colors, you can create your own colors.

Solid citizens

When you choose either the Stroke Color or Fill Color tool, Flash opens the *current color palette,* which is the active set of colors that Flash uses.

Creating new colors or editing existing colors

Flash provides two ways for you to specify your own colors:

✔ Choose the Stroke Color or Fill Color tool in the Tools panel and click the Colors Window button in the upper-right corner of the palette to open the Color dialog box.

✔ Choose Window➪Color to open the Color panel.

These two methods duplicate each other; here, we explain how to use the Color panel, which is shown in Figure 3-17.

Figure 3-17: Use the Color panel to create your own colors.

If you select an object before you use the Color panel, the object's color changes immediately when you change the color in the panel.

To create a new color or edit an existing color, follow these steps:

1. **Click the Options menu icon in the upper-right corner of the Color panel to open the pop-up menu, and then choose the color mode.**

   RGB specifies a color according to red, green, and blue components; *HSB* specifies a color by hue, saturation, and brightness. You can also define a color by using *hexadecimal notation,* which is the color system used on the Web: Just type the hexadecimal code in the Hex box of the Color panel.

2. **Click the Stroke Color or Fill Color icon to specify which color you want to change — stroke or fill.**

   Click the icon to the left of the Stroke Color or Fill Color box — not the box itself. (If you click the box, you open the color palette.)

3. **Type the color specs in the text boxes, use the sliders (click the down arrow) to drag to the desired color, or find a color in the color space that's close to the one that you want. Then click that color.**

4. **Set the level of opacity/transparency (also called *alpha*) by using the Alpha slider or by typing a number in the Alpha box.**

   A setting of 0% is completely transparent and 100% is opaque.

5. **If you want to create a new color swatch, click the Options menu icon and choose Add Swatch.**

   Flash adds the new color to the color palette so that you can access it from the Stroke Color or Fill Color boxes on the Tools panel, the Property inspector, and the Swatches panel.

Managing colors

If you've added or changed colors, you can save this new palette. (A *palette* is a set of colors.) You can then save the palette for use in other Flash movies or import a color palette from another Flash movie (so that you don't have to bother creating the colors again). Color palettes are saved as .clr files and are called *Flash color set* files. To save a color palette, choose Save Colors in the Swatches option menu. (Choose Window⇨Swatches to open the Swatches panel and click the Options menu icon in the upper-right corner of the panel to display the menu.) In the Export Swatch dialog box, choose a location for the file, name it, and click Save.

Adobe Fireworks and Photoshop use Color Table files (.act files), and Flash can save and import these as well. To save your color palette as an .act file, choose Color Table (*.act) in the Save as Type drop-down list in the Export Swatch dialog box.

To import a color palette that you've saved, use the Options menu of the Swatches panel. Choose Add Colors if you want to append this imported palette to an existing palette. Choose Replace Colors if you want the imported palette to replace an existing palette. You can use the same Swatches panel Options menu to manage your color palettes. Choose from the following options:

- **Duplicate Swatch:** Creates a duplicate of a swatch. Do this when you want to create your own color and use an existing color as a basis.

- **Delete Swatch:** Deletes a color.

- **Load Default Colors:** Replaces the active color palette with the Flash default palette.

- **Save as Default:** Saves the active color palette as the default palette for any new Flash movies that you create.

- **Clear Colors:** Clears all colors except black and white — for when you really want to start from scratch.

- **Web 216:** Loads the Web-safe, 216-color palette.

- **Sort by Color:** Sorts the display of colors by luminosity.

Gradient colors

So you're bored with solid colors and want something more interesting. *Gradients* are combinations of two or more colors that gradually blend from one to another. Flash can create gradients of as many as 16 colors — quite a feat. Gradients are always used as fills. The gradient can be linear or *radial* (concentric), as shown in Figure 3-18. Because the figure isn't in color, it can't begin to show you the glory of gradients.

Figure 3-18: Linear and radial gradients make your graphics more interesting than plain solid colors.

Linear gradient   Radial gradient

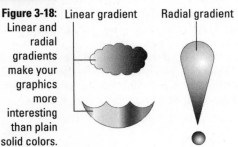

Flash offers a few standard gradients that you can find at the bottom of the color palette. But you often need a more customized look, and Flash has the tools to create just about any gradient you want.

Radial gradients look best on curved objects. A circle can suddenly look like a sphere when you fill it with a radial gradient. If you put white at the center of a radial gradient, it gives the impression of light highlights. Linear gradients look best on straight objects.

To create your own gradient, follow these steps:

1. **Choose Window⇨Color to open the Color panel (refer to Figure 3-17). Then choose Linear or Radial in the Fill Style drop-down list.**

   You see a gradient bar with color pointers that specify the colors of the gradient and where the gradient changes from one color to the next.

   If you select a fill before you use the Color panel, the object's fill color changes immediately when you change the gradient in the Color panel.

2. **To use an existing gradient as a starting point, click the Fill Color box on the Tools panel and choose a gradient from the bottom of the color palette.**

   You can also choose Window⇨Swatches to open the Swatches panel and choose a gradient from the bottom of the color palette there.

3. **To specify the color for each color pointer, click and hold the pointer and then release the mouse button (this is like a long mouse click). When the color swatches appear, select a color.**

   You can click the Fill Color box and select an existing color from the color palette or specify a new color by using the methods we describe in the earlier section, "Creating new colors or editing existing colors."

   Note that when you click a pointer, its point turns black to indicate that it's the active pointer. The square beneath the point displays the color pointer's current color.

4. **To change the number of colors in the gradient, add or delete color pointers.**

   To add a color pointer, click where you want the pointer to appear, just below the gradient bar. To delete a color pointer, drag it off the gradient bar.

5. **To adjust where the color changes, drag a color pointer to the left or right.**

6. **To add control over how colors are applied to a selected shape beyond the gradient, select one of the following *overflow modes* in the Overflow drop-down list:**

   ✔ **Extend:** Extends the last or outermost gradient color past the end of the gradient

   ✔ **Reflect:** Fills the shape by mirroring the gradient pattern

   ✔ **Repeat:** Repeats the gradient from beginning to end

   To use these effects, fill a shape with a gradient and then use the Gradient Transform tool to reduce the size of the gradient so that it no longer completely fills the shape. (We discuss the Gradient Transform tool in Chapter 4.) Then try out the three overflow modes to see the results.

   Select the Linear RGB check box to create a gradient that complies with Scalable Vector Graphics (SVG) standards. SVG is an XML language for describing 2-D graphics.

7. **To save the gradient, click the menu icon in the upper-right corner of the Color panel and choose Add Swatch.**

The new gradient now appears in the color palette of the Fill Color box on the Tools panel and in the Swatches panel. Go ahead and fill something with it!

You can also move a gradient's center and focal points, change its width and height, rotate it, scale it, skew it, and tile it. See Chapter 4 for more on editing gradients.

Bitmap fills

You can create the coolest, weirdest fills by importing a bitmap graphic and using the bitmap to fill any shape. For a hypothetical Web site protesting genetically engineered foods, for example, we could find a bitmap of a bug (representing the Bt bacteria genetically engineered into corn) and use it to fill a graphic of corn. Figure 3-19 shows the result.

To use a bitmap graphic to fill a shape, follow these steps:

1. **Create the object or shape that you want to fill.**

2. **Select the object.**

3. **If you haven't already imported the bitmap, choose File⇨Import⇨ Import to Library, choose the bitmap you want, and then click Open/Import.**

We explain more about importing graphics in the section "The Import Business — Using Outside Graphics," at the end of this chapter.

Figure 3-19:
You can fill
any shape
with a
bitmap,
repeated
over and
over and
over.

4. **In the Color palette, chose Bitmap from the Type drop-down list and choose your bitmap from the swatches.**

   Flash applies the bitmap as a fill for the selected object. You may need to scale the bitmap. See the section on transforming fills in Chapter 4 for details.

For either method of choosing a bitmap, you can choose the Brush tool (instead of using the Paint Bucket tool) and then brush with the bitmap. Use a brush size that's thick enough to clearly show the bitmap.

Locking a fill

Flash has another trick up its sleeve for gradient or bitmap fills. A *locked fill* looks as though the fill is behind your objects and the objects are just uncovering the fill. As a result, if you use the same fill for several objects, Flash locks the position of the fill across the entire drawing surface instead of fixing the fill individually for each object. Figure 3-20 shows an example of a locked fill. In this figure, you see some windows and portholes filled with a locked bitmap of the sky. Doesn't it look as though the sky is really outside the windows?

Figure 3-20:
When you
lock a fill,
the fill's
pattern
continues
across the
Stage but
appears
only where
you use it.

 To lock a fill, choose the Brush tool or the Paint Bucket tool with a gradient or bitmap fill, as we explain in the two preceding sections. Then click the Lock Fill modifier in the Options section of the Tools panel. Start painting where you want to place the center of the fill and continue to other areas.

Drawing Precisely

If drawing in Flash seems too loosey-goosey to you, you need to know about a few features that can help you draw more precisely. Other programs do offer more precise tools, but Flash might have the tools you need.

The ruler rules

To help you get your bearings, you can choose View⇨Rulers to display the Flash ruler along the top and left side of the Stage, as shown in Figure 3-21.

 To give yourself more room to work while you create drawing objects on the Stage, you can hide the Timeline by choosing Window⇨Timeline. Do the same to display the Timeline again when you need to work with layers or start animating your work.

By default, the ruler is measured in *pixels*. Computer screens are measured by how many pixels they display horizontally and vertically. Pixels are useful for Web site work because Web browsers work with only this unit. A pixel, however, is not a fixed physical size because it depends on the resolution capacity and settings of your screen. You might find it easier to think in inches or millimeters.

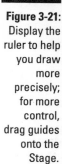

Figure 3-21:
Display the
ruler to help
you draw
more
precisely;
for more
control,
drag guides
onto the
Stage.

You can set the ruler to the unit of measurement that is most helpful to you. Choose Modify➪Document to open the Document Properties dialog box. In the Ruler Units drop-down list, choose one of the units (pixels, inches, points, centimeters, or millimeters) and then click OK.

When the ruler is displayed, lines appear on the top and side rulers whenever you drag an object — either while creating it or editing it. For example, when you drag to create a rectangle, you see a line on each ruler telling you where you started and where you ended up. If you're moving the rectangle, Flash displays two lines on each ruler indicating the outside dimensions of the rectangle. You can easily move the rectangle 1 inch — or 50 pixels — to the left by looking at the lines on the top ruler.

Using guides

Guides help you lay out the Stage more precisely. *Guides* (refer to Figure 3-21) are horizontal and vertical lines that you can use as drawing aids while you work. Don't worry — guides never appear in the published Flash Player file. To use the guides, you must display the rulers, as we describe in the preceding section. To display guides, choose View➪Guides➪Show Guides. But that action simply turns on the Guides feature; you still don't see anything!

To display the guides, you need to drag them from the rulers. Drag from the left ruler to create a vertical guide, and drag from the top ruler to create a horizontal guide.

To customize the guides, choose View➪Guides➪Edit Guides to open the Guides dialog box, where you can choose the guide color or clear all the guides. To force objects to *snap* (attach) to the guides, select the Snap to Guides check box in the Guides dialog box. You can use the Snap Accuracy drop-down list in the Guides dialog box to choose how precisely Flash snaps to the guides. To lock the guides so that they don't move while you work, choose View⇨Guides⇨Lock Guides. To remove an individual guide, drag it back to its vertical or horizontal ruler.

Working with the grid

You can display a grid on the Stage to help you draw more accurately and gauge distances. The grid exists only to guide you — it never appears when the movie is printed or published on a Web site. Simply displaying the grid doesn't constrain your objects to points on the grid. Use the grid by itself when you want a visual guide for drawing, sizing, moving, and laying out the Stage.

To display the grid, choose View⇨Grid⇨Show Grid. Use the same command to hide the grid again. You can set the size of the grid squares and change the color of the grid lines in the Grid dialog box. To open the dialog box, choose View⇨Grid⇨Edit Grid.

You can change the units of measurement used for the grid by choosing Modify⇨Document. In the Modify Document dialog box, select the unit that you want in the Ruler Units drop-down list and click OK.

Snapping turtle

When you want even more precision, you can turn on snapping. *Snapping* tells Flash to snap objects to the intersections on the grid or to other objects. Usually, you want the grid on when you use snapping so that you can see the snap points.

 To turn on snapping, choose the Selection tool and click the Snap modifier in the Options section of the Tools panel or Choose View⇨Snapping⇨Snap to Objects. To snap to the grid, choose View⇨Snapping⇨Snap to Grid. Use the same method to turn snapping off again.

Snapping pulls your cursor to the grid points and to existing objects while you work. You can take advantage of snapping both while drawing new objects and editing existing objects. When you have snapping on and select an object, Flash displays a small, black circle and snaps the circle to the grid points.

Setting snap-to-grid preferences

You can get downright picky about how Flash snaps to grid points. Do you want the end of a line (for example) to always snap, or should it snap only if it's close to a grid point or an existing object? To set your preferences, choose View⇨Grid⇨Edit Grid. In the Snap Accuracy drop-down list, select one of the options, which range from Must Be Close to Always Snap.

Setting snap-to-objects preferences

Because snapping applies to objects as well as grid points, you can separately set how Flash snaps to objects. Choose Edit⇨Preferences (Windows) or Flash⇨Preferences (Mac) and then click the Drawing category. In the Connect Lines drop-down list, select Must Be Close, Normal, or Can Be Distant. Although Flash calls this the Connect Lines setting, it affects rectangles and ovals as well as the lines you draw with the Line and Pencil tools.

This setting also affects how Flash recognizes horizontal and vertical lines and makes them perfectly horizontal or vertical. For example, the Can Be Distant setting adjusts a more angled line than the Must Be Close setting.

Pixel, pixel on the wall

If the grid isn't precise enough, you can snap to pixels. Choose View⇨ Snapping⇨Snap to Pixels to toggle snapping to pixels on and off. If Snap to Pixels is on, Flash automatically displays the pixel grid when you zoom in to 400 percent or higher. With Snap to Pixels on, you can snap all objects that you create or move to the pixel grid.

When Snap to Pixels is on, you can press the C key to temporarily turn off pixel snapping. In the same situation, you can hold down the X key to temporarily hide the pixel grid (but not while you're in the process of drawing).

You can also precisely align existing objects. For more information, see Chapter 4.

The Import Business — Using Outside Graphics

So maybe you're the lazy type — or totally without artistic talent — and you really need help. Flash hasn't given up on you completely. Rather than create your own graphics, you can use the work of others. Although Flash creates vector-based graphics, it can import both bitmap and vector graphic files.

When using others' artwork, be careful about copyright issues. For example, some graphics available on the Web can be used for personal, but not commercial, purposes. Most Web sites that offer graphics for downloading have a written statement explaining how you can use their graphics.

Importing graphics

To import a graphic file, follow these steps:

1. **Choose File⇨Import⇨Import to Stage.**

   The Import dialog box opens.

2. **In the dialog box, locate and choose the file that you want.**

3. **Click Open/Import to open the file.**

   The file appears on the Stage. If the file is a bitmap, it also goes into the Library. To import a graphic file directly into the Library without displaying it on the Stage, choose File⇨Import⇨Import to Library.

A cool feature of Flash is its capability to recognize and import sequences of images. If the image file that you choose in the Import dialog box ends with a number and other files in the same folder have the same name but end with consecutive numbers (for example, an1, an2, and so on), Flash asks whether you want to import the entire sequence of files. Click Yes to import the sequence. Flash imports the images as successive frames on the active layer so that you can use them as the basis for animation. (Chapter 9 explains more about frames and animation.) Table 3-1 provides a list of the types of files you can import into Flash.

Table 3-1	Files That Flash Can Import	
File Type	*Windows*	*Mac*
Adobe Illustrator (.ai) through version 10	X	X
All PostScript, including Acrobat PDF (.eps, .pdf, .ai)	X	X
AutoCAD DXF (.dxf); 2-D only	X	X

File Type	Windows	Mac
Bitmap (.bmp)	X	X*
Enhanced Metafile (.emf)	X	
Flash Player 6/7 (.swf)	X	X
FreeHand (.fh*); versions 7 to 11	X	X
FutureSplash Player (.spl)	X	X
GIF/animated GIF (.gif)	X	X
JPEG (.jpg)	X	X
MacPaint (.pntg)*	X	X
Photoshop (.psd)*	X	X
PICT (.pct, .pic)		X
PNG (.png)	X	X
QuickTime image (.qtif)*	X	X
Silicon Graphics Image (.sgi)*	X	X
Targa (.tga)*	X	X
TIFF (.tif)*	X	X
Windows Metafile (.wmf)	X	

Only if QuickTime 4 or later is installed

You can also simply copy and paste graphics. From the other application, copy the graphic to the Clipboard; then return to Flash and choose Edit⇨ Paste. However, in some cases, you might lose transparency when using this method. See Chapter 13 for details on exporting objects.

Flash CS3 offers new controls for importing Photoshop and Illustrator files. For Photoshop files, you can import the layers intact. When you import the file, a dialog box opens where you can specify which layers you want to. You can convert layers to Flash layers or to keyframes. For each layer decide whether to import the layer with editable layer styles or as (simple) image. For Illustrator files, you can maintain the ability to and paths in Flash. These and other controls give you a huge a power over the result of the import. Choose Edit⇨ Preference PSD File Importer or AI File Importer to set default settings these files. You can change these settings whenever you

Using imported graphics

Vector graphics from any drawing program become a grouped object that you can use like any other Flash object. The .wmf format, which is a Windows vector graphics format, also imports in this way. These formats work especially well when imported into Flash. You can sometimes find .wmf graphics in clip art collections and on the Web.

You can import text from a text editor, and Flash turns it into a Flash text object so that you can edit and format it within Flash. See Chapter 5 for more on text.

When you import a bitmap graphic, you often need to take some steps before you can use the graphic in your Flash file. You can manipulate your graphics in several ways to make them more Flash friendly:

- **Delete the background:** Some files may include a rectangular background you don't want. To get rid of that background, deselect the imported object, select just the rectangular background, and press Delete. If that doesn't work, read on.

- **Ungroup the graphic:** Ungrouping separates grouped elements into individual elements. Ungrouping retains most of the features of your graphic. Select the graphic and choose Modify⇨Ungroup. If you find that you still can't work with your graphic properly, read the next item.

- **Break apart the graphic:** Break imported graphics to separate them into ungrouped, editable elements. Breaking apart is useful for reducing the file size of graphics that you import. Breaking apart converts bitmaps to fills, converts text to letters and outlines, and breaks the link between an OLE (Object Linking and Embedding) embedded object and its source application. In other words, the Break Apart command is a powerful tool. Select the graphic and choose Modify⇨Break Apart. You may have to repeat the process to break the graphic completely apart.

- **Trace the bitmap:** Flash can work magic. If you want total control within Flash, convert a bitmap to a vector graphic.

To trace a bitmap, follow these steps:

1. **Import the bitmap — don't deselect it or perform any other action on it.**

2. **Choose Modify⇨Bitmap⇨Trace Bitmap.**

   The Trace Bitmap dialog box opens.

3. **In the Color Threshold text box, type a number to represent the threshold.**

   The higher the number, the fewer the colors you get in the final vector graphic. For close results, try a value of 10.

4. **In the Minimum Area box, type a number to represent the number of nearby pixels that Flash considers when assigning a color to a pixel.**

   For greatest fidelity, try a value of 1.

5. **In the Curve Fit drop-down list, select an option to represent how smoothly Flash draws the outlines.**

   For the most exact results, select Pixels.

6. **In the Corner Threshold drop-down list, select an option to represent how Flash reproduces sharp edges.**

   For sharpest results, choose Many Corners.

7. **Click OK to close the Trace Bitmap dialog box, and then deselect the graphic to see the result.**

When you import a bitmap graphic, Flash places it in the current movie's Library. For best results, don't delete the original graphic from the Library, even if you have modified it. Flash continues to refer to the graphic after you have converted it to a symbol. (Chapter 2 explains all about the Library. See Chapter 7 for our total wisdom on symbols.)

Whether you created your graphics in Flash or imported them, you probably need to edit them in many ways. Chapter 4 explains the details of editing objects.

Chapter 4

You Are the Object Editor

This chapter tells you all you need to know about editing objects. You can manipulate objects in a zillion ways to suit your artistic fancy. The Flash editing tools can give you precisely the results that you want. Sometimes you need to edit because you made a mistake (rarely, of course), but often editing is just part of the creation process. You might also find that you have to alter imported graphics so that they fit into the scheme of things.

Selecting Objects

Before you can edit any object on the Stage, you need to select it. Flash offers many ways to select objects. After you get the hang of using the Flash selection tools, you'll find them efficient and easy to use.

Selecting with the Selection tool

To select an object, click the black Selection tool and click the object. That sounds pretty basic. But just when you thought it was safe to skip the rest of this section, we add some ifs and buts, so read on.

What is an *object?* If you draw a shape that includes an outline (also called a *line* or a *stroke*) and a fill, such as a filled-in circle, you have two objects — the outline and the fill.

Most of these selection pointers don't work when you use the object-drawing model for creating objects. When you use the object-drawing model to draw an object, such as a rectangle, both the stroke and the fill are considered one object, so you can't select the stroke or the fill individually. (We explain the object-drawing model in Chapter 3.)

Here are some pointers for selecting objects:

✔ **If the object doesn't have an outline and is just a fill,** you're home free. Click the object with the Selection tool, and it's selected.

✔ **If the object has an outline and a fill,** clicking the fill selects only the fill. The outline remains deselected. To select both the fill and the outline, double-click the object.

✔ **To select the entire object,** you can use the Selection tool to create a selection box. Click at one corner and drag to an opposite corner, making sure that the bounding box completely encloses the object or objects that you want to select, as shown in Figure 4-1.

Figure 4-1:
You can create a bounding box by using the Selection tool to select one or more objects.

✔ **To select just an outline,** click the outline with the Selection tool. Still, you never know when an outline is really several objects, like the one in

Figure 4-1, which is made up of several curves. To select the entire outline, double-click it.

✔ **To select several unconnected objects,** select one object, press and hold the Shift key, and select additional objects. When you press Shift, you can add to already selected objects and select as many objects as you want.

To deselect selected objects, click any blank area.

So you're happily drawing away, using the various drawing tools. Then you want to select one of the objects, but you forget to change to the Selection tool. Oops! You draw another object by accident. Immediately choose Edit➪ Undo. Then use one of the Flash shortcuts:

✔ Press the V key to switch to the Selection tool.

✔ To temporarily switch to the Selection tool while you're using another tool, hold Ctrl (Windows) or ⌘ (Mac) while you select an object or objects.

Lassoing your objects

For you rodeo types, you can lasso your objects so that they can't escape. The Lasso tool creates a customized selection area and selects everything inside. Use the Lasso tool when you want to select a number of objects that are near other objects that you want to remain free.

To lasso objects, click the Lasso tool on the Tools panel.

To lasso freehand, make sure that the Polygon Mode modifier (in the Options section of the Tools panel) is not selected. Click anywhere on the Stage and drag around the objects that you want to select. Flash creates a selection area while you drag. Release the mouse button close to where you started it to close the lasso's loop, as shown in Figure 4-2.

Figure 4-2:
Lasso
freehand to
select only
the objects
you want.

You might find that freehand lassoing is hard to control. If you tend to inadvertently cut across objects rather than glide around them, use the Polygon Mode modifier to draw polygons instead — like a lasso with a very stiff rope.

To lasso by using straight lines, follow these steps:

1. **Click to choose the Lasso tool.**

2. **Click the Polygon Mode modifier in the Options section of the Tools panel.**

3. **Click where you want the first line of the polygon to start.**

4. **Click again where you want the first line to end.**

5. **Continue to click, creating line segments as you go.**

6. **Double-click when you finish lassoing the objects.**

Selecting everything in one fell swoop

Suppose that you want to select or deselect all objects at one time. Flash has some handy shortcuts to help you do that:

✔ **To select everything:** Press Ctrl+A (Windows) or ⌘+A (Mac). Or choose Edit➪Select All. The Select All command selects all objects on all layers except for objects on locked or hidden layers. (See Chapter 6 for an explanation of layers.)

✔ **To select everything on one layer:** Click the layer name.

✔ **To deselect everything:** The easiest method is to click off the Stage or on any blank area of the Stage. Alternatively, you can press Ctrl+Shift+A (Windows) or ⌘+Shift+A (Mac). Or choose Edit➪Deselect All. The Deselect All command deselects all objects on all layers.

To lock a group or symbol so that it can't be selected or edited, select the group or symbol and choose Modify➪Arrange➪Lock. To unlock a group or symbol, choose Modify➪Arrange➪Unlock All. (See the section "Getting Grouped," later in this chapter, to find out about groups. Chapter 7 is all about symbols.)

Moving, Copying, and Deleting

The most common changes that you make to objects are to move them, copy them, and delete them. Usually, moving, copying, and deleting are straightforward tasks, but Flash has a few tricks up its sleeve, so keep on truckin'.

Movin' on down the road

Before you can move, you have to select. After you select your object or objects, place the mouse cursor over any selected object until your cursor displays the dreaded four-headed arrow. (Okay, most people don't dread it at all.) Then click and drag to wherever you're going. Press Shift while you drag to constrain the movement to a 45-degree angle.

Moving precisely with Snap Align

When you drag an object, you notice vertical and horizontal dashed lines when your object approaches existing objects. This Snap Align feature displays temporary dashed lines when you move objects to show you when the edges of objects are aligned, both vertically and horizontally, with existing objects.

Snap alignment is great for quickly aligning two objects without using the Align panel. While you drag a selected object, the dashed lines appear when you move an object in alignment with an existing object, as shown in Figure 4-3. You also see the lines when you drag an object close to any edge of the Stage.

Figure 4-3: Snap alignment visually displays alignment between objects while you move them.

To turn on snap alignment (although it is on by default), choose View➪ Snapping➪Snap Align. You see a check mark next to the Snap Align item. Repeat the process to turn off snap alignment.

You can customize your snap alignment settings. Choose View➪Snapping➪ Edit Snapping to open the Edit Snapping dialog box. Then click the Advanced button to expand the dialog box, as shown in Figure 4-4.

In the Edit Snapping dialog box, you can also turn on snap alignment for the centers of objects, for easy centering of objects, by selecting both check boxes in the Center Alignment section.

Flash assumes that a border exists around the edge of the Stage. To change the border width, type a different number in the Stage Border box. To change the accuracy for alignment between objects, type a number in the Horizontal and Vertical boxes in the Object Spacing section of the dialog box. Click OK when you're finished to close the dialog box.

Figure 4-4:
The Edit Snapping dialog box makes your snap alignments snap to your orders.

You can also use the grid and turn on the snapping feature for moving and copying objects. (See Chapter 3 to find out about the grid and snapping.) For example, you can attach one object to another by moving your first object until it snaps to the second, using the small black circle at the cursor as a guide.

The snap align feature aligns objects by their edges. Object snapping aligns objects by their transformation point. See the "Changing the Transformation Point" section, later in this chapter, for more information.

You can also use the four arrow keys on your keyboard to move a selected object or objects. Each press of an arrow key moves the selection one screen pixel in the direction of the arrow. Press Shift plus an arrow key to move the selection by 10 screen pixels.

Moving with the Clipboard

You can move an object by cutting to the Clipboard and pasting if you want to move the object to another layer, scene, file, or application. After you select the object or objects, choose Edit⇨Cut. Alternatively, press Ctrl+X (Windows) or ⌘+X (Mac). Choose another layer or scene or open another file and do one of the following:

- ✔ **To paste the selection in the center of the display:** Choose Edit⇨Paste, or press Ctrl+V (Windows) or ⌘+V (Mac).

- ✔ **To paste the selection in the same position relative to the Stage:** Choose Edit⇨Paste in Place, or press Ctrl+Shift+V (Windows) or ⌘+Shift+V (Mac).

Moving with the Property inspector

If you want to place objects precisely, use the Property inspector. After you select an object or objects, choose Window⇨Properties, as shown in Figure 4-5.

Figure 4-5:
Use the Property inspector to place objects precisely — down to the pixel, if necessary.

Use the X and Y text boxes to specify the location. The X setting specifies horizontal distance; the Y setting specifies vertical distance — both are measured from the top-left corner of the Stage.

Moving with the Info panel

You can also use the Info panel to specify the X and Y positions of objects. Choose Window⇨Info to open the panel, as shown in Figure 4-6. You can use the grid next to the X and Y text boxes to specify if you're measuring either from the upper-left corner or the center of the selection — just click in the desired reference point on the grid. Flash uses the units you specify in the Document Properties dialog box. (See the section in Chapter 3 on drawing precisely for information on setting the units.) Then enter the desired X and Y location in the X and Y text boxes.

Figure 4-6:
The Info panel.

Remember that moving an object onto another existing object on the same layer either joins it (if the objects are the same color) or cuts it out (if the objects are different colors) — unless you drew the object in object-drawing mode or you used a primitive shape (oval or rectangle). See the section in Chapter 3 on mixing and matching shapes for more information.

Aligning objects with the Align panel

The Snap Align feature, as we explain in the "Moving precisely with Snap Align" section, earlier in this chapter, is the quick way to align objects. However, for more options and precision, use the Align panel. The Align panel gives you the tools to line up two or more objects vertically or horizontally and also lets you put equal space between three or more objects. Align and space objects to make your Flash movie look professional, as opposed to something that you might create at 3 a.m. when your vision is too blurry for you to see straight.

To align objects, select the objects and choose Window➪Align to open the Align panel, as shown in Figure 4-7.

Figure 4-7: Use the Align panel to line up and evenly distribute objects.

In the panel, choose the option that you want to align objects or distribute them. For example, you can align objects along their tops, their left sides, or any other direction. You can match the size of objects by using the Match Size buttons or make the spaces between objects the same with the Space buttons. Experiment with the options in this panel until you get the results that you want.

To perfectly center one object on the Stage, select it and open the Align panel. Click the To Stage button. Click both the Align Vertical Center and the Align Horizontal Center buttons. Flash centers the object on the Stage. A quicker way is to cut and paste the object because Flash automatically pastes objects at the center of the display (which is at the middle of the Stage if you haven't panned or scrolled the display).

If you use the To Stage button, be sure to deselect it when you're finished because it can cause unexpected results the next time you use it.

Copying objects

After you spend loads of time creating a cool graphic, you might want to copy it all over the place. The easiest way is to clone it directly by dragging. Just select the object and press Ctrl (Windows) or Option (Mac) while you drag. Flash makes a copy and moves it wherever you drag.

You can also copy objects to the Clipboard. Select an object or objects and choose Edit⇨Copy or press Ctrl+C (Windows) or ⌘+C (Mac). You can paste the selection on the same layer or move it to another layer, scene, or file by using one of these techniques:

- ✔ **To paste the selection in the center of the display:** Choose Edit⇨Paste, or press Ctrl+V (Windows) or ⌘+V (Mac).

- ✔ **To paste the selection in the same position relative to the Stage:** Choose Edit⇨Paste in Place. If you're on the same layer, scene, and file, you now have two copies, one on top of the other. The new object is selected, so you can immediately drag it to a new location.

Because Flash pastes objects from the Clipboard to the exact center of the display, cutting and pasting is a great technique for centering objects on top of each other. For example, if you want to create two concentric circles, one on top of the other, create the circles in separate locations. Cut and paste the larger circle first, and the smaller circle second. You now have perfect concentric circles, and you can move them together to the desired location. This technique works only if the Stage is at the center of your display — that is, if you haven't scrolled the display.

When you paste a new object, be sure to move the new object right away if it covers an existing object on the same layer. If you deselect the new object, it either joins the existing object (if the objects are the same color) or cuts it out (if they're different colors). Of course, that might be your intention. See the section in Chapter 3 on mixing and matching shapes for more information, including how to avoid this joining and cutout behavior.

Makin' objects go away

Making objects go away is easy. Just select them and press Delete or Backspace (Clear on the Mac).

Making Shapes More Shapely

Suppose that you created an object and now you want to tweak it a bit. Flash has many techniques to help you perfect your artwork, and you can modify both lines and fills.

Reshaping shapes and outlines

The Selection tool can do more than select objects — it can also reshape them — as long as you didn't create them by using the object-drawing model or a primitive shape. When you reshape with the Selection tool, you do *not* select the object.

 To reshape an outline or a fill, choose the Selection tool and place the mouse cursor near the object or on the edge of the object:

- ✔ If you see a corner next to the cursor, you can move, lengthen, or shorten an end point, as shown on the left side of Figure 4-8.

- ✔ If you see a curve next to the cursor, you can reshape a curve, as shown on the right side of in Figure 4-8.

Figure 4-8: The Selection tool modifies end points and curves.

Click and drag in the desired direction. Flash temporarily displays a black drag line to show you what the result will look like when you release the mouse button. If you don't like the result, choose Edit⇨Undo — or press Ctrl+Z (Windows) or ⌘+Z (Mac) — and try again.

As with drawing, you might find it helpful to increase the zoom factor. Try editing at 200 or 400 percent.

Using the Subselect tool

You can use the Subselect tool to reshape individual strokes or fills created by using the Pen, Pencil, Brush, Line, Oval, or Rectangle tools. When you use the Subselect tool, you move *anchor points,* which are small circles that appear on the object. To use Subselect, follow these steps:

1. **Choose the Subselect tool (the white arrow in the Tools panel).**

2. **Click the stroke (outline) or fill to display the anchor points.**

3. **Drag the anchor points to modify the shape.**

4. **To change the direction of a curve, click any anchor point to display tangent lines and drag the tangent line handles (the little dots at the ends of the tangent lines).**

The tangent lines indicate the direction of the curve. See the section in Chapter 3 on drawing curves with the Pen tool for information on anchor points and tangent lines.

If you use the Subselect tool to click a graphic and points aren't displayed on its edges, you might have grouped the graphic, as we describe later in this chapter, or you may have created it with the object-drawing model, or maybe you didn't create it with the Pen, Pencil, Brush, Line, Oval, or Rectangle tool. Try choosing Modify⇨Ungroup or Modify⇨Break Apart and then using the Subselect tool.

You can also delete anchor points. Flash reshapes the shape without that anchor point. Select the object with the Subselect tool, select an anchor point, and press Delete or Backspace.

When you use the Subselect tool on an oval or rectangle primitive, you can only change its parametric properties. For example, you can change the corner radius of a primitive rectangle. For a primitive oval, you can change the inner radius, start angle, and end angle.

Adjusting curves with the Pen tool

You can make adjustments to objects that you drew with the Pen tool. Click the Pen tool and then click the object. You now see anchor points along the curves and lines. Here's what you can do:

- ✔ **Add an anchor point:** Hover the cursor over any place that doesn't already have one. You see a little plus sign. Just click wherever you want to add the point. Alternatively, click and hold the Pen tool to display the flyout and choose the Add Anchor Point tool.

- ✔ **Delete an anchor point:** Hover the cursor over any anchor point. You see a little minus sign. Click the anchor point. Alternatively, click and hold the Pen tool to display the flyout and choose the Delete Anchor Point tool.

- ✔ **Convert an anchor point:** Anchor points can be curve points or corner points. To convert from one to the other, click and hold the Pen tool to display the flyout and choose the Convert Anchor Point tool. Then click any object you created with the Pen tool and click an anchor point. If you're converting to a curve point, immediately drag to position the tangent line handles.

Freely transforming and distorting shapes

For way-cool distortions and reshapings, use the Free Transform tool, with its Distort & Envelope options. The Free Transform tool can work its magic on objects, groups, instances, or text blocks. In addition to its special ability to create distortions, it's flexible enough to move, rotate, scale, and skew objects. Flash has other tools that rotate, scale, and skew — we cover them later in this chapter.

 To use the Free Transform tool, select an object, symbol instance, group, or text block. (See Chapter 7 for more about symbols. We discuss groups later in this chapter.) Click the Free Transform tool in the Tools panel. The object displays a bounding box with handles and a *transformation point,* shown as a circle at the center of the bounding box, as shown in Figure 4-9.

Figure 4-9:
We love
the Free
Transform
tool!

You can perform the following commonly used transformations on the selected object:

 ✔ **Move:** Place the cursor on the object itself; when you see the four-headed arrow, click and drag to move the selected object.

 ✔ **Set the center for rotation and scaling:** Place the cursor on the transformation point; when you see the small circle, you can drag the circle at the center of the bounding box to move the transformation point. The *transformation point* is the base point used for the current rotation or scaling operation.

✔ **Rotate:** Place the cursor just outside any corner handle; when you see the circular arrow, drag the object to rotate it around the transformation point.

Press Shift while you drag to constrain the rotation to 45-degree increments. Press Alt (Windows) or Option (Mac) while you drag to rotate around the diagonally opposite corner from your cursor.

 ✔ **Scale both dimensions:** Place the cursor on any corner handle; when you see the broken, two-headed arrow, drag inward or outward. Press Shift while you drag to ensure that the object is scaled proportionally without being distorted.

You can select as many objects as you want, and Flash scales them all. When you select more than one object, Flash places the handles around an imaginary bounding box that encompasses all the objects. Sometimes you might not get exactly the result you want with this method, so check carefully.

✔ **Scale one dimension:** Place the cursor on any side handle; when you see the two-headed arrow, drag inward or outward to scale in the direction that you're dragging.

✔ **Skew:** Place the cursor anywhere on the bounding box except the handles; when you see the parallel lines, drag in any direction. (We cover skewing in more detail in the "Getting skewy" section, later in this chapter.)

In the following sections, you find out about the more exciting transformations that you can create with the Free Transform tool.

Tapering objects

You can turn a square into a trapezoid by tapering. When you *taper,* you use the Free Transform tool to drag a corner handle. While you drag, the adjoining corner moves an equal distance in the opposite direction, as shown in Figure 4-10. You can taper any shape except rectangle and oval primitives — but adjoining corners are always simultaneously stretched in opposite directions.

Figure 4-10:
Tapering turns a square into a trapezoid.

To taper, press Ctrl+Shift (Windows) or ⌘+Shift (Mac) while you drag on a corner handle of the bounding box. You can also use the Distort option of the Free Transform tool: Click the Distort button and press Shift while you drag any corner handle. (This technique is ideal for people who have trouble pressing both Shift and Ctrl or ⌘ at the same time.)

Distorting objects

For even weirder effects, you can *distort* shapes (objects) — but not primitives, symbols, symbol instances, text, or groups. When you distort an object, you change the shape of the bounding box, and the shape gets stretched in the same amount and direction as the bounding box, as shown in Figure 4-11.

Figure 4-11:
Drag the
bounding
box into a
new shape;
the object
follows suit.

To distort shapes with the Free Transform tool, press Ctrl (Windows) or ⌘ (Mac) and drag either a corner or a side handle on the bounding box. To use the menu, choose Modify➪Transform➪Distort.

Stretching the envelope

You can make even more-refined changes in the shape of the bounding box by using the Envelope command. With this option, the bounding box takes on editing points like you see when you use the Pen tool. As you drag the points, tangent lines appear, as shown in Figure 4-12.

Figure 4-12:
The oval is
like taffy
when you
push the
envelope.

To use the Envelope command, select an object — a shape — but not a symbol, instance, text, or group. Choose Modify➪Transform➪Envelope. Drag any of the points in or out and then drag the end of any of the tangent lines to change the direction of the curve.

Instead of using the menu, click the Free Transform button on the Tools palette and then click the Envelope button in the Options area.

To end a free transformation, click anywhere off the selected object.

Straightening lines and curving curves

Just like you can straighten and smooth strokes by using the Straighten and Smooth modifiers of the Pencil tool, respectively, you can straighten and smooth strokes and fills of existing objects. (See Chapter 3 for more about the Pencil tool.)

You can activate the Straighten and Smooth modifiers repeatedly and watch while Flash slightly reshapes your strokes or fills each time. Eventually, Flash reaches a point where it can't smooth or straighten anymore.

Choose Edit⇨Preferences and then choose the Drawing category to adjust how Flash calculates the straightening and smoothing. Change the Smooth Curves and Recognize Shapes settings.

To straighten a stroke, first select the object. With the Selection tool active, click the Straighten Modifier button in the Options section of the Tools panel. Flash straightens out curves and recognizes shapes, if appropriate.

To smooth a curve, first select the object. With the Selection tool active, click the Smooth Modifier button in the Options section of the Tools panel. Smooth softens curves and reduces the number of segments that create a curve.

Modifying line endings

You can use *line caps* to customize the ends of lines that you draw. (See the section on setting the stroke type in Chapter 3 for details on caps.) You can change existing line caps. You can also choose a join style for the meeting point of two lines. Select a line and display the Property inspector (choose Window⇨Properties⇨Properties). Select a new option in the Cap or Join drop-down list. You'll notice the effect more with wide lines.

Optimizing curves

Flash offers a technique for curves called optimizing. *Optimizing* reduces the number of individual elements in a curve, thus reducing the size of your file and resulting in faster download times on your Web site. You can optimize repeatedly, just as you can with smoothing and straightening. Optimizing works best for complex art created with many lines and curves. The visual result is somewhat like smoothing but might be subtler.

To optimize, select the object or objects and choose Modify⇨Shape⇨Optimize. Flash opens the Optimize Curves dialog box, as shown in Figure 4-13.

As you can see in the dialog box, you can choose how much you want Flash to optimize curves. If you mangle your work too much on the first try, undo it and try again with a different setting. You can generally leave the other settings as they are. For a slower but more thorough optimization, mark the Use Multiple Passes (Slower) check box. And it's helpful to see the totals message that shows you how many curves Flash cut out and the percentage of optimization that number represents, so select the Show Totals Message check box. Click OK to optimize.

Figure 4-13:
Optimize to reduce the number of curves.

Be careful to check the results after optimizing. Flash sometimes eliminates small objects that you may want to retain. If you don't like the results of optimizing, choose Edit➪Undo.

Expanding and contracting filled shapes

You can expand and contract shapes. Expanding and contracting works best on shapes with no stroke (outline) because Flash deletes the outline when executing the command. If you want to expand or contract a shape with a stroke, scale it. We explain scaling later in this chapter in the "Scaling, scaling . . ." section. The advantage of expanding and contracting is that you can specify a change in size in terms of pixels.

To expand or contract a shape, select it and choose Modify➪Shape➪Expand Fill. The Expand Fill dialog box appears, as shown in Figure 4-14. Type a number in the Distance box, using the units that you have set for the entire movie. By default, movies are measured in pixels. (See the section in Chapter 3 on drawing precisely for the details on setting movie units.)

Figure 4-14:
The Expand Fill dialog box.

To expand a shape, select the Expand option. To contract a shape, select the Inset option. Then click OK.

Softening edges

Softening edges is another shape-modification tool. You can soften edges of a shape to get a graphic to look like you created it in a bitmap image editor, such as Adobe Photoshop. Figure 4-15 shows some text before and after its edges are softened. Note that adding softened edges can increase your file size.

Figure 4-15:
Soften the edges of objects to create cool effects.

You can create this effect by breaking apart the text twice before softening the edges. We discuss breaking apart objects later in this chapter; Chapter 5 explains more specifically about breaking apart text into editable shapes.

To soften edges, select the object or objects and choose Modify➪Shape➪ Soften Fill Edges. Flash opens the Soften Fill Edges dialog box, as shown in Figure 4-16.

Figure 4-16:
The Soften Fill Edges dialog box softens up your boss . . . uh, graphics.

To soften edges, follow these steps:

1. Set the distance, which is the width of the softened edge.

The distance is measured in pixels unless you have changed the document units. (See the section in Chapter 3 on drawing precisely for information on setting the units in the Document Properties dialog box.)

2. **Select the number of steps, which means the number of curves that Flash uses to create the softened edge.**

   Try the Flash default first and change it if you don't like the result. You can increase the number to get a smoother effect.

3. **Select the Expand option to create the softened edge outside the shape or the Inset option to create the softened edge within the shape.**

4. **Click OK to create the softened edge.**

   Your shape is still selected, so click anywhere outside it to see the result. If you don't like it, press Ctrl+Z (Windows) or ⌘+Z (Mac) and try again using different options.

You can create soft edges also by using gradients that blend into the Stage color or with partially transparent colors. Chapter 3 explains more about using colors. Flash also has a blur filter that you can use on text, movie clip symbols, and buttons. Chapter 7 describes filters.

Converting lines to fills

Flash offers lots of great ways to fill a shape — for example, with gradients and bitmap images. But what about those boring strokes or outlines? You can convert lines to fills and make them fun, fun, fun. (See Chapter 3 for an explanation of fills, including gradients and bitmap images.)

Mind you, there's not much point in converting a line to a fill if it's so thin that no one would ever see a fill in it. Figure 4-17 shows some waves we created by using the Pencil tool and a 10-point-wide line. We converted the line to a fill and then used the Paint Bucket tool to fill the line with a gradient.

Figure 4-17:
Change the line to a fill and use the Paint Bucket tool to change the fill.

To convert a line to a fill, select the line and choose Modify⇨Shape⇨Convert Lines to Fills. You don't see any visible difference when you deselect the line, but now you can change the fill to anything you want.

Transforming Fills

The Gradient Transform tool offers a unique way to edit gradient and bitmap fills. You can perform the following changes to a fill:

- ✔ Move its center point
- ✔ Change its width or height
- ✔ Rotate it
- ✔ Scale it
- ✔ Tile it
- ✔ Change the radius of a radial gradient
- ✔ Move the focus of a radial gradient
- ✔ Skew (slant) it

From this list, you can see that there's no point in fiddling with solid fills. They would look the same no matter what direction, size, or scale they were. (See the section in Chapter 3 on colors for colorful coverage of gradient and bitmap fills.)

 To edit a fill, choose the Gradient Transform tool. This tool is well hidden; you'll find it by clicking the Free Transform tool on the Tools toolbar to open a sub-menu. Click any gradient or bitmap fill. Flash places an editing boundary and editing handles around the fill, as shown in Figure 4-18. The editing boundary varies with the type of fill — bitmap, linear gradient, or radial gradient.

Figure 4-18:
The Gradient Transform tool places an editing boundary around the fill.

After you have a fill with an editing boundary, you're ready to go ahead and fiddle with the fills. Here's how to make changes:

- ✔ **Move the center of a fill:** Drag the center point, marked by a small circle at the center of the fill. You can move a center fill to move the center of a radial gradient, move the stripes of a linear gradient, or place a bitmap off center.

✔ **Move the focal point of a fill:** Drag the focal point, marked by a triangle along the center line of a radial gradient. Moving the focal point can make the apparent direction of light move from side to side in a radial gradient with a lightly colored center.

✔ **Change the width of a fill:** Drag the square handle on one side of the editing boundary. To change the height of a fill, drag the handle on the bottom of the editing boundary. If a fill doesn't have one of these handles, you can't edit the fill that way. Changing the width of a linear fill that's perpendicular to the direction of its stripes is the same as scaling the fill — the stripes get wider (or narrower).

✔ **Rotate a fill:** Drag the rotation handle, which is a small circle just outside the corner of the editing boundary. On a radial gradient, use the bottom of the three handles on the circumference of the boundary. Figure 4-19 shows a linear gradient rotated 45 degrees.

When rotating a fill, you can press and hold the Shift key while you drag to constrain the rotation of the fill to multiples of 45 degrees.

Figure 4-19:
Rotate a
linear fill to
create
diagonal
fills.

✔ **Scale a bitmap fill:** Drag the square handle at the corner of the editing boundary — inward to scale down and outward to scale up. To scale a circular gradient, drag the middle circular handle on the editing boundary. Figure 4-20 shows a bitmap gradient at its original size and scaled down. Flash tiles the bitmap if you scale down significantly.

If you scale down a bitmap so that you see many tiles, the next time that you want to edit the bitmap, Flash places an editing boundary around each tile so that you have to edit each one individually. That could take a long time! If you want to edit a bitmap in several ways, save scaling down for last.

Figure 4-20:
You can scale a bitmap fill to make it larger or smaller.

> ✔ **Skew (slant) a fill:** Drag one of the rhombus-shaped handles on the top or side of the editing boundary. You can skew only if the fill is a bitmap. Skewing is different from rotating because the bitmap is distorted. Figure 4-21 shows an example of a skewed bitmap.

Figure 4-21:
You can skew a bitmap fill for really weird results.

Later in this chapter, we explain how to rotate, scale, and skew entire objects.

Transferring Properties

You can use the Eyedropper tool to copy outline and fill properties from one object to another. (See the section on bitmap fills in Chapter 3 for instructions on using the Eyedropper tool to create bitmap fills.)

To transfer properties, follow these steps:

1. **Click the Eyedropper tool.**

2. **Select an outline or a fill.**

   If you select an outline, Flash activates the Ink Bottle tool. If you select a fill, Flash activates the Paint Bucket tool and turns on the Lock Fill modifier. (For more information on the Lock Fill modifier, see the section in Chapter 3 that discusses locking a fill.)

3. **Click another outline or fill.**

   Flash transfers the properties of the original outline or fill to the new object.

Finding and Replacing Objects

One way to change an object is to change its properties. You can find graphics objects by color or bitmap and then replace the color or bitmap. For example, you can easily change every blue fill or stroke to red if your Web color scheme changes.

You can find and replace according to color, bitmap, text, and font (Chapter 5); sound; or video (Chapter 11). You can also find and replace symbols (Chapter 7).

To find and replace objects, choose Edit⇨Find and Replace to open the Find and Replace dialog box, as shown in Figure 4-22.

Figure 4-22:
The Find
and Replace
dialog box
finds lost
sheep and
can change
their color.

In the Search In drop-down list, choose to search in the entire Flash movie document or only in the current scene. (See Chapter 9 for a full explanation of scenes.)

In the For drop-down list, select what you want to find: text, font, color, symbol, sound, video, or bitmap. The dialog box changes according to the choice you make. For example, to find and replace a color, follow these steps:

1. **Click the top Color button and select a color that exists in your document.**

2. **Click the Replace with Color button and select the replacement color that you want.**

3. **Mark one or more of the three check boxes — Fills, Strokes, and Text — to define what type of objects you want to find.**

4. **Click Find Next to find the next occurrence of the color or click Find All to find every object with that color.**

5. **Click Replace to replace the color of the currently selected object or click Replace All to replace the color of every object.**

6. **Click the Close button of the dialog box to return to your movie.**

Find and Replace is an efficient way to make mass changes of color, text, symbols, sound, video, or bitmaps.

Transforming Objects

Earlier in this chapter, in the "Freely transforming and distorting shapes" section, we explain how you can use the Free Transform tool to reshape objects. You can do many of the same tasks by using the Transform command.

To scale, rotate, and flip objects, choose Modify⇨Transform and then choose one of the submenu commands. When you scale, rotate, or skew an object, Flash kindly remembers the object's qualities so that you can return the object to the state it was in before you fiddled around with it.

Scaling, scaling . . .

Most of the time, scaling by using the Free Transform tool (as we describe earlier in this chapter) is the easiest, fastest way to go. When you want more precision, however, scale the selected object in the Property inspector. (Choose Window⇨Properties⇨Properties. Change the value in the W (width) box, the H (height) box, or both.

To make sure that the proportions of the object stay the same, click the padlock next to the W and H text boxes so that it looks locked. When you change either the W or the H text box, the other box adjusts proportionally.

For yet more scaling options, select an object and choose Window⇨Transform to open the Transform panel, as shown in Figure 4-23.

Figure 4-23:
The Transform panel lets you scale, rotate, and skew objects with great precision.

The controls in the Transform panel work only if an object is selected. If you forgot to select an object, you don't need to close the panel; just select an object

To scale the selected object or objects, type a scale value between 1 and 1000 in the Width (left) text box. Any value less than 100 reduces the size of the object, so a value of 10 creates a new object at 10 percent of the original object, and a value of 1000 multiplies the object's size by a factor of 10. Then press Enter or Return. By default, the Constrain check box is selected, so changing the width also changes the height.

To make a copy of an object at a scaled size, click the Copy button (the left button in the lower-right corner of the panel) instead of pressing Enter or Return. The copy appears on top of the original object but is selected so that you can move it immediately if you want. Figure 4-24 shows an example of how you can use scaling and copying together to create the impression of objects at varying distances. After you make the copy, just move it to a new location. When you're finished, click the Close button of the Transform panel to close it.

Figure 4-24:
The brain creatures are attacking!

'Round and 'round and 'round we rotate

Most of the time, you can probably use the Free Transform tool to rotate objects, as we explain earlier in this chapter. If you want to rotate something by an exact number of degrees, such as 20 degrees, use the Transform panel. Select the object and choose Window⇨Transform to open the Transform panel (refer to Figure 4-23).

To rotate the selected object or objects clockwise, type a value between 1 and 359. To rotate counterclockwise, type a value between −1 and −359. Then press Enter or Return.

If you don't like the results, click the Reset button (the right button in the lower-right corner of the panel) and try again.

To make a copy of an object at a different rotation, click Copy (the left button in the lower-right corner of the panel). The copy appears on top of the original object but is selected so that you can immediately move it.

If you want to rotate a section by 90 degrees by using the menu, do the following:

✔ **To rotate right (clockwise):** Choose Modify⇨Transform⇨Rotate 90° CW.

✔ **To rotate left (counterclockwise):** Choose Modify⇨Transform⇨Rotate 90° CCW.

When you rotate, Flash rotates the object around its center. To rotate around a different point on the object, you can convert the object to a group or symbol and change its *registration point,* the point on an object that Flash references when rotating. See the section later in this chapter on changing the registration point.

You can create groovy circular patterns by using the rotate and copy functions, as shown in Figure 4-25. Unless the object you're working with is completely symmetrical, you need to change the registration point.

Figure 4-25: By rotating and copying an object at the same time, you can add flower power to your Web site.

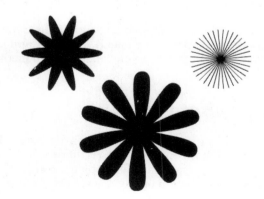

Getting skewy

Skewing is a variation of rotating. Rather than rotate an entire object, you slant it horizontally, vertically, or both. Skewing a square creates a rhombus (diamond). In Figure 4-26, you see a simple arrow before and after skewing.

Figure 4-26:
A skewed arrow looks like it's in a hurry.

The easiest way to skew objects is by using the Free Transform tool. Just select an object, choose the Free Transform tool, and drag along one of the sides of the boundary.

Usually, you can eyeball the skewing process. If you want precision or to combine skewing with scaling, use the Transform panel. Select the object and choose Window➪Transform to open the Transform panel. To skew the selected object or objects, click the Skew option.

Use the left box to skew horizontally. To skew clockwise, type a value between 1 and 89. To skew counterclockwise, type a value between –1 and –89. Then press Enter or Return.

To skew vertically, type a value in the right box. Positive values skew clockwise, and negative values skew counterclockwise. If that sounds confusing, just try something out and see whether you like it. If you don't, click Reset (the right button in the lower-right corner of the panel) and try again.

To make a copy of an object at a skewed angle, click the Copy button (the left button in the lower-right corner of the panel). The copy appears on top of the original object but is selected so that you can move it immediately.

Flippety, floppety

Flipping reverses an object so that you have a mirror image of your original object. You can flip both horizontally (left to right or vice versa) and vertically (up to down or vice versa). Flash flips objects about their center so that they stay in their original position on the Stage.

Figure 4-27 shows a curlicue design in its original form, flipped horizontally, and flipped vertically. If you flip an object horizontally and then vertically, you end up with an object that has been mirrored in both directions.

Original

Flipped vertically

Flipped horizontally

Flipped both horizontally and vertically

Figure 4-27:
You can flip objects vertically, horizontally, or both.

To flip an object, select it and choose Modify⇨Transform⇨Flip Vertical or Flip Horizontal. To flip an object in both directions, flip it in one direction and then in the other.

To create symmetrical objects, you need to change the object's registration point from the center to one side or corner. Later in this chapter, in the "Changing the Transformation Point" section, we explain how to use flipping to create symmetrical objects.

Combining Objects

You can combine objects in various ways to create new and more interesting shapes. You can perform the following actions:

✔ **Union:** Combines two objects into one object. The effect is similar to grouping objects, which we cover in the next section of this chapter. (In fact, you can use the Ungroup command to separate the objects again.) Combining two objects puts a boundary around them, like the boundary you see when you use the object-drawing model. To combine objects, select them and choose Modify⇨Combine Objects⇨Union.

See the section on keeping objects safe and secure in Chapter 3 for more information on how to use the object-drawing model.

- ✔ **Intersect:** Creates a shape that is the intersection of two overlapping shapes; the shape that remains is from the top object. However, this works only with objects that you create by using the object-drawing model. (We explain the object-drawing model in Chapter 3.)

- ✔ **Punch:** Removes the object on top from an object beneath it. This operation requires two objects that you drew by using the object-drawing model. If you put a smaller circle on top of a larger circle, the Punch feature is like punching a hole in the larger circle (but it doesn't hurt). Select two overlapping objects and choose Modify➪Combine Objects➪Punch.

- ✔ **Crop:** Creates a shape that is the intersection of two overlapping shapes that you created by using the object-drawing model; the shape that remains is from the bottom object. Select two overlapping objects and choose Modify➪Combine Objects➪Crop.

Getting Grouped

When you know how to create objects, you can get carried away and create so many objects on the Stage that they're hard to manage. You might want to move a number of objects at once. Although you can select them all and move them, that technique might not be enough. For example, you might inadvertently leave behind one piece and discover that it's hard to move that piece in the same way that you moved the rest. That's why Flash provides *grouping*. You select multiple objects and group them once. From then on, you can select them with one click. If you move one of the grouped objects, the rest come along for the ride.

In Flash, grouping has an additional advantage: If you put objects on top of each other, they merge if they're the same color or create cutouts if they're different colors, unless you draw them using the object-drawing model or a primitive shape. One way that you can avoid such friendly behavior and keep the integrity of objects is to group them. (You can also put them on different layers, as we explain in Chapter 6, or turn them into symbols, as we explain in Chapter 7.)

Grouping objects is easy. Select them and choose Modify➪Group. You shortcut types can press Ctrl+G (Windows) or ⌘+G (Mac). When you group objects and select them, all the objects are surrounded by one blue selection border.

After you group objects, you can ungroup them at any time. Select the group and choose Modify➪Ungroup. You can also break apart a group. See the discussion later in this chapter on breaking apart objects.

If you want to edit an element of the group without ungrouping first, Flash lets you do so. To edit without ungrouping, follow these steps:

1. **Using the Selection tool, double-click any object in the group.**

 Flash dims other objects on the Stage and displays the Group symbol above the layer list.

2. **Edit any of the group components.**

3. **Return to regular editing mode.**

   Double-click any blank area on the Stage with the Selection tool, click the current Scene symbol to the left of the Group symbol, or click the Back arrow to the left of the scene symbol. You can also choose Edit➪ Edit All.

Changing the Transformation Point

When Flash rotates or scales an object, it uses a *transformation point* as a reference. This point is generally the center of the object. For positioning and certain transformations of lines and shapes, Flash uses the upper-left corner. You might find that the point Flash uses isn't suitable for your needs. For example, you might want to rotate an object around its lower-left corner. For a single rotation or scaling of a simple graphic object, use the Free Transform tool and drag the transformation point — the little circle — to the desired location. If you deselect and reselect the object, you see that the circle has returned to its original central position.

Changing the transformation point is useful when you want to create symmetrical objects by flipping. To use flipping to create symmetrical objects, follow these steps:

1. **Select the object.**

 2. **Click the Free Transform tool and drag the transformation point to one edge of the object, from where you want to mirror the object.**

3. **Choose Edit➪Copy to copy the object to the Clipboard.**

4. **Choose Edit➪Paste in Place to paste the copy on top of the original.**

5. **Choose Modify➪Transform➪Flip Vertical or Flip Horizontal.**

   You see your original and the copy. The copy has been flipped so that it's a mirror image of its original.

6. **(Optional) To create a four-way symmetrical object, group the original and mirrored objects (as we explain in the previous section), and change the transformation point to one side of the combined group. Then repeat Steps 3, 4, and 5, this time flipping in the other direction.**

Figure 4-28 shows a weird creature created by copying, changing the transformation point, and then flipping.

Figure 4-28:
Create scary, symmetrical creatures by manipulating the transformation point.

Groups, symbol instances, text, and bitmaps have a *registration point,* which Flash uses to animate and transform these objects. When you use the Free Transform tool to move the circle on these objects, the circle keeps its position even after you deselect and reselect it. To move an object's registration point, follow these steps:

1. **Select a group, symbol instance, text object, or bitmap.**

2. **Click the Free Transform tool.**

   Flash displays a small circle at the transformation point.

3. **Drag the circle to the desired location.**

4. **Click anywhere else on the Stage to hide the registration point.**

To return the registration point to its original position, double-click it.

Breaking Apart Objects

With the Break Apart command, you can break apart text, groups, instances of symbols, and bitmaps into separate objects that you can edit individually. To break apart one of these types of objects, select it and choose Modify⇨ Break Apart.

What happens to your objects when you break them apart? Do they splatter all over the Stage? Here's what happens when you break apart the following objects:

✔ **Text:** Flash divides the words into individual letters, each one a separate object. If you use the Break Apart command a second time on one of the letters, the letter becomes a shape that you can modify like any other shape.

Break apart blocks of text and then use the Distribute to Layers command to animate individual letters. See Chapter 5 for more information about text and Chapter 6 for more on layers.

- ✔ **Shapes created in the object-drawing model:** The shape loses its object-drawing model status, as if you had drawn it without using the object-drawing model.

- ✔ **Groups:** Flash breaks up the group into its component parts. The result is the same as ungrouping.

- ✔ **Instances of symbols:** The symbol becomes a shape. (Symbols are covered fully in Chapter 7.)

- ✔ **Bitmaps:** Flash converts the bitmap to a fill. You can then erase parts of it.

Establishing Order on the Stage

Flash stacks objects in the order in which you create them. If you draw a circle and then an overlapping square, the square looks like it's on top of the circle because you created it more recently.

If you place an object on top of another object, the two objects become one if they're the same color. If they're different colors, the top object cuts out the underlying object.

One exception is if you use the object-drawing model to draw the objects. Oval and rectangle primitives are another exception. A different way to keep the integrity of objects is by grouping them or turning them into symbols. (Symbols are covered in Chapter 7.) Groups, object-drawing model shapes, primitives, and symbols are always stacked on top of regular objects. Therefore, to move objects above existing groups or symbols, you need to group them or convert them to a symbol. You might also need to turn some imported graphics into a symbol or group before you can move them in the stack.

If you draw an object and it immediately disappears beneath another object, it's often because you tried to draw the object on top of a group, primitive, or symbol. Group the object or change it to a symbol if it must be on top.

Another way to reorder objects is to put them on different layers. You can then reorder the objects by reordering their layers. (See Chapter 6 for the details.)

As long as you have objects that can maintain their integrity, you can change their stacking order. You can move them up or down in the stack or from the top or bottom of the stack — all within the same layer. To change the stacking order of an object, select the object and choose Modify➪Arrange. Then choose one of these options:

- ✔ **Bring to Front:** Brings the selected object to the tippy-top of the stack.
- ✔ **Bring Forward:** Brings the selected object up one level.
- ✔ **Send Backward:** Moves the selected object down one level.
- ✔ **Send to Back:** Sends the selected object down, down, down to the bottom of the stack.

Figure 4-29 shows an example of two objects stacked in different ways.

Figure 4-29:
The big, old-fashioned bitmap star and the small, up-and-coming vector star vying to be in front.

Undoing, Redoing, and Reusing

Sometimes you do something in Flash and decide that it's a mistake. Oops! For this situation, you can undo actions. You can even redo the actions that you undid. Finally, if you're environmentally conscious, you can reuse earlier actions to avoid wasting any more of your energy.

Undoing actions

To undo your last action, choose Edit➪Undo or press Ctrl+Z (Windows) or ⌘+Z (Mac). You can continue this process for a very long time. This is the familiar — and default — type of undo, and Flash calls it *document-level undo*.

To set the number of undo steps that Flash remembers, follow these steps:

1. Choose Edit➪Preferences (Windows) or Flash➪Preferences (Mac).

   The Preferences dialog box appears.

2. **Click the General category.**

3. **In the Undo drop-down list, select Document-level Undo.**

4. **In the text box just below the Undo drop-down list, enter the number of undo actions you want Flash to track.**

   The default is 100, and the maximum is 300.

Later in this chapter, in the "Reusing actions with the History panel" section, we explain another way to undo actions.

Redoing actions

Maybe you were right the first time. After you undo an action, suppose that you want to redo it. You can do that, too. To redo actions, choose Edit⇨Redo or press Ctrl+Y (Windows) or ⌘+Y (Mac).

If you haven't undone anything, you can use the same command (and keyboard shortcut) to repeat your last action, in which case it's called the Repeat command.

Using object-level undo and redo

Generally, undos and redos apply to every action you take in Flash. But sometimes you might find object-level undo and redo more helpful.

Object-level undo applies only to editing symbols, which we cover in Chapter 7. When you use object-level undo and redo, Flash remembers actions by symbol. Therefore, when you're editing a symbol, using the Undo command applies only to changes that you made to that symbol, even though you have made other changes to your movie in the meantime. If you use a lot of symbols, object-level undo offers you more flexibility. Object-level redo works in the same way.

You can use only one type of undo and redo at a time. To use object-level undo and redo, choose Edit⇨Preferences (Windows) or Flash⇨Preferences (Mac). Select the General category. In the Undo drop-down list, select Object-level Undo. You see a message explaining that switching from one type of undo to another will delete your current undo history. Flash can keep track of only one stream at a time. Click OK to close the message and click OK again to close the Preferences dialog box.

Deleting your current history is not generally a problem. But if you are in the middle of a long, complicated experiment and might need to undo many steps, choose another time to switch.

Reusing actions with the History panel

If you make several changes to an object and would like to make the same changes to other objects, you can save time and increase accuracy by saving and reusing the steps for the operations that you perform. Flash tracks the steps in the History panel.

The History panel lists every command that you perform in Flash during one session. When you save and close the file, the history list isn't saved for the next time. To open the History panel, choose Window➪Other Panels➪History, as shown in Figure 4-30. The shortcut is Ctrl+F10 (Windows) or ⌘+F10 (Mac).

Figure 4-30:
The History
panel keeps
track of
everything
you do.

You can use the History panel to troubleshoot recent steps, repeat steps, undo steps, or save steps as commands for future use.

By default, Flash records up to 100 steps in the History panel. You can change the number of steps recorded by choosing Edit➪Preferences (Windows) or Flash➪Preferences (Mac) to open the Preferences dialog box. On the General tab, change the value for Undo levels. Valid settings are from 2–300. If you want to be able to go back and save earlier steps as commands, you probably need to record more than 100 steps.

Undoing steps

One of the simplest things that you can do in the History panel is to undo one or more operations. You can also undo operations by choosing Edit➪Undo, but you can see more specific descriptions of the operation. For example, the Move operation appears in the History panel as Move {x:0, y:-103.6}. To view the specifics, right-click (Windows) or Control+click (Mac) any history item and choose View➪Arguments in Panel. With these details, you can more easily predict the result of undoing an operation.

You undo steps by using the slider on the left side of the History panel:

- ✔ **Undo the last operation that you performed:** Drag the slider up one step.

- ✔ **Undo several steps:** Drag the slider to the step above the first step that you want to undo. For example, if you want to undo three steps, drag the slider up three steps — it's now next to the step previous to the one that you undid. This is the last step that has still been executed. You can also click to the left of a step. The slider scrolls up to that step and undoes all the later steps.

When you undo a step, the step appears dimmed in the History panel.

Replaying a step

You can repeat any command from any time during a Flash session. For example, if you filled an object with a specific color, you can fill another object with the same color, even if you have performed other operations in the meantime.

To replay a step, click the step itself (not the left side of the step above the slider) in the History panel. Then click the Replay button. If you want to replay the step on a different object, first select that object, and then click the Replay button.

Copying steps

You might want to keep a list of certain steps or use them in a different movie. Select one or more steps in the History panel and click the Copy Selected Steps to the Clipboard button.

To use these steps in another Flash movie, open the movie and choose Edit⇨ Paste. To apply the steps to an object, select the object first.

Flash copies the step or steps as JavaScript code. Therefore, when you paste the step or steps into a word processor or text editor, you see the JavaScript code, which looks more complex than the step listed in the History panel. Usually, you can figure out what it means, even if you don't know JavaScript. For example, `Fill Color: '#0000ff'` appears as `fl.getDocumentDOM().setFillColor('#0000ff');`.

Saving commands

If you want to save a step or set of steps to use the next time that you open the movie, save a command. Saving a command is even useful if you want to re-execute some steps several times later in the same session because scrolling back to find the exact steps that you want to reuse can be time consuming.

To save a command, follow these steps:

1. **In the History panel, select the steps that you want to save.**

   You can drag along the step names (not along the left side, where the slider is). You can also use the usual methods of selecting multiple objects in a list — click the first object, press Shift and click the last, or press and hold Ctrl (Windows) or ⌘ (Mac) and click each step that you want to select.

To see more details about the commands, click the Options menu button (in the upper-right corner of the panel), and choose View ⇨ Arguments in Panel.

2. **Click the Save Selected Steps as a Command button.**

   This button is in the lower-right corner of the History panel. The Save As Command dialog box opens.

3. **Enter a name for the command.**

   You can simply summarize the steps. For example, you might name a command `fill blue, rotate 90`.

4. **Click OK to close the dialog box.**

When you save a command, it appears on the Commands menu. The menu in Figure 4-31 shows the command `fill blue, rotate 90`, which fills any selected shape with blue and rotates the shape 90 degrees. To use that command, you simply select a shape and then choose Commands⇨Fill Blue, Rotate 90. Presto! It's all finished. As you can imagine, you can combine complex commands and save them to automate the authoring process of creating Flash movies.

Figure 4-31:
Saved
commands
appear
on the
Commands
menu.

Clearing the History panel

If you don't want the History panel to record everything that you do — perhaps it makes you feel as if you don't have any privacy left anymore — you can clear the history list. Clearing the history list doesn't undo any steps. To clear the History panel, click the Options menu button at the upper-right corner of the panel, and choose Clear History. Then click Yes.

For good Commands menu housekeeping, choose Commands⇨Manage Saved Commands to open the Manage Saved Commands dialog box. In this dialog box, you can delete or rename a command. When you're finished, click OK to close the Manage Saved Commands dialog box.

Chapter 5

What's Your Type?

In This Chapter

▶ Creating, editing, and formatting text

▶ Using cool text effects

*W*e assume that occasionally you want to say something on your Web site, so this chapter covers text in all its forms and formats. You can use Flash to create the text for your Web pages if you want (although you don't have to). But if you want flashy text effects, Flash is definitely the way to go.

Typography is the art or process of arranging text on a page, and basically that's what this chapter is all about. Many graphics programs call text *type*. We use the words interchangeably here — we don't care what you call it.

Presenting Your Text

The majority of text on most Web sites is formatted by using HyperText Markup Language (HTML) coding that sets the font, size, and color of the text. Using HTML code is ideal for larger amounts of text because the HTML is simple to code and loads quickly.

For smaller amounts of text that you want to have special formatting or effects, Flash offers more options than HTML. Of course, if you want to animate your text, you can use Flash. For example, an animated logo usually includes not only the graphic art but also the name of the organization, which is, of course, text.

Here are some innovative things you can do with text:

✔ Rotate, scale, skew, or flip text without losing the ability to edit the text.

✔ Turn text into shapes and modify them any way you want. However, after you turn text into shapes, you can't edit the text characters by simply typing. Figure 5-1 shows some text that was modified in this way.

✔ Create transparent type.

✔ Create hyperlinked text that sends the user's browser to another Web page when the user clicks the text.

✔ Enable viewers to control some aspect of the movie by entering text in a text box

✔ Load text, such as sports scores or current weather, dynamically from a server.

Figure 5-1:
You can turn text into a shape and edit it to your heart's content.

Spring

Creating text

Creating text in Flash is simple. Follow these steps:

T

1. **Click the Text tool on the Tools panel.**

2. **Specify the text starting point on the Stage.**

   • To specify the width of the text, click the Stage in the left edge where you want your text to start and drag to the right until you have the width that you want. Flash places a square block handle in the upper-right corner of the text block.

   • To create a text block that expands while you type, just click the Stage at the desired starting point. Flash places a round block handle in the upper-right corner of the text block.

3. **Start typing.**

   To force a return to the left margin after you type one or more lines, press Enter or Return. Otherwise, if you specified a width, the text wraps to the next line when it fills up that width.

4. **After you finish typing, click anywhere off the Stage to deselect the text.**

Congratulations — you've just said something! We hope it was worthwhile.

Editing text

After you type text, it never fails that you want to change it. Editing text is easy in Flash, but first you have to select the text. Here are the selection techniques:

- ✔ **To edit an entire text block:** Click the Selection tool and then click the text. Flash places a selection border around the text. You can move, rotate, and scale all the text in a text block this way, just as you would with any other object. For example, you can use the Free Transform tool to scale the text.

- ✔ **To edit the content of the text itself:** Double-click the text with the Selection tool active. (Or click the Text tool and then click the text.) Flash switches to the Text tool automatically and places the text cursor where you clicked or double-clicked the text, more or less.

- ✔ **To select a character or characters individually:** Click the Text tool and drag across one or more characters. Do this when you want to edit only those characters.

- ✔ **To select a word:** Click the Text tool and double-click any word to select it.

- ✔ **To select a string of words or block of text:** Click the Text tool, click at the beginning of the text you want to select, and then Shift+click at the end of the desired selection.

- ✔ **To select all the text in a text block:** Click the Text tool, click in a text block, and then press Ctrl+A (Windows) or ⌘+A (Mac).

To change the content of the text, select the characters or words that you want to change, as we explain in the preceding list. Type to replace the selected text. Other text-editing techniques are the same as in your word processor. For example, you can press the Delete key to delete characters to the right of the text cursor or press the Backspace key (Windows) or Delete key (Mac) to delete characters to the left of the cursor.

Checking spelling

Spell checking works like the spell checker in your word processor, so you'll probably find it easy to use. This feature shows Adobe's commitment to reducing typos on the Web!

The first step is to set up the parameters for spell checking. Choose Text⇨ Spelling Setup to open the Spelling Setup dialog box, as shown in Figure 5-2. If the Check Spelling item isn't available on the Text menu, you need to open this dialog box and close it again.

The Spelling Setup dialog box has three sections:

- **Document Options:** Choose which parts of a movie that you want to check. For example, you may not want to spell check symbol and bitmap names.

- **Personal Dictionary:** You can change the location of the file that holds words that you add to the dictionary. Click the Edit Personal Dictionary button to add words directly. Otherwise, you add words when you are checking the spelling of specific text.

- **Checking Options:** Set options that define how spell checking works. For example, you can choose to ignore words in uppercase or with numbers.

You can also choose which dictionaries you want to use in the Dictionaries list. When you're finished, click OK to return to your movie. You're now ready to check spelling.

To check spelling, you can select text if you want to check just that text or leave all the text deselected to check the entire movie. Choose Text➪Check Spelling to open the Check Spelling dialog box, as shown in Figure 5-3.

Figure 5-3:
The Check
Spelling
dialog box.

If you selected text, Flash checks that text first and then asks whether you want to check the rest of the document. Click Yes to continue or No to end the spell check. For each misspelled word, you can do one of the following:

- ✔ Choose one of the suggestions and click Change to change that instance of the word.

- ✔ Choose one of the suggestions and click Change All to change all instances of the word.

- ✔ Click Ignore to go to the next misspelled word.

- ✔ Click Ignore All to ignore all instances of that word and go to the next misspelled word.

- ✔ Click Delete to delete the word.

- ✔ Click Add to Personal to add the word to the Personal Dictionary so that it won't appear as misspelled in the future.

To finish spell checking, click Close. You may see a message asking whether you want to start from the beginning of the document. Click Yes to do so. When spell checking is complete, you see a Spelling Check Completed message. Click OK to return to your movie.

Finding and replacing text

If you need to change all instances of the word *big* to *large,* for example, you're in luck. The Find and Replace feature comes to the rescue. In Chapter 4, we discuss how to find and replace color. Here we explain the steps (which are similar) for finding and replacing text:

1. **Choose Edit➪Find and Replace.**

   The Find and Replace dialog box appears.

2. **In the For drop-down list, choose Text.**

3. **In the Search in Text box, enter the text that you want to find.**

4. **In the Replace with Text box, enter the replacement text.**

5. **(Optional) Enable one or more of the three check boxes on the left to define what type of text you want to find: Whole Word, Match Case, and Regular Expressions.**

Regular expressions are formulas you use to locate specific text patterns in a text string. Regular expressions are beyond the scope of this book, but you can find a good tutorial at `www.regular-expressions.info/tutorial.html`.

6. **(Optional) Select one or more of the check boxes on the right to define where you want Flash to look for text.**

   - **Text Field Contents** searches text objects.

   - **Frames/Layers/Parameters** looks for frame labels and scene names (see Chapter 9), layer names (see Chapter 6), and component parameters (see Chapter 10).

   - **Strings in ActionScript** looks for text strings in ActionScript.

   - **ActionScript** looks for all ActionScript code.

7. **To edit each object on the Stage, select the Live Edit check box.**

8. **Click the appropriate button as needed:**

   - Click **Find Next** to find the next occurrence of the text.

   - Click **Find All** to find all occurrences of the text.

   - Click **Replace** to replace the currently selected object.

   - Click **Replace All** to replace all instances of that text.

When Flash finds the specified text, the box at the bottom of the Find and Replace dialog box displays its location and type along with the entire text so that you can see the context of the text you're replacing. You can resize the Find and Replace dialog box as well as the columns in the list of found items. When you're finished, click the Close button in the Find and Replace dialog box to return to your movie.

Setting character attributes

Of course, you don't always want to use the Flash default font and size for your Web site. Boring! You can set the attributes before you start typing or edit the attributes of existing text. To edit existing text, double-click the text block and then select the characters or words you want to format. To either set or edit attributes of text, choose Window⇨Properties⇨Properties to open the Property inspector.

Figure 5-4 shows the expanded Property inspector when some static text is selected. (Static text is normal text that just sits there and looks pretty.) The Property inspector changes slightly depending on which type of text you select. See "Creating input and dynamic text," later in this chapter, for more information about the various types of text.

Setting the font, font size, and font style

Usually, the first step in formatting text is selecting a font. To select a font for your text, simply choose one in the Font drop-down list in the Property inspector. Flash changes the font of the selected text.

You can change the font characteristics that control specific properties of the font, such as size and style:

✔ **To select a font size:** Type a font size in the text box or drag the slider to the desired value.

✔ **To select a font style:** Click Bold, Italic, or both. Flash applies the style to the selected text.

You can also select fonts, font sizes, and font styles directly from the Text menu. This menu is devoted entirely to helping you format your text.

Figure 5-4: The Property inspector is the place to liven up your text.

You can create vertical text, where letters flow downward rather than across. Okay, so the purpose is mostly for languages that are often written vertically, such as Chinese. Vertical text must be static and can go from either left to right or right to left. (We explain static, input, and dynamic text later in this chapter.) Figure 5-5 shows some vertical text.

D
o
w
n

w
e

g
o

Figure 5-5: Try vertical text for a change of direction.

To create vertical text, follow the instructions for creating normal text, but before clicking the Stage to place the text, select the Vertical, Left to Right or the Vertical, Right to Left option from the Change Orientation of Text button on the Property inspector (refer to Figure 5-4).

Specifying text color

Black is the Flash default color, but you have lots of additional options. The first concern is that the text is legible against its background. For example, yellow text looks great in front of a black background, but it's almost invisible against white. Also consider that text is often unreadable in front of complex graphic images, no matter what the color.

To set text color, select the text that you want to change if you've already created the text. In the Property inspector, click the Text Color button (refer to Figure 5-4) to open the color palette, and select a color. (For more information on colors, see Chapter 3.) If you haven't created the text yet, choose the Text tool, select the color, and then create the text. Click anywhere else to deselect the text so that you can see the new color.

To create transparent (or semitransparent) text, select the text and choose Window⇨Color Mixer to open the Color Mixer panel. In the Alpha text box, type a new Alpha percentage and press Enter or Return. A 100-percent alpha setting results in opaque text. Text with a 0-percent alpha setting is completely transparent. A setting of 50 percent results in text that looks somewhat transparent but is still visible. You can also set the transparency after you choose the Text tool but before you type anything.

Adjusting kerning and tracking

Kerning reduces the spacing between certain letters, such as *V* and *A*. Because of the diagonal line on the *A* and *V,* without kerning, the letters might look too far apart. Figure 5-6 shows an example of text with and without kerning.

Figure 5-6:
The first line uses kerning; the second line doesn't.

VACATION
VACATION

By default, Flash uses a font's kerning information, which is embedded in the font definition. Sometimes with smaller font sizes, kerning can make text hard to read, so you can turn it off. Without kerning, text takes up slightly more space. To turn off kerning, select the characters that you want to adjust and clear the Auto Kern check box in the Property inspector.

You can adjust the spacing between all the letters, a process called *tracking*. Perhaps you need the text to fit into a tight space or you want to stretch it out without changing the font size. Figure 5-7 shows some text with various tracking settings. To change tracking in the Property inspector, type a value in the Letter Spacing text box or drag the slider bar to the desired value.

Figure 5-7:
Stretched and condensed text.

Split the scene and leave it clean	**Split the scene and leave it clean**
Split the scene and leave it clean	Split the scene and leave it clean

Making text selectable

Do you want users to be able to select text and copy it to the Clipboard? If so, you should make the text selectable. To do so, select the text (naturally), and click the Selectable button in the Property inspector. Deselect this button to prevent users from selecting text.

Hyperlinking text

You can create text that acts as a link to other Web pages. Flash underlines linked text, following the global convention on Web sites. To create text with a hyperlink, follow these steps:

1. **Select the text.**

2. **Choose Window⇨Properties⇨Properties.**

   The Property inspector appears.

3. **In the URL text box, type the URL (Uniform Resource Locator, or Web address) of the Web page that you want to use.**

   When you complete the URL, a dotted line appears below the text to indicate that it's a hyperlink. When your Flash movie appears on a Web site (or even when you test the movie on your own computer), clicking the hyperlinked text displays the URL you specified.

   The dotted line below the text doesn't appear when you test or publish the movie.

4. **In the Target drop-down list, choose one of the window targets for the URL.**

   The two most commonly used are `_blank`, which opens the URL in a new browser window, and `_self`, opens the URL in the same window and is the default.

Getting the best text appearance

Flash usually stores outlines of the text in your movie when you publish or export it, so your audience will see your fonts in your movie even if they're not installed on your audience's computer. However, not all fonts displayed in Flash can be stored as outlines when you publish or export your movie.

To test whether Flash can export a font with a movie, choose View⇨Preview Mode⇨Antialias Text. If the text appears jagged, Flash cannot export the text with the movie.

Anti-aliasing is a method of making text look smoother — reducing the jaggies that sometimes create stairlike lines on text. Anti-aliasing is especially helpful for smaller font sizes. If you're worried about the jaggies, try choosing the Anti-alias for Readability option in the Font Rendering Method drop-down list in the Property inspector.

The way that your type looks on the Stage is only an approximation of how it will look when you publish or export your movie. To see a more accurate rendering of how your type will look when you publish or export it, view your movie by choosing Control➪Test Movie.

If you want to use type in a font that Flash can't export, you can break apart the type into shapes, as we describe at the end of this chapter. However, this option increases the size of your movie file and makes the text no longer editable.

If you'd like a space-saving alternative to storing your text as outlines in your Flash movie, you can use Flash's three *device fonts* that the Flash Player always converts to the closest available font on the local computer:

- ✔ _sans: A sans serif font similar to Arial (Windows) and Helvetica (Mac).

- ✔ _serif: A serif font similar to Times New Roman (Windows) and Times (Mac).

- ✔ _typewriter: A font that looks like it has been typed on a typewriter. (Are you old enough to remember what that is?) It's similar to Courier New (Windows) and Courier (Mac).

When you use device fonts, your resulting published movies are smaller, so download time is shorter. With device fonts, your text also might be more legible in text sizes below 10 points. To use device fonts, specify one of the device fonts and then deselect the text. Then select Use Device Fonts in the Font Rendering Method drop-down list in the Property inspector. (This setting applies only to horizontal static text.) When you publish your movie, select the Device Font check box on the HTML tab (Windows only) of the Publish Settings dialog box. Chapter 13 tells you more about publishing settings.

Setting up paragraph formats

You can set paragraph attributes such as alignment, margins, indents, and line spacing. Use these settings whenever you type more than one line of text. (You are getting long winded, aren't you!)

Setting text alignment

You can align text along the left margin or right margin of the text block. You can also center text. You can create an even edge along both margins, called *full justification* or *justified text*. By default, text is left aligned.

To align text, select it and display the Property inspector (choose Window➪ Properties➪Properties to open the Property inspector (refer to Figure 5-4) or click its title bar if its collapsed). Then click the Align Left, Align Center, Align Right, or Justify button.

Setting margins and indents

The *margin* is the space between the text block border and your text. By default, the margin is 0 pixels. You can increase the margin to guarantee some space around the text. You can set only the left and right margins (not the top or bottom ones).

To set the left margin, select the paragraph and click the Edit Format Options button in the Property inspector to open the Format Options dialog box, as shown in Figure 5-8. Type a value in the Left Margin text box or click the arrow and use the slider to specify a value. Then press Tab or Enter (Windows) or Return (Mac) to see the result right away. To set the right margin, use the Right Margin text box.

Figure 5-8:
Use the
Format
Options
dialog box
to whip your
text into
shape.

Format Options

Indent: 0 px
Line spacing: 2 pt
Left margin: 0 px
Right margin: 0 px

OK
Cancel

Indentation creates an indented first line. It's equivalent to placing a tab at the beginning of a paragraph. (Remember your sixth-grade teacher who told you to always start each paragraph with an indent?) To indent the first line, select the paragraph and type a value in the Indent text box in the Format Options dialog box or click the arrow and drag the slider bar.

Specifying line spacing

Line spacing determines the space between lines. Flash measures line spacing in points ($\frac{1}{72}$ of an inch) because font size is measured in points. For example, if your text is 18 points high and you want to double-space the lines, use a line spacing of 18 points so that a space exactly one line high exists between each line of text. To set the line spacing, select the paragraph, click the Edit Format Options button in the Property inspector to open the Format Options dialog box, and type a value in the Line Spacing text box or click the arrow and drag the slider bar. Press Tab or Enter (Windows) or Return (Mac).

Click OK (Windows) or Done (Mac) when you're finished with the Format Options dialog box.

Flash remembers paragraph properties from movie to movie. When you change paragraph properties for one movie, the properties rear their ugly heads in your next movie. If your text automatically indents at the beginning of paragraphs or comes out double-spaced, check out the Format Options dialog box.

Creating input and dynamic text

You can create three kinds of text in Flash:

- **Static text:** Regular text that doesn't change or do anything, although you can animate it.

- **Input text:** Text that viewers can enter, as in a text box. You can use input text, for example, for forms and surveys or to interactively create values that affect the movie.

- **Dynamic text:** Text that changes based on data coming from an external source (such as a Web server), an internal source (such as ActionScript), or input text in the movie. Dynamic text is often used for data such as sports scores, current weather, and stock prices.

To choose the type of text, use the Text Type drop-down list in the Property inspector. (It's a good thing the Flash creators didn't call it the Type Type drop-down list.)

Several text settings in the Property inspector apply only to input or dynamic text (and therefore don't appear if you use static text):

- **Instance Name:** This text box appears under the Text Type drop-down list when you select input or dynamic text. An instance name identifies the text object so that you can refer to the text in ActionScript. (See Chapter 10 for the scoop on ActionScript.) Instance names are handy because with input or dynamic text, the contents of the text field can change while your Flash movie is playing; but if you give your text field an instance name, you can always refer to it in your ActionScript, even though you don't know the contents of the text field ahead of time.

- **Line Type:** Defines how text is displayed.

  - **Multiline** displays the text in multiple lines.

  - **Single Line** displays the text as one line.

- **Multiline No Wrap** displays text in multiple lines that break only if the last character is a breaking character, such as Enter (Windows) or Return (Mac).

- **Password** displays asterisks.

✔ **Render Text as HTML:** Preserves formatting, such as fonts and hyperlinks, with certain HTML tags. You need to create the formatting by using ActionScript.

✔ **Show Border Around Text:** Displays a black border and white background for the text field. This border helps users know where to enter text in an input text block.

✔ **Variable:** Enables you to enter a variable name for the text field. You can use variable names similarly to instance names, but your options are more limited.

✔ **Maximum Characters:** Specifies the maximum allowable characters that users can input in a text box. For example, you could limit a zip code to five digits.

✔ **Embed:** Opens the Character Embedding dialog box, where you can select options for embedding font outlines. Choose one or more of the options (such as Uppercase and Lowercase). You can press Ctrl (Windows) or ⌘ (Mac) and click several options. Or click the Don't Embed button if you don't want to embed font outlines. When you're finished, click OK. The font outlines you chose are exported when you publish the movie to ensure a smooth appearance. Limiting the font outlines you export helps to make the file size smaller.

Creating Cool Text Effects

Flash wouldn't be worth its salt if you couldn't create some flashy effects with text. You can manipulate text in several ways:

✔ **Transform text just like other objects.** In other words, you can scale, rotate, skew, and flip type. Figure 5-9 shows an example of skewed text.

✔ **Convert type to shapes by breaking it apart.** Select the text and choose Modify➪Break Apart. The first time that you use the Break Apart command, words are broken up into individual letters. Use this command again, and letters are turned into shapes so that you can then edit the text in the same way that you edit shapes. However, you can no longer edit the text as text, so check your words before converting them! (Refer to Figure 5-1 for an example of text turned into shapes.)

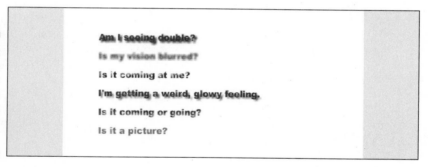

Figure 5-9:
This text is
skewed to
match the
angles of
the skewed
rectangles,
creating a
3-D effect.

Grapple with enigmas and master our mysteries!

Grow your brain with our brain teasers!
Unravel baffling riddles, and cut your teeth on curious conundrums!

Crack our fascinating puzzles and decipher our codes!

✔ **Apply special graphic effects to text, called *filters*.** Select the text and click the Filters tab of the Property inspector. Click the Plus (+) icon and choose one (or more) of the following filters: Drop Shadow, Blur, Glow, Bevel, Gradient Glow, Gradient Blur, or Adjust Color. Each filter has a number of settings that you can adjust to get just the right effect. Figure 5-10 shows these effects in the order listed here.

Figure 5-10:
Filters are
shortcuts to
cool looking
(but not
necessarily
legible) text.

Am I seeing double?

Is my vision blurred?

Is it coming at me?

I'm getting a weird, glowy feeling.

Is it coming or going?

Is it a picture?

You can animate text to your heart's content. To animate text, you usually break it apart so that you can move letters individually. You can then use the Modify➪Timeline➪Distribute to Layers command to put each letter on a separate layer. After that, you can animate each letter. (See Chapter 9 for the details on animation.)

Chapter 6

Layering It On

· ·

· ·

*F*lash lets you organize objects on the Stage in layers. *Layers* keep objects separated from each other. Flash either combines or creates cutouts when two objects overlap if you don't use the object-drawing model (as we explain in Chapter 3). But by placing the two objects on different layers, you avoid this behavior yet retain the appearance of overlapping objects. In addition, by rearranging your layers, you can easily rearrange the order of your objects — that is, which objects appear to be on top and which appear to be on the bottom.

Layers are also necessary for error-free animation. To move one object across the Stage in front of other objects, such as a background, you need to put the object on its own layer. If you want to animate several objects across the Stage, put each object on a separate layer.

You can hide layers. Flash doesn't display objects on hidden layers. Hidden layers are great for hiding some objects temporarily while you figure out what to do with all the rest of the stuff on the Stage.

Finally, layers are great places to put sounds and ActionScript code. For example, you can name a layer *Music* and put your music there. Then you can easily find the music if you want to change it. Layers provide a great way to keep the various components of your movie organized. (See Chapter 10 to find out more about ActionScript.) In this chapter, you get all the information you need to use layers effectively.

Creating Layers

Flash lists layers at the left side of the Timeline. New movies start out with one layer, named Layer 1. You can, and should, change the name of this layer and new layers to something more descriptive, as shown in Figure 6-1.

Figure 6-1:
Flash
keeps you
organized
by listing all
your layers.

If you're the organized type, you should think about your animation in advance and decide which layers you need. However, animations often don't work out the way you plan, and you might find yourself creating layers after you've created objects. Either way, your method for creating layers is the same.

To create a layer, click the Insert Layer button, at the bottom of the layer list (or choose Insert➪Timeline➪Layer). Flash displays the new layer above the active layer and makes the new layer active. To name the layer, double-click its name, type something meaningful, and then press Enter (Windows) or Return (Mac).

Using layers

Any object that you create goes on the active layer. You can tell which layer is active because it's highlighted and has a pencil icon next to its name (refer to the Resources layer in Figure 6-1). To change the active layer, just click any inactive layer's name. You can also click anywhere in the layer's row on the Timeline.

To help make your work easier, Flash automatically changes the active layer to match any object that you select. So, if you're working on a layer that you named *Text* and select a shape on a layer that you named *Shapes,* Flash automatically activates the Shapes layer. Any new objects that you create are now on the Shapes layer. Of course, if that's not the layer you want, you can switch to any other layer at any time by clicking its name.

If you click a layer to make it active, Flash selects all the objects on that layer that exist in the current frame. (Even if a layer is already active, you can click its name to select all of its objects.) This feature is helpful for working with all the objects on a layer and discovering which objects a layer contains. If you don't want the objects selected, click anywhere that there's not an object.

Because in many cases, each animated object needs to be on its own layer, you often need to distribute objects to their own layers. Select the objects and choose Modify⇨Timeline⇨Distribute to Layers. This command saves lots of work!

Changing layer states

Besides being active or inactive, layers have three states that determine how objects on that layer function or look; you can show or hide a layer, lock or unlock it, or display objects on a layer as outlines. Use these states to help you organize how you work. The more objects and more layers that you have, the more you need to use these layer states.

Above the layer list, on the right side, you see an eye, a lock, and a box. These aren't mystical symbols. The following sections explain what they are and how to use them.

Show/Hide

Use the Show/Hide icon (as shown at the left) to hide all objects on a layer (also called *hiding a layer*), reducing clutter while you work. To hide a layer, click below the Show/Hide icon on that layer's row. Flash places a red X under the eye icon. All the objects on that layer disappear. Keep in mind, however, that you can't work on a hidden layer. Click the X to get them back again. To hide (or show) all the objects on the Stage, click the Show/Hide icon itself.

Don't forget hidden layers because they do appear in your published movies.

To show or hide all layers *except* one, Alt+click (Windows) or Option+click (Mac) below the Show/Hide icon on that layer's row. You can also right-click (Windows) or Control+click (Mac) on a layer and choose Hide Others in the shortcut menu.

Lock/Unlock

Use Lock/Unlock to prevent objects from being edited by locking their layers. Lock a layer when you want to avoid changing objects by mistake. To lock a layer, click below the lock icon on that layer's row. Flash places a lock in the layer's row. Click the lock to unlock the layer again. The lock disappears, and you can now edit objects on that layer. You can lock *all* layers by clicking the lock icon directly. Click the lock icon again to unlock all the layers.

To lock or unlock all layers *except* one layer, Alt+click (Windows) or Option+click (Mac) below the lock icon on that layer's row. You can also right-click (Windows) or Control+click (Mac) a layer and choose Lock Others in the shortcut menu.

Outlines

 Use Outlines to display objects as outlines of different colors. *Outlines* help you see which layer objects are on because each layer uses a different color, as shown in Figure 6-2. (Okay, you can't *really* see the colors in a black-and-white book, but you can probably tell by the variations in gray that the objects aren't all the same color.) To display outlines, click below the Outlines (box) icon on that layer's row. Flash puts a colored box in the layer's row, and all objects on that layer are now shown as outlines in that color. (Text is still filled in, however.) Click the box to display objects on that layer normally. To display *all* layers as outlines, click the Outlines icon directly. Click it again to see your objects as normal. You can work on outlined layers, but all new objects appear as outlines, so telling how they appear when displayed normally is difficult.

Figure 6-2:
All the objects on the Stage are shown as outlines except for text that hasn't been broken apart.

Thanks to Polly Wickstrom, www.tomatotree.com, for this Flash movie.

In Figure 6-2, some text has been broken apart for animation and is therefore outlined like other objects.

To display all layers as outlines except for one layer, Alt+click (Windows) or Option+click (Mac) below the Outline icon on that layer's row.

Getting Those Layers Right

Good layer housekeeping can help keep you sane. Delete layers that you no longer need. Rename layers when their content changes. Copy layers with their entire contents rather than re-create them from scratch. Here we explain how to keep control over layers.

You can select more than one layer at a time. To select a contiguous group, click the first layer, hold down the Shift key, and click the last layer in the group. To select more than one layer when they're not all together in a group, click the first layer, press and hold Ctrl (Windows) or ⌘ (Mac), and click any additional layers that you want to select.

Deleting layers

When you work, you might find that a layer no longer has any objects. It's a layer without a purpose in life, so delete it. Select the layer and click the Trash can icon at the bottom of the layer list. You can also drag the layer to the Trash can.

When you delete a layer, you delete everything on the layer. However, some objects on a layer might not be visible, because you see only what exists on the Stage in the current frame. For example, if you introduce a circle in Frame 15 of a layer named Circle but you're in Frame 1, you don't see that circle. Deleting the Circle layer, however, deletes the circle, although you can't see it. (We discuss frames in more detail in Chapter 9.)

To check for objects on a layer, right-click the layer and choose Hide Others in the shortcut menu. Click the first frame on the Timeline and press Enter (Windows) or Return (Mac) to run any existing animation. Objects on that layer appear during the animation if they exist.

Copying layers

You can copy a layer, along with its entire contents, throughout all frames. If you've created a great bouncing ball and now want two balls, copy the layer. You can then modify the position of the second ball throughout the Timeline without having to re-create the ball itself. Now you have two bouncing balls.

To copy and paste a layer, follow these steps:

1. **Click the layer name to select the layer.**
2. **Choose Edit➪Timeline➪Copy Frames.**
3. **Click the Insert Layer button to create a new layer.**
4. **Click the new layer to make it active.**
5. **Choose Edit➪Timeline➪Paste Frames.**

Renaming layers

Rename a layer whenever you want. By default, Flash names layers Layer 1, Layer 2, and so on. When you use a layer, rename it to reflect its contents. To rename a layer, double-click the layer name and type a new name. Then press Enter (Windows) or Return (Mac).

Reordering layers

In Chapter 4, we explain how to change the order of objects on the Stage when they're on the same layer. When objects are on different layers, a new rule applies. The order of the layers indicates the display order of objects on the Stage. Therefore, objects on the uppermost layer in the list are always on top, objects on the second layer appear one level down, and so on. Objects on the last layer in the list appear on the bottom level of the Stage, behind everything else.

In fact, a simple and effective way to control object stacking is to put objects on different layers and then move the layers higher or lower in the layer list. To move a layer, just click and drag it within the layer list to the desired position. Figure 6-3 shows an example before and after moving a layer. The ball and the oval are on different layers. The left image looks a little odd, but when you reorder the layers, their objects are reordered as well, and you can then see a ball and its shadow.

Figure 6-3:
By changing the order of the layers, you change the order of the objects on those layers.

Changing the layer order can help you more easily select and edit objects that are covered up by other objects. Simply drag the layer to the top of the list, and the objects in that list then appear on top. When you finish editing the objects, drag the layer back to its original location.

Organizing layers

Sometimes layers can get out of hand. You might have several layers with sounds on them or several layers for each animation. Tame those layers by putting them into *folders*. Instant organization! For example, you can create a Sounds folder and folders for each animation group.

 To create a folder, click the Insert Layer Folder icon below the layer list. You see a new folder just above the active layer. Name the folder in the same way that you name a layer: Double-click it, type the name, and press Enter (Windows) or Return (Mac). You can distinguish a folder from a layer by its folder icon.

After you have a folder, you fill it up with layers by dragging layers into it. Click and drag a layer onto the folder's row, and then release the mouse button. At the same time, the layer's name becomes indented so that you can easily tell that it's in a folder, as shown in Figure 6-4.

Figure 6-4:
Put your
layers into
folders
to keep
yourself
organized.

You can even put folders in folders. Just drag one folder into another. A folder within a folder is a *nested* folder, and the folder that it's in is the *parent* folder.

Here are some other things that you can do with folders:

- ✔ **Remove a folder from a folder:** Drag the nested folder above its parent folder.

- ✔ **Remove a layer from a folder:** Drag the layer above the folder name or to another location where it doesn't darken a folder.

- ✔ **Collapse or expand individual folders:** Click the folder's arrow, at the left of its icon.

✔ **Expand or collapse all folders:** Right-click (Windows) or Control+click (Mac) and choose Expand All Folders or Collapse All Folders in the shortcut menu.

✔ **Hide or lock an entire folder and its layers:** You can hide or lock a folder just like you hide or lock a layer. (See the "Changing layer states" section, earlier in this chapter.) Click below the eye (Show/Hide) or lock (Lock/Unlock) icon on the folder's row.

✔ **Reorder folders:** You can change the order of folders, which automatically changes the order of the layers that they contain. Just drag any folder up or down. For more information, see the preceding section.

✔ **Copy the contents of a folder to another folder:** To make a quick shortcut for copying layers and their contents, you can copy folders. Collapse the folder and click the folder name. Choose Edit⇨Timeline⇨Copy Frames. Create a new folder. With the new folder active, choose Edit⇨Timeline⇨ Paste Frames.

✔ **Delete folders:** You can delete folders in the same way you delete layers. Select the folder and click the Trash can icon.

Deleting a folder deletes all layers in the folder and everything on those layers. Luckily, Flash warns you before you take the plunge.

Modifying layer properties

You can use the Layer Properties dialog box, shown in Figure 6-5, to change certain layer properties, such as the color used for the layer's outlines and the layer height. Most settings, however, are easily accessible from the layer list. Select a layer (or a folder) and choose Modify⇨Timeline⇨Layer Properties to open the Layer Properties dialog box.

Figure 6-5: The Layer Properties dialog box lets you fine-tune layer settings.

Here's how to use this dialog box to get the most from your layers:

✔ **The Name text box displays the current name of the layer.** You can rename the layer here if you want.

✔ **Change the layer states by selecting (or deselecting) the appropriate check boxes.** Usually, you change these states directly in the layer list, as we explain earlier in this chapter, in the "Changing layer states" section.

✔ **You can change the type of layer (guide or mask) by choosing from the list of layer types.** We cover guide and mask layers later in this chapter.

✔ **You can change the color that Flash uses when the layer is displayed as outlines.** Click the Outline Color swatch and choose another color in the color palette.

✔ **Select the View Layer as Outlines check box to turn on outlines.** As we explain earlier in this section, you can accomplish this task easily from the layer listing.

 ✔ **You can change the layer height to two or three times the normal height.** One reason to change the height of a layer is to more easily view sound waves on a layer that contains a sound. Another is to see larger previews of your keyframes in the Timeline — you can adjust the layer height by clicking the drop-down list in the upper-right corner of the Timeline and choosing Preview or Preview in Context in the pop-up menu.

After you finish using the Layer Properties dialog box, click OK.

Creating Guide Layers

A *guide layer* is a layer that's invisible in the final, published animation. You can use guide layers for several purposes:

✔ **Animation:** You can place a path on a guide layer to control the motion of an object during animation. Figure 6-6 shows a guide layer that contains a motion guide for the skateboarder. When animated, the skateboard does two flips, following the motion guide. (Read through Chapter 9 for the lowdown on how to create a motion guide.)

✔ **Layout:** Although you can display guides on the screen to help you draw precisely (as we describe in Chapter 3), you can also place gridlines on guide layers to help you lay out the Stage. Graphic designers use these types of gridlines to figure out how to create a balanced, pleasing effect in their art.

Figure 6-6:
A guide layer
controls the
motion of
an object
during
animation.

✔ **Drawing:** You can import a bitmap graphic onto a guide layer and draw over the graphic on a regular layer by using the Flash drawing tools. This technique of drawing over a graphic can be a big help when creating your artwork.

Of course, you could use a regular layer and then erase whatever you don't want to appear in the final movie. But if you need to go back and make changes, you would have to create the guide layer again. Using a guide layer gives you the flexibility of keeping the layer in the movie file, knowing that it will never appear in the published animation.

Hidden layers appear in the published .swf file, but guide layers don't appear.

To create a guide layer, create a new layer. Then right-click (Windows) or Control+click (Mac) and choose Guide in the shortcut menu. The layer is now a guide layer. Use the same procedure to convert a guide layer back to a regular layer. The Guide item on the menu is a toggle, so when you click it again, Flash removes the guide status of the layer.

When you use a guide layer as a motion guide, you must link the guide layer to a layer that contains the objects you want to guide. The layer with the guided objects is called a *guided layer*. In Figure 6-6, the loops are on a guide layer, and the skateboarder is on a guided layer. All objects on a guided layer automatically snap to the path of the motion guide on the guide layer. To link a layer to a guide layer, creating a guided layer, you can do any of the following:

✔ Create a new layer under the guide layer

✔ Drag an existing layer under the guide layer

✔ Choose Modify⇨Layer and choose Guided in the Layer Properties dialog box

Flash indents the guided layer below the guide layer to help you see that they're linked. If you want to unlink a guided layer, drag it above the guide layer or choose Modify⇨Timeline⇨Layer Properties and select the Normal option in the Layer Properties dialog box.

Opening Windows with Mask Layers

A *mask layer* hides every object on its related layers except those inside a filled shape or text object. You can use mask layers to create peepholes or spotlight effects. Figure 6-7 shows a keyhole shape on a mask layer that hides the entire garden scene except for the part within the keyhole. The garden scene is a rectangle much larger than the section displayed through the keyhole.

Figure 6-7:
You can use a mask layer to create a hole through which you can see the layer or layers below.

Creating a mask layer

Follow these steps to create a mask layer, the object on the mask layer, and the objects behind the mask layer:

1. **Create the objects that you want to show through the hole in the mask layer.**

   These objects can be on one or more layers. Place all the layers that you want to be masked next to each other and at the top of the layer list.

2. **Select the topmost layer in the layer list and click the Insert Layer button to create a new layer at the top of the list.**

   This layer will become the mask layer.

3. **Create, insert, or import one filled shape, text, or an instance of a symbol on the new layer. (See Chapter 7 for more about symbols.)**

   The filled part of the shape, text, or instance becomes the hole — in other words, it's transparent. Unfilled portions of the object become opaque, so everything becomes the opposite of its current state.

4. **Right-click (Windows) or Control+click (Mac) the layer's name and choose Mask in the shortcut menu.**

   Flash turns the layer into a mask layer and locks the mask layer as well as the layer just below it in the layer list. The masked layer is indented. You see the mask effect displayed. (To link more than one layer to the mask layer, see the next section, "Editing mask layers.")

Editing mask layers

Because Flash locks both the mask layer and the layer or layers that are masked, you cannot edit them until you unlock them. Click the lock icon above the layer list to unlock all the layers, or unlock the mask and masked layers only. Flash removes the mask effect. After you finish editing the layers, lock them again to redisplay the mask effect.

When you create a mask layer, Flash links only the layer directly below it to the mask layer. A layer linked to a mask layer is masked. If you place objects that you want to be masked on several layers, you need to change the property of all those layers from normal to masked.

All the layers that you want to be masked must be directly under the mask layer.

You can link a layer to a mask layer in several ways:

✔ If you drag a normal layer directly below a mask layer, Flash links it to the mask layer in addition to existing masked layers.

✔ Right-click (Windows) or Control+click (Mac) the layer and choose Properties. Select the Masked option in the Layer Properties dialog box.

Similarly, you can unlink a layer from its mask layer by using one of these methods:

✔ Drag the linked layer above the mask layer.

✔ Right-click (Windows) or Control+click (Mac) the layer and choose Properties. Select the Normal option in the Layer Properties dialog box.

Animating mask layers

Mask layers are more fun when you animate them. You can move them, change their sizes, and change their shapes. If you create a keyhole like the one shown in Figure 6-7, you can move the keyhole past the masked layers, revealing what lies beneath while the keyhole moves. You can use the same technique to create an effect of a spotlight moving around a stage, revealing whatever it lights up. The only thing you can't do is animate the mask layer objects along motion paths. (Chapter 9 explains how to animate masks and other objects.) You can create more complex mask animations by using ActionScript. For the steps to do this, see the section on creating animated masks with movie clips in Chapter 10.

Look for ffd_reveal.fla on this book's Web site at www.dummies.com/go/flashcs3. To see the mask, open the file and unlock all the layers. *Thanks to Shane Mielke for this file. Check out Shane's fantastic portfolio at www.shanemielke.com.*

Part III
Getting Symbolic

In this part . . .

Symbols can represent the deeper levels of life, and Flash symbols let you get down deep into the mechanics of animation. In this part, you discover the three kinds of symbols — graphic symbols, button symbols, and movie clip symbols — and how to use them.

Manipulating symbols is a critical feature of Flash. Symbols enable you to easily place duplicate graphics in your movie without significantly increasing the movie's size, and symbols are necessary when you start to animate. This part of the book also gives you the lowdown on buttons, which are central to the Web lifestyle in the 21st century. Flash lets you create buttons that change when you pass the mouse cursor over them and again when you click them. You can even make animated buttons. Part III provides you with the basis for creating great animations.

Chapter 7

Heavy Symbolism

Flash offers a way to simplify your work, using symbols. A *symbol* can be any object or combination of objects, animation, or a Web button. When you create a symbol, the objects (or animation or Web button) become one object. Sounds like grouping, yes? (If you've already read Chapter 4, you know what we mean.) The difference is that Flash stores the definition of the symbol in the Library. From the Library, you can now effortlessly insert multiple copies of the symbol into your movie. Each copy is called an *instance*.

Besides making your life easier when you want to use a set of objects more than once, the use of symbols significantly reduces the size of your files. Instead of storing each instance that you use, Flash stores one definition for the symbol and refers to that definition each time you display an instance of the symbol. You can place symbols inside other symbols, which is called *nesting*. Used this way, symbols are the building blocks for complex graphics and animation. Motion-tweened animation requires symbols, groups, or text, so you often create symbols when preparing to animate. (Chapter 9 explains tweened animation.)

So, symbols are all-around good guys, and you should use them as much as possible.

Understanding Symbol Types

Flash offers four types of symbols: graphic, movie clip, button, and font. Each type is made up of one or more objects or animation, but each type has a different purpose. Understanding these types is important to understanding symbols and Flash animation in general.

Using graphic symbols

Graphic symbols are the simplest and most obvious type of symbol. When you create a Flash movie, you create objects on the Stage. Some objects may remain still, such as backgrounds. Other objects are animated — after all, what would Flash be without animation? Use graphic symbols for collections of static objects or for simple animation. Figure 7-1 shows a graphic symbol created from several curves and circles.

Figure 7-1:
A graphic symbol, created from several objects, has a single selection border.

You create graphic symbols to reduce the size of your file and to make it easier to add multiple copies of a graphic to your movie. Symbols are stored in the Library and are available to not only the movie in which you created them but also to any other movie. You don't have to re-create the wheel.

Flash ignores sounds and ActionScript inside graphic symbols. ActionScript code (which we explain in detail in Chapter 10) is the key to creating interactive movies. For that reason, don't use graphic symbols if you want to use ActionScript to directly control them — use movie clips instead.

Using movie clip symbols

A *movie clip* is like a movie within your movie that you can manipulate by using interactive controls (which you can read about in Chapter 10). Movie clips are crucial for complex animation and especially for interactive animation. A movie clip has its own Timeline independent of the movie's main Timeline. For example, you can go to a movie clip at any point in the movie, play it, and then return to where you left off on the Timeline. You can also attach movie clips to buttons. We explain how to create movie clips in this chapter; Chapter 8 discusses using movie clips with buttons. Chapter 9 covers using movie clips in animation, and Chapter 10 explains how to use and control movie clips by using interactive controls.

Flash comes with a library of *components,* which are special movie clips that allow you to add user-interface elements — such as radio buttons, check boxes, and scroll bars — to your movies. Choose Window⇨Components and drag one of your choices to the Stage. Then choose Window⇨Component Inspector to set the parameters of the component. For example, you can insert a list box and then add all the items (called *labels* on the Component Parameters panel) that you want on the list. For more information on components, see Chapter 12.

Using button symbols

Button symbols create *buttons* — those little graphics that you click on Web pages to take you to other pages on the site or the Internet. In Flash, you can use buttons for this type of navigation, but you can also use buttons to interact with your site. For example, you can let viewers decide whether they want to see a movie — when they click the button, the movie starts. You can also use advanced scripting to create buttons that control interactive games and other viewer activities. However you want to use buttons, button symbols are the way to start. You can add movie clips and interactive controls to buttons. Find out about buttons in Chapter 8.

Using font symbols

A *font symbol* exports a font for use in multiple Flash movies. This is great whenever you use the same font in more than one Flash movie on a Web site: Your audience needs to download the font information only oncerather than every time for every single Flash movie. This makes your Flash movies smaller and the user's loading time faster. We show you how to use font symbols in Chapter 12.

Creating Symbols

For graphic symbols and button symbols, usually you create the objects that you need and then turn them into a symbol. The same is true of movie clips if they are static and you use ActionScript to control them. However, when you use a movie clip as a type of animation, you can use one of two approaches:

- ✔ Create an animation on the Stage and then convert it to a movie clip symbol
- ✔ Create the movie clip symbol, create the initial objects, and then create the animation

In the next few sections, we explain the various ways of creating symbols, for whichever purpose you want to use them.

Each type of symbol has its own icon that's used in the Library. The following table shows what type of symbol each icon represents:

Symbol	What It Represents
	Movie clip
	Button
	Graphic

Creating symbols from existing objects

To create a symbol from unanimated objects you've already created, follow these steps:

1. **On the Stage, select the objects that you want to convert to a symbol.**

2. **Choose Modify⇨Convert to Symbol or press F8.**

   The Convert to Symbol dialog box opens, as shown in Figure 7-2.

Figure 7-2:
The Convert to Symbol dialog box.

3. **In the Name text box, type a name for the symbol.**

   A common convention is to name the symbol in a way that's unique and also indicates the symbol type. For example, `help_btn` could be the name for a button symbol that will become a Help button on a Web site.

4. **In the Type list, select the type of symbol you want to create: graphic, button, or movie clip.**

   For slightly different results when scaling a movie clip, you can enable 9-slice scaling. To do so, click the Advanced button in the Convert to Symbol dialog box. In the expanded dialog box, select the Enable Guides for 9-Slice Scaling check box. When you're finished, you can see special guides on the symbol in the Library. This feature is not available for graphic or button symbols. For information on how to use this feature, see the "Editing symbols" section, later in this chapter.

5. Click OK to create the symbol and close the dialog box.

The objects that you selected become one object, indicated by a single selection border around all the objects. Flash also stores the symbol in the Library. (Chapter 2 explains how to use the Library.)

Creating empty symbols

Rather than create a symbol from existing objects, you can create an empty symbol and then create the objects for the symbol. If you know in advance that you want to create a symbol, you can use this method.

To create an empty symbol, follow these steps:

1. With no objects selected, choose Insert⇨New Symbol.

The Create New Symbol dialog box opens.

2. In the Name text box, type a name for the symbol.

3. In the Type list, select the type of symbol you want to create — graphic, button, or movie clip — and then click OK.

Flash switches to symbol-editing mode, which we describe in the section "Editing symbols," later in this chapter.

4. Create the objects or animation for the symbol in the same way you do in regular movie-editing mode.

5. Choose Edit⇨Edit Document to leave symbol-editing mode and return to your movie.

Your new symbol disappears! Don't worry — Flash saved the symbol in the Library. To find out how to insert an instance of the symbol on the Stage, see the "Inserting instances" section.

Converting an animation to a movie clip symbol

You can create a movie clip symbol by converting regular animation to a movie clip. Use this method when you already have the animation created on the Timeline. To convert an animation on the Stage to a movie clip symbol, follow these steps:

1. On the layer listing, select all frames in all layers containing the animation by clicking the first layer and pressing Shift while you click the last layer in the group.

Alternatively, you can press Ctrl (Windows) or ⌘ (Mac) and click additional layers.

 2. **On the Timeline, right-click (Windows) or Control+click (Mac) and choose Copy Frames to copy all the frames of the animation to the Clipboard.**

Alternatively, you can choose Edit⇨Timeline⇨Copy Frames.

 3. **With no objects selected (click off the Stage to be sure that no objects are selected), choose Insert⇨New Symbol.**

The Create New Symbol dialog box opens.

 4. **In the Name text box, type a name for the movie clip.**

 5. **In the Type list, select Movie Clip as the type of symbol. Then click OK.**

Flash switches to symbol-editing mode so that you can edit the symbol.

 6. **Click the first frame of the Timeline to set the start of the movie clip symbol.**

 7. **Choose Edit⇨Timeline⇨Paste Frames to paste the animation into the Timeline and create the symbol.**

 8. **To return to the main movie and Timeline, choose Edit⇨Edit Document.**

 9. **To delete the animation from the main movie (now that you've saved it in a movie clip), select all layers as you did in Step 1 and choose Edit⇨Timeline⇨Remove Frames.**

You can delete the animation from the main movie because your Library now has a movie clip that contains that animation. When you choose the movie clip in the Library panel, you can click the small Play button to play the animation in the Library panel's window.

Creating a symbol by duplicating a symbol

One more way to create a graphic, button, or movie symbol is to duplicate an existing symbol. To duplicate a symbol, follow these steps:

 1. **Open the Library (choose Window⇨Library).**

 2. **Select the symbol that you want to duplicate.**

 3. **Click the Options menu in the upper-right corner of the Library window and choose Duplicate.**

Flash opens the Duplicate Symbol dialog box.

4. **In the Name text box, type a name for the duplicate. Select the type of symbol that you want to create if you want a different kind from the original.**

5. **Click OK to close the dialog box and create the duplicate symbol.**

Modifying Symbols

Flash is a master of flexibility, and sometimes you need to make changes. Of course, you can change symbols after you create them. Here we explain the procedures you need to know.

Changing the properties of a symbol

You might need to change a symbol's properties. For example, you might create a graphic symbol and then realize that you need it to be a movie clip. No problem!

To change the properties of a symbol, follow these steps:

1. **Choose Window⇨Library to open the Library.**

2. **Right-click (Windows) or Control+click (Mac) the symbol's icon (not its name) and choose Properties.**

   The Symbol Properties dialog box opens.

3. **If the symbol is a graphic, button, or movie clip, select the type of symbol that you want in the Type list and then click OK.**

Look on our companion Web site at www.dummies.com/go/flash8 for ffd_reveal.fla — a good example of a short movie with lots of symbols. *(The Flash movie is courtesy of Shane Mielke. You can see his other work at www.shanemielke.com)*

Editing symbols

An *instance* is a copy of a symbol that you insert into your movie. Part of the power of symbols lies in their control over instances. If you edit a symbol, Flash updates all instances of that symbol in the movie. You can change a symbol once and save yourself the time of creating the same change for every instance of that symbol. For that reason, it's worthwhile to make a symbol whenever you want to use a certain shape or group of shapes more than once.

You can edit a symbol in three modes:

- ✔ **Edit in symbol-editing mode:** Switches you to symbol-editing mode. You see only the symbol. Right-click a selected symbol and choose Edit.

- ✔ **Edit in place:** Lets you edit a symbol while still viewing other objects on the Stage. Other objects are dimmed while you edit the symbol. Double-click a selected symbol and choose Edit in Place.

- ✔ **Edit in a new window:** Opens a new window where you can edit your symbol. You see only the symbol. Right-click a selected symbol and choose Edit in New Window.

The value of editing in place is that you can see how your change works with the rest of the objects that you have on the Stage. For example, if you want to make your symbol bigger, you may need to make sure that it doesn't obscure some nearby text. However, if you have lots of stuff on the Stage, editing in symbol-editing mode or in a new window can help you focus more easily on the symbol itself.

Editing a movie clip's 9-slice scaling guides

Movie clips can have 9-slice scaling enabled to control how they scale. Sometimes, when you scale a symbol, you don't really want it to scale equally throughout; instead, you may want the corners to remain unscaled. The 9-slice scaling feature, new for Flash CS3, allows you to scale everything but the corners, which remain unscaled.

We explain how to enable 9-slice scaling for movie clips in the "Creating symbols from existing objects" section. Here we explain how to edit the guides to get the results you want:

1. **Right-click the movie clip and choose Edit.**

   You enter symbol-editing mode. You cannot edit the guides in any other mode. You see the symbol, with two vertical and two horizontal guides, as shown in the figure.

2. **Drag the guides so that they border the corners of the symbol according to your needs.**

   The sections of the symbol outside each set of vertical and horizontal guides (the corners) will not resize when you scale the symbol.

3. **Choose Edit➪Edit to return to the main Stage.**

   For information about scaling objects, including symbols, see Chapter 4. When you scale the movie clip symbol, you'll see that although the entire symbol changes size, the corners remain unchanged.

To see the effect, try creating a shape with curved corners and duplicate it. Turn the first shape into a movie clip and enable 9-slice scaling. You can leave the default positioning of the guides or use the procedure we just described to move the guides. Then scale up both the movie clip and the duplicate. You'll see how the corners of the movie clip don't change when scaled, and you'll clearly see the difference between the two shapes.

To edit a symbol, follow these steps:

1. **Select any instance of the symbol on the Stage.**

2. **Right-click (Windows) or Control+click (Mac) the instance and choose Edit, Edit in Place, or Edit in New Window.**

   (Choosing Edit puts you into symbol-editing mode.) Flash displays the symbol name above the Timeline. If you choose Edit in Place, other objects are dimmed, as shown in Figure 7-3.

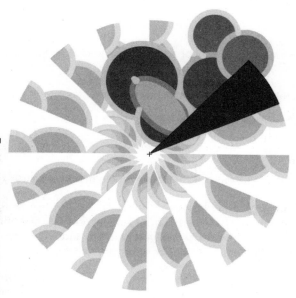

Figure 7-3:
One symbol, which includes a wedge and some circles, is being edited.

This kaleidoscope animation is in the Ch07 folder on the companion Web site at www.dummies.com/go/flash8.

3. **Edit the symbol in any way you want.**

4. **After you finish editing, do the following:**

   • **If you chose Edit or Edit in Place, click the scene name to the left of the symbol name or choose Edit⇨Edit Document.**

   • **If you chose Edit in New Window, click the Close button.**

   You are now back in your main movie.

Using Symbols from Other Movies

After you create a symbol and store it in the Library, you can use that Library in any other movie. You can also open the Library from any other movie and use its symbols in your current movie.

If the other movie is open and its Library is open, you can access that movie's Library from within your current movie. Libraries of any open movie are available from any other open movie. Just choose that other movie in the drop-down list at the top of the Library palette. (Choose Window➪Library to open the Library.)

To use a symbol from the Library of another movie that is closed, follow these steps:

1. **Choose File➪Import➪Open External Library.**

   The Open as Library dialog box opens.

2. **Select the movie file.**

3. **Click Open.**

   Flash displays the Library of the other movie in a new Library window.

The new Library might hide your current movie's Library. Just drag the new Library by its title bar so that it rests under the current Library until it docks there. In the new Library, many Options menu items and icons are disabled to prevent you from making changes in the other movie's file.

When you have more than one Library open, the background of the listing of open movies is white. The background of Libraries from other, unopened movies is gray, so you can quickly see which Library is which.

To use a symbol from the other Library, drag the symbol onto the Stage. When you do this, Flash places a copy of the symbol in the current movie's Library. (See Chapter 2 for more information about the Library.)

You can also update or replace any graphic, button, or movie clip symbol in your movie's Library with the content of a symbol from any other Library on your hard drive or network. Accessing a symbol in this way is called *author-time sharing* of symbols or assets. On the other hand, you can also share symbols or assets at *runtime,* after you have uploaded your movie. A *font symbol* is a special type of symbol that you use at runtime. We explain runtime shared libraries (which can include sounds) in Chapter 12.

When you share a symbol while you're creating a movie (during *authoring*), the symbol in your current movie keeps its original name, but the contents take on the properties of the symbol you're sharing. If you have already replaced a symbol and the outside symbol changes (because it has been edited), use author-time sharing to update the symbol in your current drawing.

To update or replace a graphic, button, or movie clip symbol in your movie with the properties of another symbol, follow these steps:

1. **Open the Library (choose Window⇨Library) and select the symbol you want to update or replace.**

2. **In the Library menu, choose Properties.**

   The Symbol Properties dialog box opens.

3. **Click Advanced, if necessary, to see the expanded dialog box. In the Source section, click Browse.**

   The Locate Adobe Flash Document File dialog box opens.

4. **Navigate to the movie (`.fla`) file that contains the symbol you want to use. Select it and click Open.**

   The Select Source dialog box opens. You see a list of the symbols in the movie that you selected.

5. **Choose a symbol and click OK.**

   When you choose a symbol, you see a preview in the preview box, so you can easily find the symbol you want. When you click OK, you're back in the Symbol Properties dialog box.

6. **In the Source section of the Symbol Properties dialog box, select the Always Update Before Publishing check box if you want to automatically update the symbol if the original has changed.**

   Enable this check box to create a link between the source symbol and the symbol in your current movie.

7. **Click OK.**

You now have a symbol in your Library that has its original name but looks like the symbol you chose from the other movie.

Using the Flash Library

Flash comes with three common libraries you can use. To access these libraries, choose Window⇨Common Libraries and then select the one you want. Flash includes buttons, learning interactions (interface items for creating online courses), and classes (building blocks for developing ActionScript applications). These libraries are also a good place to pick up ideas and see what you can create in Flash.

Using the Flash For Dummies Library

The Flash Libraries contain some good examples, but they miss many basic shapes and simple objects, some of which are hard to draw in Flash. We decided to fill in the gaps! We created a Library of art, geometric shapes, and fun shapes that you can use in your movies, with some new shapes designed especially for this edition — a 3-D helix, a cone, and a pyramid. You'll find 79 items in all! The *Flash For Dummies* Library is named `Flash CS3 For Dummies Library.fla`. You can find it at `www.dummies.com/go/flashcs3`.

To use this Library, go to `www.dummies.com/go/flashcs3` and download `Flash For Dummies Library.fla`. In Windows, download it to the `Program Files\Adobe\Adobe Flash CS3\en\Configuration\ External Libraries` folder on your hard drive. On the Mac, download it to the `Applications/Adobe Flash CS3/Configuration/Libraries` folder on your hard drive.

After that, you can always open this Library the same way you open other common Libraries: Choose Window⇨Common Libraries⇨Flash CS3 For Dummies Library.fla. We hope you enjoy it!

Working with Instances, for Instance

After you create a symbol, you can use it in many ways. You can insert it in your movie, inside other symbols, or even in other movies. Each copy of the symbol is called an *instance.* You can change the properties of an instance so that it differs from its parent symbol. For example, you can change the color of an instance — the original symbol remains unchanged.

Inserting instances

To insert an instance of a symbol, follow these steps:

1. **Choose Window⇨Library (Ctrl+L or F11 for Windows or ⌘+L or F11 for the Mac) to open the Library, as shown in Figure 7-4.**

2. **In the layer list, choose the layer where you want the instance to be placed.**

   See Chapter 6 for the full story on layers.

Figure 7-4:
Insert an
instance of
a symbol by
dragging it
from the
Library.

3. **Click a keyframe on the Timeline where you want the instance to be placed.**

   Flash places instances only in keyframes. If you don't select a keyframe, Flash puts the instance in the first keyframe to the left of the current frame. (See Chapter 9 for more about keyframes.)

4. **Drag the symbol from the Library to the Stage.**

   You can drag from the list of items or directly from the preview at the top of the Library.

When you insert a graphic instance, you need to consider how it fits in your entire animation. For example, the instance might be the starting point for some animation, or it might be part of the background that remains static throughout the animation. Perhaps you want the instance to suddenly appear at some point in the animation. If the instance contains animation, you need to insert it at its proper starting point. (Chapter 9 explains how to copy graphics across any number of frames to create a static background and covers the entire topic of animation in detail.)

A movie clip instance, however, takes up only one frame on the Timeline. It plays and loops automatically unless you create ActionScript code to control it. (Chapter 10 talks about ActionScript.)

Editing instances

A symbol's children don't have to be carbon copies of their parents, thank goodness. Instances of a symbol can differ from their parent symbol by color, type, and play mode. You can also rotate, scale, or skew an instance, leaving the parent symbol unchanged.

When you edit an instance, Flash remembers the changes. If you later edit the symbol, Flash doesn't forget the changes you made to the instance. Suppose that you create a red circle graphic symbol, and then you create several instances of it and change one instance to pink. Then you edit the (still red!) circle symbol to change it to an oval. All the instances are now ovals, but the one you turned pink is still pink. The instance's shape has been updated, but the pink color remains.

In the Property inspector (choose Window⇨Properties⇨Properties), you can change an instance's color (or tint), brightness, or transparency, giving you some useful control over the appearance of your instances. To change an instance's color, brightness, or transparency, follow these steps:

1. **Select the instance.**

2. **Choose Window⇨Properties⇨Properties to open the Property inspector.**

3. **In the Color drop-down list, select one of these options:**

   - **None:** Adds no color effect

   - **Brightness:** Changes the lightness or darkness of the instance

   - **Tint:** Changes the color of the instance

   - **Alpha:** Changes the opacity/transparency of the instance

   - **Advanced:** Changes both the color and the alpha

4. **Make the desired changes, as we explain in the next few sections.**

   You see the changes that you make in the Property inspector immediately in your selected instance.

Changing brightness

When you choose Brightness in the Color drop-down list, a text box and a slider appear. Type a brightness percentage or drag the slider and see the result in the symbol instance. High brightness makes the image light, and 100-percent brightness makes the instance white. (It disappears if you have a white background!) Low brightness makes the image dark; 0-percent brightness turns the instance black.

Changing tint

When you choose Tint in the Color drop-down list, you can choose the color and then the amount of the color (the tint), by percentage, that you want to apply. Figure 7-5 shows the controls for this option. You can select a color by clicking the Tint Color button and choosing from the color swatches or by typing red, green, and blue values (if you know them).

Specify the percentage of the color you want to apply by typing a value in the percent text box or by clicking the drop-down arrow and dragging the slider to choose a percentage. When the percentage is set to 100%, the instance changes to the color you specified. If the percentage is set to 0%, Flash leaves the instance unchanged.

The Flash method of specifying a color gives you great flexibility and precision. You can choose a color and use the tint control to create a meld of the current color and your chosen color.

If you want to stick to the 216 Web-safe color palette, just select a color swatch from the ones displayed when you click the Tint Color button and then slide the tint control all the way up to 100%.

Changing transparency

Choose Alpha in the Color drop-down menu to change the transparency of an instance. (*Alpha* enables levels of transparency, and you can think of the term as somewhat synonymous to *opacity*.) Use the slider or type a value in the text box. A value of 0 means that your instance becomes completely transparent — in that case, when you return to the Stage, all you see is the selection border and the small plus sign that marks the symbol's registration point. When you deselect the instance, you see absolutely nothing! (Chapter 4 explains more about a symbol's registration point, including how to move it. See the section on groups.)

Partial transparency lets your background show through. A partially transparent instance blends in with your background, creating a softer effect. However, transparency is a complex feature and can slow down the loading and playing of a movie.

Changing color and transparency at the same time

Select Advanced in the Color drop-down menu to change both the color and the transparency at the same time by using red, green, and blue values. The Settings button appears on the Property inspector. Click Settings to open the Advanced Effect dialog box. Figure 7-6 shows the controls, which are complex.

Figure 7-6:
The Advanced Effect dialog box.

Use the controls on the left to specify the color or transparency as a specific percentage of the current value. Use the controls on the right to change the color or transparency to a specific, absolute amount. Flash calculates the new color value by multiplying the current value by the percentage you specified and then adding the value from the right side. As you can see, this method provides lots of control — but it might make you crazy first.

To simply change both the color and the transparency of an instance, choose Tint from the Color drop-down list to change the color and then just change the left Alpha setting in the Advanced Effect dialog box.

Adding filters and blends

You can apply special graphic effects called *filters* to text, buttons, and movie clips. Select the item and click the Filters tab of the Property inspector. Click the plus (+) icon and choose one (or more) of the following filters: Bevel, Drop Shadow, Glow, Blur, Gradient Glow, Gradient Blur, or Adjust Color. The Filters tab then displays further controls so that you can specify how you want the filter to look. You can get some cool effects this way. You can even add multiple filters to an object.

To apply filter settings from one object to another, you can copy and paste one or more filters.

To copy and paste filters, follow these steps:

1. **Select the object that has the filter (or filters) that you want.**

2. **On the Filters tab of the Property inspector, select all the filters that you want to copy.**

3. **Click the Copy Filters button. In the drop-down menu, choose Copy Selected or Copy All.**

4. **Select the object that you want to have the filters.**

5. **Click the Paste Filters button.**

You can also apply *blend modes* to movie clips. Blend modes determine how movie clips that overlap blend with each other at the point of overlap. To apply a blend, select a movie clip instance and adjust the color and transparency as we explain in the previous sections. Then choose a blend mode in the Blend drop-down list in the Property inspector. The names of the blend modes are not self-explanatory, so you need to try them out to see their effect.

Changing an instance's type

The instance type — graphic, movie clip, or button — comes from the symbol type, but you might want to change it. For example, if you created some animation and saved it as a graphic symbol, you might want to use it as a movie clip. Rather than change the symbol type, you can change only the type of the instance that you have inserted.

To change the instance type, follow these steps:

1. **Select the instance.**

2. **Choose Window⇨Properties⇨Properties to open the Property inspector.**

3. **In the Instance Behavior drop-down list, select one of the following types:**

   • **Graphic:** If the graphic contains animation, select Graphic in the Behavior drop-down list and then determine how the animation will run in the Options for Graphics drop-down list on the Property inspector. You have three choices:

   Loop plays the animation contained in the instance over and over during the frames occupied by the instance.

   Play Once plays the animation one time from the frame you specify.

Single Frame displays any one frame of the animation. In other words, the animation doesn't play; you specify which frame the movie displays.

- **Button:** Select the Button option to determine how the button is tracked in the Tracking Options section. In the Options for Buttons drop-down list, select Track as Button when you're creating single buttons. Select Track as Menu if you're creating pop-up menus.

- **Movie Clip:** Select the Movie Clip option and specify an Instance name in the Name box. You use this name with certain ActionScript controls so that you can refer to and control the instance. (For more information about ActionScript, see Chapter 10.)

If you select a movie clip or button instance, you can select the Use Runtime Bitmap Caching check box in the Property inspector. Runtime bitmap caching optimizes playback of a Flash movie in a browser. Use bitmap caching only when you have a complex background whose content remains the same. By storing the background as a bitmap, the Flash player can play the animation faster and more smoothly because it doesn't have to redraw the image throughout the movie.

Replacing an instance

Suppose that you create a complex animation with bouncing bunnies all over the Stage. Suddenly your boss decides that some of the bouncing bunnies should be bouncing squirrels instead. Meanwhile, you had already edited all the bunnies to make them different sizes and colors. You need a way to replace some of the bunnies with squirrels without losing their sizes and colors.

To replace an instance, follow these steps:

1. **Create the squirrel symbol (or whichever new symbol you need).**

   Flash stores the new symbol in the Library.

2. **Select an instance of the bunny — that is, your original instance — on the Stage.**

3. **Choose Window⇨Properties⇨Properties to open the Property inspector.**

4. **Click the Swap button to open the Swap Symbol dialog box.**

5. **In the dialog box, select the squirrel or any other symbol.**

6. **Click OK to swap the symbols and close the Swap Symbol dialog box.**

   Flash retains your color effects and size changes but changes the symbol.

Unfortunately, you must repeat this process for all the bunnies you want to change on the Stage, but it's better than reinserting all your instances and re-creating the instance changes.

If your boss actually wants you to change all the bunnies to squirrels, your job is much simpler. Just edit the bunny symbol (as we describe in the "Editing symbols" section, earlier in this chapter) to replace the bunny image with a squirrel. Then all the instances of that symbol instantly change to squirrels yet retain the color effects and size changes that you gave them while they were still bunnies.

Duplicate a symbol when you want to use one symbol as a springboard for creating a new symbol. Follow the instructions in the "Creating Symbols" section, earlier in this chapter. Make any changes that you want to the new symbol and place instances on the Stage.

Breaking apart an instance

You can break apart an instance into its component objects. The original symbol remains in the movie's Library. You might want to use the instance as a starting point for creating a completely new symbol, or you might want to animate the components of the symbol so that they move separately. Other instances remain unchanged.

To break apart an instance, select it and choose Modify⇨Break Apart. If an instance contains symbols or grouped objects within it, you can use the Break Apart command again to break apart those internal objects as well.

Chapter 8

Pushing Buttons

When you view a Web page, you click buttons to move to other pages or sites. As you probably know, these buttons are graphical images, but they're hyperlinks as well. If you start to pay attention to these buttons, you see that some of them change when you pass your mouse cursor over them. They change again when you click them. Sometimes they make a sound when you click them.

Flash can create these types of buttons and more. You can animate Flash buttons so that they move or rotate when viewers pass their cursors over them or click them. You can add interactive controls (actions) to buttons so that passing over or clicking them starts other movies or creates other effects.

In this chapter, you find out how to create buttons that look the way you want. You also discover how to make more complex buttons that include sounds, movie clips, and simple ActionScript. To discover more about ActionScript and interactivity, see Chapter 10.

Creating Simple Buttons

Before you create a button, stop and think about what you want the button to accomplish on a Web page and how you want it to look. When designing a Web site's navigation, designers often create a series of similar buttons that lead to pages within a site. This similarity provides a coherent style for the site. Buttons usually include some text to identify the button's purpose.

But you can use buttons for lots of other, more advanced purposes than navigating around Web pages. A button can control the play of music, indicate a choice in a survey, or control a game.

A *button* is a symbol that responds to a mouse. (See Chapter 7 for the low-down on how to create and edit symbols.) In this chapter, we cover the entire process of creating buttons.

Understanding button states

A button has four states that define characteristics of the button:

- ✔ **Up:** What the button looks like when the mouse pointer is not over the button. The viewer initially sees the Up state of a button.

- ✔ **Over:** What the button looks like when the pointer is over the button but it hasn't been clicked.

- ✔ **Down:** What the button looks like when it is clicked.

- ✔ **Hit:** The area of the button that responds to the mouse. The user doesn't see this area — it's invisible. When you pass the pointer over the hit area, the pointer is considered to be over the button. When you click anywhere in the hit area, the button works.

Figure 8-1 shows a button in its four states. A typical, simple button might show a lit-up effect for the Over state and an indented look (as though the button is pressed in) for the Down state. In this example, the Down state moves the highlight to the right, giving the impression of movement when the user clicks the button.

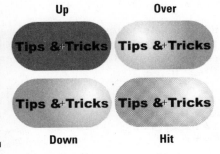

Figure 8-1:
The four states of a button: Up, Over, Down, and Hit.

Radial gradients are useful for creating a lit-up or pushed-in look. Use a light color or white to create the appearance of a highlight. Use a dark color or black to create an indented look. Just changing the color of the fill (often to a lighter color) is enough to make it seem lit up.

The button shown in Figure 8-1 is on the companion Web site at www.dummies. com/go/flashcs3. Look for capsule.fla. To try out the buttons in this movie, choose Control⇨Test Movie.

Making a basic button

To create a simple button, follow these steps:

1. **Choose Insert⇨New Symbol to open the Create New Symbol dialog box.**

2. **In the Name text box, type a name for the button.**

   When you have many symbols in a movie, it helps to name them accord-ing to their type and purpose. For example, if a button will be labeled *Submit a Resource,* you might name it btnSubmitResource.

3. **In the Behavior section, select the Button option.**

4. **Click OK.**

   You're now in symbol-editing mode. Flash displays the special Timeline for buttons, with four frames: Up, Over, Down, and Hit, as shown in Figure 8-2. Note the dot in the Up frame, indicating that the frame is a keyframe. (For more information about keyframes, see Chapter 9.) The word *Up* is highlighted, indicating that the Up frame is active.

Figure 8-2:
The Flash symbol-editing mode for buttons displays a Timeline with four frames.

5. **Create the graphic for the Up state.**

   You can use the Flash drawing tools, an imported graphic, or an instance of a graphic or movie clip symbol. You can create as many layers as you want for the button. For an animated button, use a movie clip symbol. We explain how to create an animated button in the "Adding a movie clip to a button" section, later in this chapter.

   If you want the button image for the four states to be in the same place, place the graphic in the center of the display and build the other states in the center as well. To do this, cut and paste the graphic. (See Chapter 4 for more about centering objects on the display.) If the button images aren't in the same place, the button appears to shift when the viewer passes the cursor over or clicks the button.

6. **Right-click (Windows) or Control+click (Mac) the Over frame and choose Insert Keyframe from the contextual menu.**

   Flash inserts a keyframe in the Over frame of the button. You can also choose Insert⇨Timeline⇨Keyframe or press F6. The graphic for the Up state remains on the Stage.

7. **Create the graphic for the Over state.**

   You can use the graphic for the Up state as a starting point and change it (or leave it the same if you don't want the button to change when the mouse pointer passes over the button). You can also delete the graphic and put a new one in its place. If you have more than one layer, place a keyframe on each layer before creating the artwork for that layer.

8. **Right-click (Windows) or Control+click (Mac) the Down frame and choose Insert Keyframe.**

9. **Create the graphic for the Down frame.**

   Repeat as in Step 7. Note that if the button functions as navigation to another page, your viewer will see this state for only a split second.

10. **Right-click (Windows) or Control+click (Mac) the Hit frame and choose Insert Keyframe.**

11. **If necessary, create the shape that defines the active area of the button.**

    This shape should completely cover all the graphics of the other state. Usually, a rectangle or circle is effective. If you ignore the Hit frame, Flash uses the boundary of the objects in the Up frame, which might be what you want.

   If you use text for the button, viewers have to click the letters precisely unless you create a rectangular hit area around the text. To cover an area of text, create a filled-in shape on a new layer.

12. **Click the scene name above the layer list (or the Back arrow to the left of the scene name) to return to the regular Timeline and leave symbol-editing mode.**

13. **If the Library isn't open, choose Window⇨Library and drag the button symbol that you just created to wherever you want it on the Stage.**

    You just created a button!

A button is a symbol, but when you want to place a button on the Stage, you must drag the button from the Library to create an instance of the symbol. See Chapter 7 for a full explanation of symbols and instances.

Putting Buttons to the Test

After you create a button, you need to test it. You can choose from several methods. The fastest way to test a button is to enable it on the Stage. An enabled button responds to your mouse as you would expect — it changes as you specified when you pass the mouse over it or click it. To enable the buttons on the Stage, choose Control⇨Enable Simple Buttons. All the buttons on the Stage are now enabled. Have fun with your button! Pass the mouse over it, click it, and watch it change.

After you test your button, suppose that you want to select the button to move it. You try to click it to select it, and it only glows at you, according to the Down frame's definition. Choose Control⇨Enable Simple Buttons again to disable the buttons. Now you can select a button as you do any other object. In general, you enable buttons only to test them.

However, if you really want to select an enabled button, you can do so with the Selection tool by dragging a selection box around it. You can use the arrow keys to move the button. If you want to edit the button further, choose Window⇨Properties⇨Properties to open the Property inspector and edit the button's properties, as we explain in Chapter 7.

If you have other animations on the Stage, you can play an animation with the buttons enabled. Choose Control⇨Play or press Enter (Windows) or Return (Mac). By playing the animation, you can see how the buttons fit in with the rest of your movie.

Another way to test a button is to test the entire movie. Choose Control⇨Test Movie. Flash creates an .swf file just as it would if you were publishing the movie based on default publishing settings. Any animation plays, and you can test your buttons as well. When you're finished, click the Close box of the window.

If your button contains movie clips, you must use this method of testing the button because the animation doesn't play on the Stage.

Creating Complex Buttons

Buttons can do more than just change color or shape. You can enhance a button in three ways:

- ✔ **Add a sound:** For example, you can add a clicking sound to the Down frame of a button so that users hear that sound when they click the button.

- ✔ **Add a movie clip:** To animate a button, you add a movie clip to it. You can animate the Up, Over, and Down frames, if you want.

- ✔ **Add an action (interactive control):** To make a button do something, you need to add an action to it by using ActionScript. Actions are covered in Chapter 10, but we discuss some of the basic concepts here.

Adding a sound to a button

For fun, you can add a sound to a button. Usually, sounds are added to the Over or Down frame — or both, if you want. Chapter 11 explains lots more about sound, but in this section, we explain how to add a simple sound to a button.

On the companion Web site at www.dummies.com/go/flashcs3, look for click.wav. You can add this sound to the Down frame of a button.

To add a sound to a button, follow these steps:

1. **Create the button symbol.**

2. **Choose File⇨Import⇨Import to Library to open the Import dialog box.**

3. **Select the sound file (in .wav, .aiff, or .mp3 format) and click Open.**

   Flash stores the file in the Library.

4. **Choose Window⇨Library to open the Library.**

5. **If you aren't in symbol-editing mode, double-click the button's icon in the Library to enter symbol-editing mode.**

6. **Click the Insert Layer button at the bottom of the layer list to add a new layer.**

   See Chapter 6 for a full explanation of layers.

7. **Name the new layer *Sound* or something similar.**

8. **In the new layer, right-click (Windows) or Control+click (Mac) the frame where you want to place the sound — for example, the Down frame — and choose Insert Keyframe.**

9. **Display the Property inspector.**

   Choose Window⇨Properties⇨Properties to open the Property inspector if it's not already open. If necessary, expand the Property inspector to its full size.

10. **In the Sound drop-down list, select the sound file that you want.**

    Flash lists all the sounds you've imported into the Library. When you select the sound file, you see the sound wave indicator on the sound's layer in the frame where you inserted the sound, as shown in Figure 8-3.

11. **With the new keyframe still selected, click the Sync drop-down list in the Property inspector, and choose Event.**

    The Event setting synchronizes the sound to the occurrence of an event: in this case, the clicking of the button. Event is the default setting.

12. **Click the scene name in the upper-left area of the layer list or the back arrow to the left of the scene name.**

    Flash returns you to the regular Timeline and leaves symbol-editing mode.

Figure 8-3:
When you
add a sound
to a button,
the sound
wave
appears in
the Timeline.

13. Drag the button symbol that you just created from the Library to wherever you want the button on the Stage.

You're finished! Now test the button as we explain in the earlier section, "Putting Buttons to the Test."

Be sure to look in Chapter 11 for more information on adding sounds to buttons and movies.

If you've already added the sound to another movie, choose File⇨Import⇨ Open External Library and choose the other movie. Click the desired keyframe and drag the sound from the Library to anywhere on the Stage. Flash places the sound in the selected keyframe.

Adding a movie clip to a button

If you think that simple buttons are b-o-r-i-n-g, you can animate them. To animate a button, you must create a movie clip symbol and then insert the movie clip into one of the frames. Generally, button animation is localized in the area of the button. If you want to make an elaborate button, you can animate all three frames — Up, Over, and Down.

To add a movie clip to a button, first create the movie clip. Chapter 7 explains how to create a movie clip symbol, and Chapter 9 explains how to create the animation to put in the movie clip. See Chapter 10 for an example of how to use a button to play a movie clip.

For the following steps, you can use the movie clip that we provide on the companion Web site at www.dummies.com/go/flashcs3. Open flower power.fla. It's a blank movie whose Library contains the symbols necessary to create a button with a movie clip.

If you've never created a button, review the steps in the "Making a basic button" section, earlier in this chapter. Then to create a button with a movie clip, follow these steps:

1. **If you're using the movie file included on the Web site, open flower power.fla; otherwise, open any new movie file.**

2. **Choose Insert⇨New Symbol to open the Create New Symbol dialog box.**

3. **In the Name text box, type a name for the button.**

4. **In the Type list, select the Button option. Then click OK.**

5. **Create the graphic for the Up state.**

   If you're using the movie from the Web site, choose Window⇨Library and drag the graphic symbol named Flower to the Stage. Press the arrow buttons on the keyboard (left, right, up, and down, as necessary) to center the flower symbol's registration point (shown by a little plus sign) exactly over the registration point (also a plus sign) on the Stage (see Figure 8-4). You can also cut and paste the symbol to center it. The flower graphic symbol is static, not animated.

6. **Right-click (Windows) or Control+click (Mac) the Over frame and choose Insert Keyframe from the contextual menu.**

   Flash inserts a keyframe.

7. **Create the graphic for the Over state.**

   For this example, delete the graphic on the Stage (it's still there from the Up frame) and drag the movie clip called Flower Rotating to the center of the Stage. Click the Stage and use the arrow keys to perfectly center the flower. The Flower Rotating movie clip animates the flower by rotating it.

8. **Right-click (Windows) or Control+click (Mac) the Down frame and choose Insert Keyframe.**

9. **Create the graphic for the Down state.**

   In this example, delete the graphic on the Stage and drag the Flower Light graphic symbol to the exact center of the Stage.

10. **Right-click (Windows) or Control+click (Mac) the Hit frame and choose Insert Keyframe.**

11. **Use the Rectangle tool and drag a square to cover the entire area of the symbol, leaving the symbol on top. Use the Selection tool to select and delete the symbol, leaving only the square.**

    If you don't perform this step, viewers must place the mouse cursor exactly over one of the petals to see the animation. By defining the Hit frame as a square, placing the cursor anywhere within that square activates the button. Your screen should look like Figure 8-4, shown with the Up frame active.

Figure 8-4:
You can use the Flower Power library to create an animated button.

12. **Click the scene name (Scene 1) above the layer list to return to the regular Timeline.**

13. **Drag the button symbol that you just created from the Library to wherever you want the button placed on the Stage.**

    Congratulations! You have just created a button with a movie clip.

To test the button that you just created, choose Control➪Test Movie. Place the cursor over the button, click the button, and watch the animation. If you used the Flower Power movie from the Web site, first save the file on your computer by choosing File➪Save As and choosing a location on your hard drive. When you test this movie, the flower rotates when you pass the cursor over it and also lightens. When you click the flower, it seems to freeze. When you're finished, click the Close box of the window.

If you want to see the final result of the preceding steps, check out `flower power final.fla` on the companion Web site at `www.dummies.com/go/flashcs3`.

Adding an action for a button

A button doesn't do anything except look pretty until you give it the proper instructions. For example, a button can link you to another Web page or start a movie. See Figure 8-5. You find out about ActionScript in Chapter 10, but in this section, we explain the basic principle of adding an action to a button — in this case, an action that links the user to another Web page.

Courtesy Macquarium Inc.

As we explain in Chapter 10, Flash CS3 includes a new version of ActionScript, called ActionScript 3.0. Although this upgrade is great for developers, because it adds programming power, it makes once simple tasks much more difficult. However, after you have the ActionScript code for a button, you can use it as a template to create your own buttons.

You add an action for a button by placing the action on the Timeline, usually in the first frame. To create ActionScript for a button, follow these steps:

1. **If you haven't already done so, drag an instance of the button onto the Stage. If the button isn't selected, select it.**

2. **Open the Property inspector (choose Window⇨Properties⇨Properties). In the Instance Name text box, enter a name for this instance of the button symbol.**

   The name can't include spaces. You can use an underscore or hyphen for readability.

   Each instance of a button symbol should have a different instance name.

3. **Click anywhere off the Stage to deselect the button.**

4. **Create a new layer, called *Actions*.**

   Chapter 6 explains how to create layers.

5. **Click the first frame of the Actions layer.**

   This instruction assumes that you want the button to appear at the beginning of the movie. If you want the button to appear later, right-click

(Windows) or Control+click (Mac) the frame where you want the button to appear and choose Insert Keyframe. When you click a keyframe of a layer, all actions that you add go in that keyframe and on that layer.

Testing your button's URL navigation

To properly test a button, you need to publish your movie, upload it to your Web page, go online, and try it out. However, you can test the button on your hard drive first so that you can be fairly sure that it will work when you put it on your Web page.

To test your button without publishing it, choose Control⇨Test Movie and click the button. If you used an absolute (complete) URL, you should have no problem. Your browser should open and display the appropriate Web page. However, a relative (local) URL might not be available. For example, if your URL is `tips.html`, the button won't work unless you have a file named `tips.html` in the same folder as the Flash movie.

You can still test a relative URL on your hard drive. Continuing with the example of a link to `tips.html`, assume that on your Web server, `tips.html` is in the same folder as the Web page containing your Flash button so that you can use this simple local URL.

To test your button's ActionScript, follow these steps:

1. **After creating the button and its ActionScript containing a URL of `tips.html` (or whatever's appropriate in your situation), choose File⇨Save to save the movie file.**

2. **Choose File⇨Publish.**

   Flash publishes the file, creating an HTML file and an `.swf` file in the same folder as your `.fla` file. (These are default settings.

See Chapter 13 for more information on publishing movies.)

3. **You need a file on your hard drive with the same URL that you used for your button. Create a file named `tips.html` (or whatever URL you used) on your hard drive in the same folder as your movie.**

   You can use either of two methods:

   ✔ Make a copy of the existing `tips.html` (if you have it on your hard drive) and move it to the folder containing your movie.

   ✔ Create a new HTML document and save it as `tips.html` in the same folder as your movie. This document can be a dummy document — you can put any text you want in it. For example, you can type **This is a test HTML document**. If you create this document in a word processor, be sure to save it as an HTML document. Otherwise, use the software that you normally use to create HTML documents.

4. **Working offline, open your browser, choose File⇨Open, and open the HTML file for your Flash movie. (It has the same name as your movie.)**

5. **Click your button.**

   You should see `tips.html` displayed. If you don't, go back and check your ActionScript.

6. **Open the Actions panel (choose Window⇨Actions). Type the following ActionScript, substituting the following:**

- Your function name for goHome

- Your instance name for btnHome

- The URL you want for the URL in the code you see here

```
function goHome(event:MouseEvent):void
{
    var targetURL:URLRequest = new
        URLRequest("http://www.ellenfinkelstein.com/")
        ;
    navigateToURL(targetURL);
}
btnHome.addEventListener(MouseEvent.CLICK, goHome);
```

This code creates a function, called goHome, that references an instance of a button, called btnHome. It "listens" for a click and then executes the function. Be sure keep the same capitalization and line endings as shown here.

If the Compiler Error panel opens when you test your button (Control⇨ Test Movie), it means that you made a mistake in your typing. Check your code, correct any errors, and try again.

7. **Close the Action panel and save your movie.**

You can add your button to an existing Web page. In such a case, the button might be the only Flash element on the page. You can also include buttons as part of an environment created completely in Flash. Either way, buttons are a valuable piece of the Flash arsenal.

Part IV
Total Flash-o-Rama

The 5th Wave By Rich Tennant

"Well, it's not quite done. I've animated the gurgling spit sink and the rotating Novocaine syringe, but I still have to add the high-speed whining drill audio track."

In this part . . .

Moving imagery is the heart and soul of Flash, and in this part you make your Flash creations come to life through the power of animation and video. You find out about moving objects, changing their shape (or *morphing* them), letting Flash create animation for you, and easy ways to integrate video into your Flash extravaganzas.

After you create your movie, you can make it interactive so that the viewer's Web experience is more meaningful and engaging. Flash ActionScript offers infinite potential, so let your imagination soar. We show you how to combine your animation with your symbols and then add ActionScript to script your entire movie.

The world is not silent, and your Flash movies don't have to be either. Find out how to add sounds and music to your movies — from the simplest sound of a button click to the majestic tones of a full-fledged symphony.

Chapter 9

Getting Animated

. . . .

. . . .

In this chapter, we explain animation and making your graphics move. Are you ready to plunge into a world where you can make almost anything seem to happen? Hold on to your hat!

We start by explaining the basics of animation, including how to prepare for animation and how to work with the Timeline. Then we go into the specific techniques — Timeline effects, frame-by-frame animation, and tweening — that you can use to create great, animated effects in Flash. We cover both motion and shape tweening and then give you the details of editing your animation. So let's get moving!

Who Framed the Animation?

The secret of animation in Flash, as in the movies, is that nothing ever really moves. A Flash movie creates the illusion of movement by quickly displaying a sequence of still images. Each still image is slightly different. Your brain fills in the gaps to give you the impression of movement.

One of the great things about Flash is that you can easily create complicated, spectacular extravaganzas of animation. And Flash stores lots of information in the super-compact vector format. Because the files can be small, they can be transmitted over the Web quickly. That's good for your Web site viewers.

Just as in a movie on film, each still image is contained in a frame. Each *frame* represents a unit of time. You create the animation by placing images in the frames. A frame can contain one object or none or many, depending on how crowded a scene you want to create.

Time is your ally in Flash because you have complete control over it. You can look at each individual image in time and tweak it to your heart's content. Then you can step on the gas, play everything back at full speed, and watch everything appear to move.

In Flash, you create animation in three ways:

- ✔ **Frame by frame:** You move or modify objects one frame at a time. This frame-by-frame animation is time consuming but is sometimes the only way to create complex animated effects. This method can certainly satisfy your appetite for total control.

- ✔ **Tweening:** You create starting frames and ending frames and let Flash figure out where everything goes in the in-between frames, which is why it's called *tweening*. Tweening is much more fun and easier than frame-by-frame animation. If you can create the animation you want by tweening, it's definitely the way to go. Flash offers two types of tweening: motion tweening and shape tweening, both of which we describe later in this chapter, in the section "The Animation Tween."

- ✔ **Timeline effects:** You choose from a list of prebuilt animations, adjust a few settings, and then instantly apply them to your text, graphics, buttons, or movie clips. Flash automatically creates the tweens for you. This cool feature of Flash takes the automatic creation of animation to a whole new level.

In tweening, the starting and ending frames are called *keyframes* because they are the key moments in time that the software uses to calculate the in-between frames. Tweening not only means less work for you but also creates smaller files (which download faster) because you're describing your animations more concisely. In frame-by-frame animation, every frame is a keyframe because every frame defines a change in the action.

Preparing to Animate

You probably want to get started animating, but you need to set the stage first so that your animation works properly. Here are the steps you need to take before you can begin creating your animation:

1. **Choose Insert⇨Timeline⇨Layer to create a new layer for your animation and put your starting graphic or graphics on that layer.**

You should always animate each object on a separate layer that has no other objects on it. Otherwise, your animated objects might erase, connect to, or segment other objects . . . with messy results. And your animation probably won't work. Refer to Chapter 6 for more information on layers.

2. **If you plan to use motion tweening, turn your object into a symbol or group; if you plan to use shape tweening, make sure that your object is a shape and not a symbol; and if you plan to do frame-by-frame animation, your graphic can be anything you want.**

   See the section "The Animation Tween," a little later in this chapter, to find out more about motion tweening and shape tweening. Your graphic absolutely must be a symbol instance, a group, or text for your motion tweening to work. (Refer to Chapter 7 for more about symbols and instances, and see Chapter 4 for the lowdown on grouping objects.) For shape tweening, the rule is the opposite of motion tweening. If your graphic is a symbol or a group or both, you can't shape tween it; so for shape tweening, just draw a shape by using the drawing tools.

   Lines and shapes can have disastrous results when used together in shape tweens. Try to stick to one or the other. Shapes seem to work the best.

3. **Set a frame rate.**

   See the later section "Turtle or hare?" for more information.

When you animate, you often need to play back your animation during the process. The simplest way is to press Enter (Windows) or Return (Mac), which plays the movie. Sometimes, however, you might want more control — perhaps to play part of your movie. In this case, the Controller is invaluable. The Controller, as shown in Figure 9-1, is a simple toolbar that looks like the controls on a tape recorder. Use it to play, rewind, fast-forward, and stop your animation.

Figure 9-1:
The
Controller.

Pressing Enter or Return or using the Controller is a quick way to see your animation. But if you have a movie clip on the Timeline, you won't see the animation within the movie clip until you choose Control⇨Test Movie.

Master of the Timeline

The *Timeline* is the map of your animation sequence. If the Timeline isn't visible, choose Window⇨Timeline. Each layer has its own Timeline row. The

Timeline has its own coding to help you understand the structure of your animation, as shown in Figure 9-2.

You can undock the Timeline from the main Flash window and resize it. First click the gripper (the two dotted vertical bars) at the upper-left corner of the Timeline (to the left of the eye icon) and drag the Timeline where you want it. Then you can resize it as an independent window by dragging the lower-right corner (Windows) or the Size box in the lower-right corner (Mac). (If you get lost with the new arrangement, you can always go back to Window⇨Workspace⇨Default.)

Half the power of the Timeline is that it divides motion into *frames* — bits of time that you can isolate and work with — one at a time. The other half of the Timeline's power is that you can organize different components of your animation into different layers.

Always animate one layer at a time.

Click any frame to make it active. Remember to click in the row of the layer containing the graphics you want to animate. By clicking any frame, you can view your animation frozen in a moment of time.

Figure 9-2:
Use the Flash Timeline to control your animations.

As you read through the examples and steps in this chapter, you'll quickly get the hang of working with the Timeline.

Hide the layers that you're not interested in (click below the eye icon) to help you visualize the animation. But don't forget to check the animation with all the layers displayed to see how everything looks together. You should also lock layers when you're finished with them to avoid unwanted changes. Refer to Chapter 6 for further instructions on hiding and locking layers.

Turtle or hare?

All you need to do to make animation work is to view your sequence of still images over time at high speed. Unless you have a remarkable attention span, one image per second is way too slow. Silent movies were typically 16 or 18 frames per second (fps). With the arrival of talkies, the speed got bumped up to 24 fps for better quality sound. On your television, the speed is roughly 30 images per second.

The smoothness of the playback of your animation depends not only on the frame rate that you specify but also on the complexity of the animation and the speed of the computer that's playing it. Generally, 12 fps is a good choice for Web animation. Luckily, that's the default rate in Flash.

To change the frame rate for your animation, follow these steps:

1. **Double-click the Frame Rate box (which displays a number and the letters fps), at the bottom of the Timeline, to open the Document Properties dialog box.**

   Alternatively, you can choose Modify⇨Document.

2. **In the Frame Rate text box in the Document Properties dialog box, type a new number (in frames per second).**

   You can set only one frame rate for all the animation in your current Flash file. You should set the frame rate before you start animating.

3. **Click OK to set the new speed and close the dialog box.**

A Flash movie's frame rate represents the maximum speed at which the movie runs. Flash animation has no guaranteed minimum speed. If your animation is lagging or bogging down, increasing the frame rate doesn't help at all; in fact, it might make things worse.

Creating Animations Instantly with Timeline Effects

You can instantly create complex animations in Flash simply by choosing from a list of Timeline effects and applying one to your art. With Timeline effects, you can use prebuilt animations to make your art spin, shrink, explode, expand, fade in or out, and do many other tricks, with just a few clicks of your mouse.

To add animation by using Timeline effects, do the following:

1. **Select an object that you want to animate.**

   You can apply Timeline Effects to a shape, text, a bitmap image, a graphic symbol, a button symbol, a group, or a movie clip.

2. **Choose Insert⇨Timeline Effects and the submenus you want.**

   For example, in the Assistants submenu, you can choose Copy to Grid or Distributed Duplicate. (These effects allow you to automatically position multiple duplicates of an object.) In the Effects submenu, you can choose Blur, Drop Shadow, Expand, or Explode. In the Transform/Transition submenu, you can choose Transform or Transition.

   The Effects Settings dialog box opens for the effect that you select. Figure 9-3 shows the Effects Settings dialog box for the Drop Shadow effect.

Figure 9-3:
You can use the Drop Shadow effect to automatically add a shadow behind your graphics.

3. **In the Effects Settings dialog box, modify any of the default settings if you want to change them and then click OK.**

   The Effects Settings dialog box disappears. Flash automatically creates a new layer. The layer has the same name as the effect but with a number appended corresponding to the number of Timeline effects that you've created so far.

   Flash also automatically puts your object inside a new symbol, which is, in turn, inside a new graphic symbol that contains all the new tweens and transformations needed for the effect. Flash transfers all this to the new layer.

4. **Choose Control⇨Test Movie to view your animation.**

   Your movie is exported to a Flash Player (.swf) window.

5. **To further adjust your Timeline effect, close the Flash Player (.swf) window and click the Edit button in the Property inspector.**

   The Effects Settings dialog box for your Timeline effect reappears.

6. **Repeat Steps 4 and 5 as desired.**

To delete a Timeline effect, follow these steps:

1. **On the Stage, right-click (Windows) or Control+click (Mac) the object with the Timeline effect that you want to remove.**

   A contextual menu appears.

2. **Choose Timeline Effects⇨Remove Effect.**

   The Timeline effect is removed, and the original layer names are restored.

Animating with Keyframes

Keyframes are the frames that are key to your animation. In frame-by-frame animation, every frame is a keyframe. In tweened animation, only the first and last frames of a tween are keyframes. By creating keyframes, you specify the duration and therefore the speed of an animated sequence.

To create a keyframe, select a frame on the Timeline and choose Insert⇨ Timeline⇨Keyframe. For faster service, right-click (Windows) or Control+click (Mac) a frame on the Timeline and choose Insert Keyframe. You can also press F6.

You can change the display of the appearance of frames on the Timeline by clicking the Frame View button in the upper-right corner of the Timeline. This action brings up the Frame View pop-up menu. With this menu, you can

✔ Set the width of frame cells to Tiny, Small, Normal, Medium, or Large.

✔ Decrease the height of frame cells by choosing Short.

✔ Turn on or off the tinting of frame sequences.

✔ Choose to display a thumbnail of the contents of each frame. This is an awesome feature, like unspooling a reel of film. If you choose Preview, the thumbnail is scaled to fit the Timeline frame; if you choose Preview in Context, the thumbnail also includes any empty space in the frame.

Frame after frame after frame

If your animation isn't a simple motion in an easily definable direction or a change of shape or color — and isn't one of the prebuilt Timeline effects — you probably need to use frame-by-frame animation.

If you must, you must. Some complex animations just have to be created frame by frame. The basic procedure is simple.

To create an animation by using the frame-by-frame technique, follow these steps:

1. **Select a frame in the row of the layer that you want to use.**

   The animation starts in that frame.

2. **Right-click (Windows) or Control+click (Mac) the frame and choose Insert Keyframe.**

   The first frame on a movie's Timeline is automatically a keyframe, so you don't have to create it.

3. **Create the graphic for the first frame.**

   You can import a graphic, paste a graphic from the Clipboard, or use the Flash drawing tools. (Refer to Chapter 3 for help with creating or importing a graphic.)

4. **Right-click (Windows) or Control+click (Mac) the next frame and choose Insert Keyframe again.**

   The next frame on the Timeline now has the same graphic as the preceding one.

5. **Modify the graphic to create the second frame of the animation.**

TIP

6. **Repeat Steps 4 and 5 until you've created all the frames that you need for your animation.**

   While you work, you can continually check your cool animation by pressing Enter (Windows) or Return (Mac) to play it back.

Figure 9-4 shows frames of an animation as the word *New!* is created from a few specks on the page.

Figure 9-4: Sometimes a complex animation must be created frame by frame.

Stillness in the night

Regular frames cannot contain changes. Therefore, if you insert a graphic in the first keyframe, the graphic remains throughout the Timeline until it reaches another keyframe.

For several reasons, you might need to copy objects over a number of frames. Sometimes, you want a still image to sit unmoving for a while on a layer of your animation — as a background image, for example — while your animation moves in front. A background gives context to your animated objects. Even animated objects often need to remain on the Stage after they've finished moving about. A key element of animation is timing, and an animated character is often still for a few moments (even in elaborately animated Disney cartoons) before taking its next action.

To create an image that remains still over a number of frames, add a new layer for your background or other unmoving object. With that layer active, create or paste your object (or objects) at the starting frame you choose. Then click your chosen ending frame, and choose Insert⇨Timeline⇨Frame (or press F5). Flash duplicates your image throughout all intermediate frames.

As a shortcut, after you have your object or objects in the starting frame, Alt+drag (Windows) or Option+drag (Mac) the frame along the Timeline until you reach the last frame that you want to contain the object. Flash copies the contents of the first keyframe through all the frames.

If you copy the objects to a keyframe, they remain on the Stage until the next keyframe.

The Animation Tween

If your animation follows some simple guidelines, you can save yourself lots of work (and reduce your file size, too) by using Flash to calculate the in-between frames for you automatically. You create just the first and last keyframes, and Flash figures out what should go in between. In animation technobabble, that's called *tweening* — a quick, fun way to create great animations.

You can do a lot with Flash's tweening capabilities, including

✔ **Motion tweening:** This is definitely the most common type of tweening. With simple motion tweening, you can move your objects in a straight line from here to there. You can use motion tweening also to animate an object along any path that you create, even one with lots of curves.

✔ **Shape tweening:** This type of tweening gradually changes any shape to another shape. You create the first and last shapes. These days, kids call it *morphing*. The results may be quite unpredictable and require a lot of computer processing but are usually interesting. You can add shape hints to try to tell Flash exactly how you want your shape to morph.

And with both motion tweening and shape tweening, you can

✔ **Change an object's size:** For example, if you make an object smaller as you move it, the object often appears to be moving away from the viewer.

✔ **Rotate an object:** You specify the amount of the rotation. Flash combines the motion or shape tweening with the rotation so that you get both effects at one time.

✔ **Change color or transparency or both:** Flash creates a gradual change in color based on your starting and ending colors.

Animating your graphic's transparency is a particularly cool effect because it lets you fade objects in and out, making them magically appear and disappear at just the right moment.

Of course, you can create several animations, one after another, to mix and match the effects. You can also combine frame-by-frame animation with tweened animation. Let your imagination soar!

From here to there — motion tweening

In motion tweening, you move an object from one place to another. The movement can be a straight line or any path that you can draw with the Pencil tool. Figure 9-5 shows a few frames from a motion tween that uses a looped path. While the animation progresses, the skateboarder image also scales down to 50 percent of its original size so that it appears to be moving away from you. In this example, the path is made visible so that you can see how the animation works. You usually hide the layer that contains the path.

Moving symbols, groups, and type

You can motion tween symbol instances, objects that you've made into a group, or type (text). You can not only move them but also change their size, rotation, and skew. And, in the case of instances, you can also motion tween their color. (To change the color of groups or text during motion tween, you have to convert them into symbols first.) See Chapter 7 for more on symbols and instances.

Figure 9-5:
You can draw any path and animate an object along the path.

To *skew* an object means to slant it along one or both axes.

To create a simple motion tween animation, follow these steps:

1. **Right-click (Windows) or Control+click (Mac) an empty frame where you want the animation to start and then choose Insert⇨Keyframe.**

   The Timeline's first frame is always a keyframe, so if you're starting from the first frame, just click the frame.

2. **Create a group or text block or drag a symbol instance from the Library.**

   Refer to Chapter 7 for the details on creating symbols and instances. Refer to Chapter 2 for the lowdown on using the Library.

3. **Create another keyframe where you want to end the animation.**

4. **Move the object to a new position.**

5. **If you want to change the object's size, rotation, or color (as we explain in the sections that follow), make the adjustments at this point.**

   See the next two sections of this chapter for details.

6. **Click anywhere in the tween before the last keyframe.**

   The first keyframe is a good place to click.

7. **Choose Window⇨Properties⇨Properties to open the Property inspector if it's not already open.**

   If necessary, expand the Property inspector to its full size.

8. **In the Tween drop-down list in the Property inspector, select Motion.**

   Flash creates the motion tween. If you want to change the object's size or rotation, specify the settings in the Property inspector, as we explain in the next section.

You're done! Click the first frame and press Enter (Windows) or Return (Mac) to play the animation.

Here's a silly phrase to help you remember the procedure for creating a motion tween:

Funny	First keyframe
Objects	Object — place it
Love	Last keyframe
Moving	Move object
In	In the middle — click between the keyframes
Tweens	Tween — select Motion in the Tween drop-down list

Scaling and rotating an animated object

Okay, so you're creative and ambitious and want to do more. Changing other properties of your graphic while you're moving it is easy. In Step 5 of the procedure in the preceding section, you can scale and rotate (including skewing) your object.

Use the Free Transform tool, located on the Tools panel, or any other method of changing size or rotation. (Refer to Chapter 4 for instructions on scaling and rotating objects.)

In Step 7 of the motion tweening procedure in the preceding section, complete the rest of the settings in the Property inspector, as shown in Figure 9-6 (and described in the following text).

Figure 9-6:
The
Property
inspector.

After you specify motion tweening, settings appear in the Property inspector, letting you specify how your motion tweening will work:

- ✔ **To put into effect any scaling changes you made, select the Scale check box.** Enabling Scale has no effect if you don't change the object's size when you create the motion tween. Clearing the Scale check box disables the scaling.

- ✔ **To rotate your graphic, select one of the Rotate options in the drop-down list.** The Auto option automatically rotates the graphic once in the direction that uses the least movement. Or you can choose to rotate it clockwise (CW) or counterclockwise (CCW) and then type the number of times that you want to rotate your graphic. These options rotate your object even if you didn't rotate it in Step 5 of the motion tweening procedure. If you did rotate the object, however, Flash adds the two rotations to end up with the rotation angle you specified.

- ✔ **To control the acceleration or deceleration of the movement, use the Easing slider.** By default, the slider is in the middle, which creates a constant rate of movement throughout all the frames. Move the slider down to start slowly and speed up at the end. Move the slider up to slow down at the end. You can create a sense of anticipation or excitement by using this technique.

> ✔ **To ensure that your graphic symbol animation loops properly, select the Sync check box.** If your animation is in a graphic symbol and the number of frames it takes up isn't an even multiple of the frames that the symbol occupies on the main Timeline, Flash synchronizes the two time-lines so that the graphic symbol loops properly in the main Timeline. (This is a cool feature.)

We explain the Snap and Orient to Path settings later in this chapter, in the section "Tweening along a path." For details on the Sound, Effect, and Sync settings on the right side of the Property inspector, check out Chapter 11.

If you're doing character animation, use the Free Transform tool to reset the symbol transformation point to the joint position. For instance, a hand would rotate from the wrist. This can save you some work. (See Chapter 4 for more info on changing the transformation point.)

Tweening colors and transparency

To change an object's color, click the keyframe on the Timeline where you want to change its color. Then click the object. If your object is a shape rather than an instance, you can simply change its color and opacity in the Color panel. (See Chapter 3 for more on the Color panel.) If your object is an instance, choose Window⇨Properties⇨Properties to open the Property inspector if it's not already open.

To expand the Property inspector to its full size, if necessary, drag the bottom-right corner of the Property inspector (Mac) or click the Maximize button near the top right of the Property inspector title bar.

Select one of the options (such as Tint or Alpha) in the Color drop-down list and make the desired adjustments. (Chapter 7 explains how to modify instances of symbols and provides much more detail about using the options in the Color drop-down list.)

You can mix and match motion animation with scaling, rotation, color, and transparency changes to create exciting effects. If an object spins and gets smaller while it moves, it can seem to be rolling away from the viewer. Animating semitransparent objects in front of each other creates interesting mixtures of color and gives a semblance of texture and depth in the 2-D world of the Web. Decreasing Alpha (opacity) during a tween makes the object appear to fade as it becomes more transparent. Try out some possibilities and come up with ideas of your own.

Color fades are less work for the computer than alpha fades. If you need an object to fade in or out, your movie loads faster on older computers if you tween to or from the background color rather than tween to or from transparency.

Tweening along a path

You can create animation that doesn't move in a straight line by motion tweening along a path that you draw. Suppose that you want to get the skateboarder shown in Figure 9-5 to do some tricks. The following steps show you how to do that.

If you want to follow along with these steps, you can download the skateboarder image (skateboarder.bmp) from the companion Web site for this book at www.dummies.com/go/flashcs3. Then choose File➪Import➪Import To Library. In the File dialog box that appears, navigate to skateboarder.bmp and click Import to Library. (We made him in Poser — a cool program for generating 3-D people, in case you're interested. You can find out more about Poser at www.e-frontier.com.)

To tween along a path, follow these steps. (The first steps are the same as the ones we provide earlier in this chapter for motion tweens, in the section "Moving symbols, groups, and type.")

1. **Create the first keyframe (if necessary).**

2. **Place your instance, text block, or group on the Stage.**

   If you're using the skateboarder, drag it from the Library to the left side of the Stage.

3. **Create the ending keyframe.**

   Don't move the object as you usually do when creating a motion tween.

4. **Click anywhere between the two keyframes.**

5. **Choose Window➪Properties➪Properties to open the Property inspector if it's not already open.**

   To expand the Property inspector to its full size, if necessary, drag the bottom-right corner of the Property inspector (Mac) or click the Maximize button near the top right of the Property inspector title bar.

6. **In the Tween drop-down list, select Motion.**

   You now have a motion tween with no motion.

7. **In the Property inspector, select the Snap check box to snap the transformation point of the object to the motion path.**

8. **If you want to rotate the object with the angle of the motion path, select the Orient to Path check box.**

   The effect of this is even more dramatic if the object's transformation point is not at its center.

9. **Choose Insert➪Timeline➪Motion Guide.**

   A new layer appears on the Timeline. It's labeled Guide and has a motion guide icon. (If you want, you can create this layer before you start the process of creating the animation.)

10. **Click the first frame in the new Guide layer to select it, and draw your path, making a few curves or loop-the-loops, if you want.**

    You can use any of the drawing tools: Pen, Pencil, Line, Circle, Rectangle, or Brush. You can also use the Straighten or Smooth modifiers if you're using the Pencil tool. (The path shown in Figure 9-5 was created by using the Pencil tool with the Smooth modifier.)

    Lock the object's layer while you're drawing the guide path so that you don't move the object by accident. Refer to Chapter 6 for further instructions on hiding and locking layers.

11. **Choose the Selection tool, click the first frame of the animation, and drag the object to the place on your path where you want your animation to start; release the mouse button when the transformation point snaps to the desired place on the path.**

12. **Click the last keyframe and drag the object to the place on the path where you want the animation to end; release the mouse button when the transformation point snaps to the desired place on the path.**

13. **Press Enter (Windows) or Return (Mac) to play the animation.**

    You should see a few moments of death-defying skateboarding (or whatever animation you've created).

You can find the completed animation, skateboarder.fla, on this book's companion Web site at www.dummies.com/go/flashcs3.

Getting your tween ready for prime time

The steps listed in the preceding section for tweening along a path provide only the basic process. You often need to make several refinements to motion animation along a path.

Not satisfied with your motion path? No problem. Here's a great feature that lets you easily modify your path. Select the motion guide layer. Choose the Selection tool and reshape the line by dragging from any point on the line. (Just be sure not to break the line apart!) Press Enter (Windows) or Return (Mac) again, and the skateboarder follows the revised path.

Want to get rid of that unsightly motion guide? That's easy, too. Click the eye column of the motion guide layer to hide it. Press Enter (Windows) or Return (Mac) to play back the animation. (Even if you don't hide the motion guide layer in this way, the motion guide isn't visible when the movie is published.)

Symbols, groups, text, and bitmap images have transformation points that are usually at the center of the graphic. When you tween along a path, you might want another point to follow the path. In the section on groups in Chapter 4, you find out how to change the transformation point to get the results you want.

What if you already have a motion guide and you want to link it to an object on a different layer? Here are two ways you can link your motion guide to your object:

✔ **Drag the layer:** Drag the layer with your graphics so that it's under the motion guide layer. The new layer appears indented under the motion guide layer, showing that it's linked to the motion guide, as shown in Figure 9-7. When the new layer appears indented under the motion guide layer, you know that the layer is linked.

Figure 9-7:
A guide
layer.

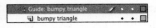

✔ **Modify Layer Properties:** Select your graphics layer and then choose Modify⇨Timeline⇨Layer Properties. In the Layer Properties dialog box, select Guided and then click OK. This links the graphics layer to the nearest motion guide layer above your graphics layer.

After dragging the layer or modifying the layer properties as just described, you need to connect your graphics to the motion guide. To do this, add an ending keyframe (if you don't already have one) in the graphics layer, and create a motion tween between the starting and ending keyframes in that layer. Then click the starting keyframe, drag your object to snap to where you want your animation to start on the path, click the ending keyframe, and snap to where you want your animation to end on the path.

Tweening shapes

In shape tweening, you change an object's shape at one or more points in the animation, and the computer creates the in-between shapes for you. You can get some great animation effects by using shape tweening. This process is often called *morphing.* You can see an example in Figure 9-8.

When shape tweening, you can combine changes in shape with changes in position as well as changes in size, color, and transparency. As with motion tweening, you should work with one shape per layer to avoid problems.

You can shape tween objects that you have created by using the Flash drawing tools.

Figure 9-8:
You can twist and deform your objects by using shape tweening, and a circle becomes a star!

You can't shape tween a symbol instance, text (type), or a group unless you break them apart into shapes by selecting them and choosing Modify⇨Break Apart. And you have to break apart text blocks twice — once to break the text block into individual letters and again to break the letters into shapes. You can also try to shape tween a bitmap image after breaking it apart, but the results are sure to be unpredictable.

If you break apart a symbol instance, text block, bitmap image, or group by using Modify⇨Break Apart, you might have a number of shapes to animate. Be sure to put each animated object on a separate layer. You can do this easily by selecting the objects and choosing Modify⇨Timeline⇨Distribute to Layers, which we explain in Chapter 6.

To create a simple shape tween, follow these steps:

1. **Right-click (Windows) or Control+click (Mac) an empty frame where you want the animation to start and then choose Insert⇨Timeline⇨ Keyframe.**

2. **Use the drawing tools to create the beginning shape.**

   You can create complex objects by merging objects of the same color or creating cutouts with objects of differing colors. (Refer to Chapter 3 for details.)

3. **Create a new keyframe after the first keyframe wherever you want it on the Timeline by using the same technique you used in Step 1.**

4. **Create the ending shape.**

   You can erase the old shape and draw a new one, or you can use the first shape, still on the Stage, and modify it. You can also move the shape and change its color or transparency or both. You can quickly change the color by using the Color modifiers in the toolbox. Use the Color panel to change opacity (Alpha). Refer to Chapter 3 for more information on colors and transparency.

5. **Click anywhere in the tween before the last keyframe.**

   The first keyframe is a good place to click.

6. **Choose Window⇨Properties⇨Properties to open the Property inspector if it's not already open.**

   To expand the Property inspector to its full size, if necessary, drag the bottom-right corner of the Property inspector (Mac) or click the Maximize button near the top right of the Property inspector title bar.

7. **In the Tween drop-down list, select Shape.**

8. **Select an Angular Blend or Distributive Blend type.**

   Select the Angular Blend type for blending shapes with sharp corners and straight lines. It preserves corners and straight lines in the in-between shapes of your animation. If your shapes don't have sharp corners, use the Distributive Blend type (the default) for smoother in-between shapes.

   Using the Angular Blend on irregular shapes may cause the animation to vanish!

9. **You're finished! Click the first frame and press Enter (Windows) or Return (Mac) to play the animation.**

Getting Flash to take a hint — using shape hints

Does the transformation of your shape animation look strange? Flash tries to figure out the simplest and most probable way to change one of your shapes into another, but this solution might not turn out the way you expect or want.

You can use the Flash shape hints feature to attempt to correct this problem. A *shape hint* is a marker you attach to a point on a shape at the beginning and end of a shape change. The shape hints signal to Flash exactly how you want this point and the area around it to move from the start to the end of the shape tweening process.

You can use up to 26 shape hints per layer. Shape hints are displayed on the Stage as small, colored circles with a letter (*a–z*) inside. On the starting keyframe, the shape hint is yellow; and on the ending keyframe, it's green. When you first insert a shape hint — before you move it onto your shape — it's red. Figure 9-9 shows an example of beginning and ending shapes with shape hints.

Figure 9-9:
Shape hints
guide Flash
as it tweens
your shape.

From this book's companion Web site, at `www.dummies.com/go/flashcs3`, you can download the Flash movie file shown in Figure 9-9. It's the `4 to 5 point star with shape hints.fla` file.

To use shape hints, follow these steps:

1. **If you haven't already done so, create a shape animation by using shape tweening.**

   Refer to the set of steps in the preceding section if you need help with this task.

2. **Click the keyframe where you want to add your first shape hint.**

3. **With the object selected, choose Modify⇨Shape⇨Add Shape Hint or press Ctrl+Shift+H (Windows) or ⌘+Shift+H (Mac).**

   Your beginning shape hint appears as the letter *a* in a small, red circle somewhere on the Stage.

4. **Click the small, red circle and drag it to the part of your graphic that you want to mark.**

5. **Click the keyframe at the end of the shape animation.**

   The ending shape hint appears somewhere on the Stage, again as the letter *a* in a small, red circle.

6. **Click the small, red circle and drag it to the point on your shape where you want your beginning point to move.**

   The ending shape hint turns green. If you go back to the first frame of the animation, the beginning shape hint turns yellow.

7. **Press Enter (Windows) or Return (Mac) to play your movie.**

You can drag shape hints off the Stage to remove them. Or choose Modify⇨Shape⇨Remove All Shape Hints to nuke them all — but the layer with shape hints must be selected. (Your animation then reverts to its original tween.) Choose View⇨Show Shape Hints to see all the shape hints in your current layer and keyframe. Choose it again to hide them. (Again, the layer and keyframe with shape hints must be selected.)

Adjusting shape hints

To tweak your animation, click the keyframe at the start or end of your shape animation and move your shape hint. Then play your animation again to see the new result. The more complicated your shape animation, the more shape hints you need to use. For more complicated shape animations, you can also add more keyframes between your original starting and ending keyframe. This creates intermediate shapes at the new keyframes that you can then tween (using plenty of shape hints, of course). In other words, you can create two or more shape tweens, one immediately following the other.

If you aren't getting the results you want, make sure that you have placed your shape hints logically. If you have a curve with shape hints *a, b,* and *c* (in that order), don't have them tween to a curve with the shape hints in *c, b, a* order unless you want some unusual effects. Flash does a better job with shape hints when you arrange them in counterclockwise order, starting from the upper-left corner of your object.

Editing Animation

You may find that you usually don't get your animation to move perfectly the first time, but fortunately Flash is quite forgiving. You can edit keyframes in assorted ways.

You can't edit tweened frames directly — you can view them, but you can edit your objects only in the keyframes, not in the in-between frames. You can overcome this restriction and edit your tweened frames by inserting a new keyframe between your beginning and ending keyframe and then editing the new keyframe. You do this by clicking a frame in the Timeline and then choosing Insert⇨Timeline⇨Keyframe (or pressing F6). Don't choose Insert⇨Timeline⇨Blank Keyframe unless you want to nuke your existing tween animation. Of course, you can always edit tweened frames by simply changing the starting or ending keyframe that defines them. When you edit a keyframe of a tweened animation, Flash automatically recalculates the entire tween.

The following sections explain some useful techniques for editing and managing your animations.

Adding labels and comments

Animation can get complicated after a while. You might find it helpful to add comments to the Timeline to explain what each part of the Timeline is doing. Also, when you start adding interactivity to your movies, you can add labels to frames and then refer to them in your ActionScript. (You can find out more about ActionScript in Chapter 10.)

To add a label or a comment to a frame, follow these steps:

1. **Select a frame.**

   See the next section for information on selecting a frame.

2. **Choose Window⇨Properties⇨Properties to open the Property inspector if it's not already open.**

   To expand the Property inspector to its full size, if necessary, drag the bottom-right corner of the Property inspector (Mac) or click the Maximize button near the top right of the Property inspector title bar.

3. **In the Frame Label text box, type the text for the label or comment and press Enter (Windows) or Return (Mac).**

   To make the text function as a comment, choose Comment from the Label Type drop-down list, below the Frame Label Text box.

Adding frame labels can be a nice way to lay out the timing of a movie, by typing what you want to happen where on your Timeline, for a kind of brief verbal storyboard. This can be particularly helpful when you're working with others on a project.

Selecting frames

Flash offers two styles of making selections on the Timeline:

✔ **Frame-based selection (the default):** In this method, if you click a frame or a keyframe, it's selected. To select a range of frames, you can click and drag over the frames that you want to select, or you can click the first frame, press Shift, and then click the last frame in the range.

✔ **Span-based selection:** In this method, if you click a frame, it selects the entire sequence containing that frame, from one keyframe to the next. Clicking and dragging moves the entire sequence (between the keyframes) along the Timeline in either direction. To select an individual frame, you need to press Ctrl (Windows) or ⌘ (Mac). (Span-based selection is a feature that many people prefer not to use.)

You can change the style of selection by first choosing Edit➪Preferences (Windows) or Adobe Flash CS3➪Preferences (Mac). Then in the General category in the Preferences dialog box, select or deselect the Span Based Selection option in the Timeline section.

Copying and pasting frames

You can copy frames that contain content you want elsewhere. Then you can paste the frames in another location.

To copy and paste frames, follow these steps:

1. **Select one or more frames.**

2. **To copy the frames to the Clipboard, choose Edit➪Timeline➪Copy Frames.**

3. **Select the first frame of your destination or select a sequence of frames that you want to replace.**

4. **To paste the frames into their new location, choose Edit➪Timeline➪ Paste Frames.**

You can also copy frames by pressing and holding Alt (Windows) or Option (Mac) while you drag the keyframe or range of frames to a new location. You see a small plus sign while you drag.

Copying and pasting motion

In Flash CS3, you can now copy motion tween information from one object to another. If you've created some nice animation for one character, for example, you can easily copy that same animation to other characters in your scene — or in another scene or movie.

To copy and paste motion from one symbol instance to another, follow these steps:

1. **In the Timeline, select the frames that contain the motion tween that you want to copy.**

   To get this to work properly, be sure to copy all the frames.

2. **To copy the motion information to the Clipboard, choose Edit⇨ Timeline⇨Copy Motion.**

3. **Select the symbol instance that you want to copy the motion information to.**

   The symbol instance should only be one frame long at this point; Flash will add the needed frames.

4. **To copy the motion information to the symbol instance you selected, choose Edit⇨Timeline⇨Paste Motion.**

   The pasted motion tween appears, starting in the frame of the Timeline that contains the destination symbol instance.

This copies all the motion tween information from one symbol instance to another — including the information about the symbol's changes in horizontal (x) and vertical (y) position, changes in horizontal and vertical scale, changes in rotation and skew, changes in color (including tint, brightness, and alpha), changes in filter values, and changes in blend modes. (See Chapter 7 for information on filters and blend modes.)

If you want to copy only some of this information, choose Edit⇨Timeline⇨ Paste Motion Special in Step 4. The Paste Motion Special dialog box appears, and you can select the check boxes for the properties you want to copy. Select the Override Target Scale Properties check box if you want the pasted scale properties to replace the target's scale properties; leave it deselected if you want the pasted scale properties to be added to the target's scale properties. Similarly, select the Override Target Rotation and Skew Properties check box if you want the pasted rotation and scale properties to replace the target's rotation and skew properties; deselect it if you want to add to the target's rotation and skew properties. Then click OK. The dialog box disappears, and the motion tween properties that you selected appear in the layer of the Timeline containing the destination symbol instance. You can now edit the new tween independently of the original — for example, you can change its length so that it doesn't remain in sync with the original.

Moving frames

You can move frames and their contents. Select the layer and place the cursor over a frame or range of frames. Then drag them to their new home, as shown in Figure 9-10.

Figure 9-10: Move frames by selecting and dragging them.

Adding frames

You can stretch out your animation by right-clicking (Windows) or Control+ clicking (Mac) and choosing Insert Frame. (Or you can select a frame and then press F5 to insert a frame.) Because you now have more frames between your first and last keyframes, the animation takes longer to complete and therefore appears to be slower. Use this technique to slow down the rate of animation.

Deleting frames

Delete frames by selecting one or more frames. Then right-click (Windows) or Control+click (Mac) one of the frames and choose Remove Frames. If you delete frames within a tweened animation, the animation is completed more quickly and appears to be faster.

Turning keyframes back into regular frames

If you don't like a keyframe, you can change it back to a regular frame by right-clicking (Windows) or Control+clicking (Mac) the offending keyframe and choosing Clear Keyframe. Changing a keyframe into a regular frame removes the change that occurred at that keyframe. You can use this technique to merge two consecutive tweens into one tween — change the keyframe in the middle to a frame.

Reversing your animation

You can make your animation play backward by selecting the relevant frames in one or more layers and choosing Modify⇨Timeline⇨Reverse

Frames. Your selection must start and end with keyframes. (This is an amazing feature.)

Changing speed

After you set up your animation, play your movie to check the speed. If one part of your tweened animation is too fast or too slow, you can slide keyframes around on the Timeline to shorten or lengthen the time between keyframes. You can do this by simply clicking a keyframe and dragging it to another point on the Timeline. This technique gives you lots of control over the timing of your animation.

If you have difficulty dragging an ending keyframe, create a new keyframe somewhere to the keyframe's right and then drag the obstinate keyframe.

Figure 9-11 shows two possible versions of the Timeline for the shape tween shown in Figure 9-9. The black dots on the Timeline are the keyframes. To create the version on the bottom, we dragged the last keyframe to the right, thereby lengthening the tween. Because the same change in shape now occurs over a longer period, the tween appears slower.

Figure 9-11: You can change the length of a tween.

The effect is even more noticeable when an object is moving across the stage during a tween. For example, if a symbol (or shape) moves from the left of the Stage to the right and you shorten the tween, the symbol (or shape) appears to move across the Stage more quickly because it must get from the left to the right in fewer frames.

Changing the animation settings

You can always go back and change some of the settings in the Property inspector. For example, you can add *easing* (acceleration or deceleration of movement) or change the blend type (angular or distributive) of a shape tween in the Property inspector. We explain these settings earlier in this chapter, in the sections "Scaling and rotating an animated object" and "Tweening shapes."

Using onion skins

To help you visualize the flow of your animation, you can turn on the onion-skinning feature. *Onion skinning* lets you see a "ghost image" of some or all of the frames in your animation. (Normally, you see only the current frame on the Stage.) Figure 9-12 shows an example of both regular and outlined onion skinning. Onion skinning displays frames as transparent layers, like the transparent layers of an onion skin.

Figure 9-12:
Onion
skinning
helps you
to see
where your
animation is
going.

 To display onion skinning, click the Onion Skin button at the bottom of the Timeline.

 To display onion skinning with outlines, click the Onion Skin Outlines button. Sometimes this makes it easier to see how your objects are animating.

When you display onion skinning, Flash places markers at the top of the Timeline around the frames that are displayed as onion skins. (See Figure 9-13.) Usually, these markers advance automatically when the current frame pointer advances. You can manually adjust the beginning and ending of the onion-skinning effect by clicking and dragging either the left or right marker to a new location on the Timeline.

Onion-skin markers

Figure 9-13: When you display onion skinning, markers are placed on the Timeline.

To edit any of the frames on the Timeline no matter where your current frame pointer is, click the Edit Multiple Frames button. If you also have onion skinning turned on, you can then edit any frame while viewing all the other onion-skinned frames.

Click Modify Onion Markers to display a menu to help you adjust the way your onion markers work:

- ✔ **Always Show Markers:** Shows onion markers even when you've turned off onion skinning.

- ✔ **Anchor Onions:** Locks the onion markers in their current position and prevents them from moving along with the current frame pointer, as they normally do.

- ✔ **Onion 2:** Applies onion skinning to the two frames before and the two frames after the *playhead* (the current frame pointer).

- ✔ **Onion 5:** Applies onion skinning to the five frames before and the five frames after the playhead.

- ✔ **Onion All:** Applies onion skinning to all the frames on your Timeline.

Hidden or locked layers never show as onion skinned. Hide or lock layers to isolate them from the layers you really want to change and to keep your onion skinning from getting out of control. Chapter 6 explains how to hide and lock layers.

Moving everything around the Stage at once

If you move a complete animation on the Stage without moving the graphics in all frames and all layers at one time, you might quickly go nuts when you discover that every little thing must be realigned. Instead, retain your sanity and move everything at one time.

To move a complete animation, follow these steps:

1. **Unlock all layers that contain the animation you want to move and then lock or hide any layers that you don't want to move.**

   To lock (or unlock) a layer, click below the lock icon on that layer's row. To hide (or unhide) a layer, click below the eye icon on that layer's row. See Chapter 6 for more information on working with layers.

2. **Click the Edit Multiple Frames button at the bottom of the Timeline.**

   If you ever need to resize a project, this button is your new best friend.

3. **Drag the onion-skin markers to the beginning and ending frames of your animation.**

   Alternatively, if you want to select all frames, click the Modify Onion Markers button at the bottom of the Timeline and choose Onion All.

4. **Choose Edit⇨Select All.**

5. **Drag your animation to its new place on the Stage.**

   If you run into difficulties making this work, in Step 3 click the Modify Onion Markers button at the bottom of the Timeline and choose Onion All, and in Step 5 use the keyboard arrows to move your animation to its new place on the Stage.

Making the Scene

Animations can get complicated fast, and one way to manage that complexity is by organizing them in layers and layer folders. (Refer to Chapter 6 for the lowdown on layers and layer folders.) Another great way to manage the complexity of your animations is to break them into chunks of time — into scenes. You can then use scenes as the modular building blocks of your movies, which you can then rearrange any way you want.

When is a good time to break up your movie into scenes? If your movie is simple, one scene might be all that you need. But if the movie gets more complex, you might want to break it up into a loading message, an introduction, the main act, the ending, and the credits.

Or if your Timeline becomes longer than one screen will hold at a time, you might want to find logical places to separate segments of your animation into scenes. If your cast of graphics characters changes at a particular time, that might be a good place to break into a new scene. And if a section of your movie can conceivably be reused elsewhere in other movies, you might have an excellent reason to break it out into its own scene.

Breaking your movie into scenes

When you create a new Flash movie file (for example, by choosing File⇨New and selecting a Flash File ActionScript 3.0 under the General tab), by default the file contains one empty scene, cleverly titled *Scene 1*. Any animations that you create then become part of Scene 1.

If you want to add a scene, choose Insert⇨Scene. The Stage clears, and the Timeline is labeled *Scene 2*.

Manipulating that scene

To keep track of your scenes, open the Scene panel by choosing Window⇨Other Panels⇨Scene, as shown in Figure 9-14. The Scene panel lists all the scenes in your movie. When you choose Control⇨Test Movie, the scenes play in order from the top of the list down.

Figure 9-14:
The Scene
panel lets
you make a
big scene.

Here's how to use the Scene panel to control your scenes:

✔ **To change the order in which scenes play:** Drag a scene's name on the Scene panel to a new place in the list.

✔ **To rename a scene:** Double-click the scene's name in the Scene panel, type the new name, and then press Enter (Windows) or Return (Mac).

To delete a scene, select that scene and click the Delete Scene button at the bottom of the Scene panel.

 To duplicate a scene, click the Duplicate Scene button at the bottom of the Scene panel.

To view a particular scene, click its name on the Scene panel. Or choose View⇨ Go To and choose the name of the scene that you want from the submenu.

Chapter 10

Getting Interactive

- -

In This Chapter

▶ Getting familiar with ActionScript

▶ Using methods to control objects

▶ Storing ActionScript in a frame

▶ Putting buttons to work with ActionScript

▶ Creating event listeners

▶ Animating masks

▶ Creating drag-and-drop animations

▶ Investigating advanced ActionScript features

- -

*T*he real fun with Flash begins when you start to make your art and animations interactive. *Interactivity* means that a computer user's input triggers
immediate changes on the computer screen, which the user can then
respond to further, as if a conversation is taking place between the user and
the computer. Examples can be as simple as clicking a button to go to
another Web page, or as complex as a video jukebox.

Flash uses a computer language called ActionScript to specify how the interactivity works. *ActionScript* statements are short instructions that tell Flash
what to do next. By combining them, you can produce complex sets of
instructions to create amazing animated graphics and to give your Flash
movies sophisticated interactive capabilities. ActionScript provides you with
tremendous flexibility in designing animations and interactivity, and only
your imagination limits what you can do.

Understanding ActionScript

Flash CS3 features ActionScript 3.0, a new version of ActionScript that has
been thoroughly redesigned to better support big, complex applications that
have lots of data.

For those just starting out with Flash, one advantage of ActionScript 3.0 is that Flash movies powered by ActionScript 3.0 can perform up to ten times faster than those using earlier versions of ActionScript.

Flash CS3 supports earlier versions of ActionScript too, but in this book all of our code is written in ActionScript 3.0 because that's the wave of the future. To run Flash movies written with ActionScript 3.0, your users need Flash Player 9 or later. At this writing, only about half of the computer users in the world have Flash Player 9, but by 2008 that number will probably rise to 90 percent or more.

ActionScript is based on the same language specification as JavaScript, the popular computer language used extensively in Web page design. ActionScript is basically a powerful version of JavaScript with extensions for controlling Flash animations. If you know JavaScript, you can use much of that knowledge when working with ActionScript, and vice versa.

Making objects work for you

ActionScript has numerous software building blocks that are ready for you to use. These building blocks are organized into *classes* that share similar properties and capabilities. (The capabilities are called *methods*.) You create instances of a class in ActionScript to use them in your Flash movies. These instances are called *objects*. Buttons, for example, are one kind of object in ActionScript, and sounds are another.

Objects such as buttons, text, movie clips, and sounds have properties and methods built into them in ActionScript, and this makes it easy to use ActionScript to control them.

Method acting

You can make an object work for you by calling on one of its built-in methods. Doing this is pretty easy: You specify the object by name, followed by the dot (.) operator, followed by the method and the parameters that you want to pass to it.

For example, if you have a movie clip with an instance named owl, you can create a variable (using the definition keyword var) named my_color that can use ActionScript's built-in ColorTransform class and its transform and colorTransform properties to transform the color of the instance:

```
var my_color:ColorTransform =
        owl.transform.colorTransform;
```

You can set `my_color` by specifying it by name, followed by the dot (.) operator, followed by the `color` property (which describes its red, green, and blue intensity), and then setting all that equal to a number for the color you want, like this:

```
my_color.color = 0x445566;
```

(In ActionScript, you specify a color by using hexadecimal format preceded by 0x.) Then you can apply the change to `owl` by specifying the name of the instance you want to change (`owl`), followed by the dot (.) operator, the `transform` property, another dot operator, and the `colorTransform` property, and then setting all that equal to `my_color` variable:

```
owl.transform.colorTransform = my_color;
```

As usual, Flash makes it easy for you to control objects and their built-in methods. As we show you in the next section of this chapter, you can just choose methods, events, and properties from a list in the Actions panel, and Flash shows you the parameters you need to fill in.

Flash lets you put ActionScript 3.0 in only two places:

- ✔ A keyframe on the Timeline
- ✔ A separate ActionScript text file

Adding ActionScript to Frames

You can add ActionScript to any frame, but to manage your Flash project more efficiently, it's a good idea to put all of your ActionScript code in one place, such as in Frame 1 in the first layer of your `.fla` file, to make it easy to find and modify.

Before we take a look at a specific example of adding ActionScript to a keyframe, let's get an overview of the process. First, you select the keyframe where you want to store the ActionScript, then you open the Actions panel (shown in Figure 10-1), and finally you add the ActionScript.

Now let's take a look at how we proceed through those steps in a simple example of using ActionScript in a frame: placing a `Stop` method at the beginning of the movie. You might want this, for example, if you provide a button that starts the movie, so that viewers can choose whether they want to see it. Then the movie loads, but the first thing that it encounters is a command to stop. Nothing happens until someone clicks a button to start the movie. (Of course, the Web page should also contain other buttons and information that viewers can use to navigate through your Web site.)

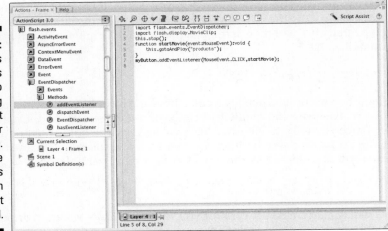

Figure 10-1:
The Actions panel is your key to adding ActionScript to your frames. Here the window is shown with Script Assist enabled.

To add the Stop method to your movie, follow these steps:

1. **Create your animation.**

2. **Choose Control⇨Test Movie and watch your animation run.**

3. **Create a new layer for your ActionScript and name it *Actions*.**

   Chapter 6 explains how to create and name layers.

4. **Click the keyframe where you want to add the ActionScript.**

5. **Choose Window⇨Actions to open the Actions panel if it isn't open already.**

   If necessary, click the Actions panel's title bar to expand the panel. And if the left pane of the Actions panel is not visible, click the tiny triangle in the middle of the left side of the Actions panel. If you don't see the Actions toolbox on the left (a list of ActionScript elements), click the tiny arrow at the bottom of the top of the left pane.

6. **Click the Script Assist button on the right side of the Actions window if it isn't already enabled.**

   In Script Assist mode, the right side of the Actions window is split into two horizontal sections so that the upper-right pane of the Actions window can display any parameters you need to type to write your ActionScript.

   Using Script Assist makes creating ActionScript much easier. We love it and leave it on almost all the time. We suggest that you do, too.

7. **In the left pane, choose flash.display⇨MovieClip⇨Methods, and then double-click Stop in the list of methods.**

   This code appears in the Script pane on the right of the Actions panel:

   ```
   import flash.display.MovieClip:
   not_set_yet.stop();
   ```

   The first ActionScript statement imports information about the MovieClip class into your Flash project so that your movie will have access to the prebuilt methods and properties of the MovieClip class. The second ActionScript statement uses the `stop` method to stop the `not_set_yet` instance. We change `not_set_yet` in the next step.

   (Each instruction in ActionScript is called a *statement*, and is written with a semicolon at the end.)

   To get an idea of the scope of ActionScript, take a peek at the many categories and subcategories that you can choose from in the left pane of the Actions window. For starters, you might browse briefly through the flash.display category and its subcategories.

8. **In the Object text box in the Actions panel, type the word** `this`.

   The word `this` refers to the currently running movie clip, which in our case is the movie defined by Flash's main Timeline. In the Script pane on the bottom right of the Actions panel, the second line of code changes to:

   ```
   this.stop();
   ```

9. **Choose Control⇨Test Movie again.**

   This time, the movie doesn't run; the `stop` method halts it.

Using ActionScript with Buttons

A common way to add interactivity is to create a button. The viewer clicks the button and something happens (or stops happening). Usually, you add text near or on the button so that your viewers know what the button is for.

If you've already worked on a Web site, you're familiar with the concept of hyperlinks. If you know HyperText Markup Language (HTML) — the language behind Web pages — you know that you can create hyperlinks by using the `<a>` tag and its `href` attribute. This tag links text or an image to another URL. When people click the text or the image, they are teleported to that URL. You can create Flash buttons that accomplish the same purpose but with much greater flair. And you can use buttons for so many other useful tasks — to start or stop animation, jump to different parts of a movie, turn music on and off, and much more.

Here's an example of how to create ActionScript that plays a movie clip when you click a button. To do that, follow these steps:

1. **Create the button and place an instance of the button on the Stage.**

   Chapter 8 tells you about creating buttons.

2. **Open the Property inspector if it isn't already open (choose Window⇨Properties⇨Properties).**

   If necessary, expand the Property inspector to its full size.

3. **In the Instance Name text box on the left side of the Property inspector, type a unique instance name for the button, such as myButton.**

4. **Create a new layer for your ActionScript and name it *Actions*. Click the first keyframe in the new layer.**

   The ActionScript that you create in the next steps is stored in this frame.

5. **Choose Window⇨Actions to open the Actions panel if it's not already open.**

   If necessary, click the Actions panel's title bar to expand the panel. And if the left pane of the Actions panel is not visible, click the tiny triangle in the middle of the left side of the Actions panel.

6. **If the Script Assist button on the right side of the Actions panel is enabled, click the button to disable Script Assist.**

7. **In the Script pane of the Actions panel, type**

   ```
   import flash.display.MovieClip:
   this.stop();
   ```

   This stops your movie on the first frame, as described in the previous section.

8. **Click the Script Assist button on the right side of the Actions window to enable Script Assist.**

9. **In the left pane of the Actions panel choose Language Elements⇨ Statements, Keywords & Directives⇨Definition Keyword⇨function.**

   Language Elements is up near the top of the list. Note the code that appears in the Script pane now, just below this.stop();

   ```
   import flash.display.MovieClip:
   this.stop();
   function not_set_yet() {
   }
   ```

10. **In the Name text box (in the Parameters area in the upper-right pane of the Actions panel), type** `startMovie`. **In the Parameters text box, type** `event:MouseEvent`. **In the Type text box, type** `void`.

Now the code in the Script pane on the right of the Actions panel looks like this:

```
import flash.display.MovieClip:
this.stop();
function startMovie(event:MouseEvent):void {
}
```

11. **In the left pane of the Actions panel, choose flash.display⇨ MovieClip⇨Methods⇨gotoAndPlay.**

Now the code in the Script pane on the right of the Actions panel looks like this:

```
import flash.display.MovieClip;
this.stop();
function startMovie(event:MouseEvent):void {
        not_set_yet.gotoAndPlay();
}
```

12. **In the Object text box (in the Parameters area of the Actions panel), type** `this`. **In the Frame text box, type a frame number (such as** `20`) **or a frame label (in quotes) — for example** `"products"`.

See Chapter 9 for information on creating a frame label.

Now the code in the Script pane on the right of the Actions panel looks like this:

```
import flash.display.MovieClip;
this.stop();
function startMovie(event:MouseEvent):void {
        this.gotoAndPlay("products");
}
```

The code creates a function named `startMovie`. When Flash runs the function startMovie, it goes to the frame labeled `"products"`. The word `this` is ActionScript shorthand for the currently running (or stopped) movie clip — in this example it's the Flash movie running from the main Timeline.

Be sure your code is within the final bracket, which is what closes the function.

13. **In the Script pane at the bottom right of the Actions panel, select the final line of code (the curly bracket). In the left pane of the**

Actions panel, choose flash.events⇨EventDispatcher⇨Methods⇨ addEventListener. In the Object text box, type myButton. **In the Type text box, type** MouseEvent.CLICK. **In the Listener text box, type** startMovie.

Now the code in the Script pane on the right of the Actions panel looks like this:

```
import flash.events.EventDispatcher;
import flash.display.MovieClip;
this.stop();
function startMovie(event:MouseEvent):void {
        this.gotoAndPlay("products");
}
myButton.addEventListener(MouseEvent.CLICK,
        startMovie);
```

This adds an event listener to myButton that "listens" for a mouse click and executes the startMovie function when it detects a mouse click on myButton.

14. **If you want to change the** MouseEvent.CLICK **parameter, click it in the lower-right pane of the Actions panel. Then in the Parameters area of the Actions panel, replace** CLICK **with another parameter, such as** MOUSE_OVER.

See Table 10-1 for more information on some of the event parameters that you can use to define when a button action goes into effect.

15. **Choose Control⇨Test Movie.**

When you click your button, your Flash movie jumps to the frame labeled "products" in your Timeline.

Table 10-1	Mouse Events
Event	*When the Action Occurs*
CLICK	When the user clicks the mouse button
MOUSE_DOWN	When the mouse cursor is over the object (or the button's hit area) and the user is pressing the mouse button
MOUSE_UP	When the mouse cursor is over the object (or the button's hit area) and the user releases the mouse button
MOUSE_OVER	When the mouse cursor moves over the object (or the button's hit area) without clicking
MOUSE_OUT	When the mouse cursor moves out of the object (or the button's hit area) without clicking
MOUSE_WHEEL	When a mouse wheel is spun over the object

The hit area of a button is the button's *active area* — the area that responds to mouse clicks and other user interactions. See Chapter 8 to find out all about buttons.

Here's a variation of the preceding ActionScript code. This version makes use of different mouse events — the MOUSE_DOWN and MOUSE_UP events. With this code, pressing the mouse button makes the movie on the current Timeline play, and releasing the mouse button stops it.

```
import flash.events.EventDispatcher;
import flash.display.MovieClip;
this.stop();
function startMovie(event:MouseEvent):void {
        this.play();}
function stopMovie(event:MouseEvent):void {
        this.stop();}
myButton.addEventListener(MouseEvent.MOUSE_DOWN,startMovie
        );
myButton.addEventListener(MouseEvent.MOUSE_UP,stopMovie);
```

Using ActionScript with Movie Clips

You use ActionScript with a movie clip in much the same way that you use it with a button; both are instances of objects that you can control with ActionScript.

You can use ActionScript with movie clips to do all kinds of things. You can use ActionScript to start or stop a movie clip from playing and to replace one movie clip with another. You can use ActionScript to make one movie clip control a second movie clip — the ActionScript could set the second movie's properties, for instance, and change its size, visibility, and so on, based on the user's interaction with the first movie clip. For example, you might make a movie clip that contains a cartoon of a dancing TV set, and add ActionScript so that each time the user clicks the movie clip, the TV shows a different cartoon.

In this section we look at two examples of how you can use ActionScript with movie clips. In the first, you make one movie clip into an animated mask that reveals another movie clip underneath it. In the second, you find out how to make a movie clip draggable.

Creating animated masks with movie clips

Flash has loads of useful methods and properties built into its objects. One is the DisplayObject class's mask method, which you can use, for example, to create an animated mask. When a mask is animated, the mask reveals the background beneath while it moves. (For more on masks, refer to Chapter 6.)

To use the mask property to make a movie clip into a mask, follow these steps:

1. **Create a movie clip and place an instance of it on the Stage.**

   This instance will be the background movie clip behind the mask. For example, you may want to make a wide movie clip a landscape. (If you need to know how to create movie clips, check out Chapter 8.)

2. **Choose Window⇨Properties⇨Properties to open the Property inspector.**

   If necessary, expand the Property inspector to its full size.

3. **In the text field near the upper-left corner of the Property inspector, enter an instance name for the movie clip (such as *background*).**

4. **Create another movie clip and place an instance of it on a new layer on the Stage. In the Property inspector, enter an instance name (such as *binoculars*) for the second movie clip.**

   This instance will be the mask movie clip. Check out Chapter 6 for information on creating new layers.

5. **Create some animation for this movie clip so that it moves over the background movie clip.**

   See Chapter 9 for information on creating animation.

6. **Create a new layer in the Timeline, and select Frame 1 of the new layer.**

7. **Choose Window⇨Actions to open the Actions panel.**

   If necessary, click the Actions panel title bar to expand the panel.

8. **Click the Script Assist button on the right side of the Actions window if it isn't already enabled. In the left pane of the Actions panel, choose flash.display⇨DisplayObject⇨Properties, and double-click mask.**

   This code appears in the Script pane to the right of the Actions panel:

   ```
   import flash.display.DisplayObject:
   not_set_yet.mask();
   ```

   The first line of code imports information about the DisplayObject class into your Flash project so that your movie will have access to the pre-built methods and properties of the DisplayObject class.

9. **In the Expression text field at the upper-right pane of the Actions panel, change not_yet_set to the first movie clip's instance name**

(such as *background*). Before the ending semicolon, type an equal sign and the mask movie clip's instance name (such as *binoculars*).

If your mask movie clip's instance name is `binoculars` and your other movie clip instance is named `background`, the code in the Actions panel should now look like this:

```
import flash.display.DisplayObject:
background.mask = binoculars;
```

10. **Choose Control⇨Test Movie and enjoy the new animation.**

Dragging movie clips

Flash lets you create objects that your audience can drag around the screen. Draggable objects are used for games, slider bars, and other fun purposes.

You can create draggable movie clips to use for games, drag-and-drop interfaces, or slider bars. Although creating draggable movie clips is an advanced function, it's too much fun to leave out of this book. To create a draggable movie clip, follow these steps:

1. **Choose Insert⇨New Symbol to create a new symbol.**

2. **In the Create New Symbol dialog box that appears, name your new symbol, select the option for the Movie Clip behavior, and click OK.**

3. **On the Stage, create an object that you want the viewer to be able to drag.**

4. **Choose Edit⇨Edit Document to return to the main Timeline.**

5. **Drag the movie clip that you created from the Library to the Stage.**

    An instance of the movie clip appears on the stage.

    To open the Library, choose Window⇨Library.

6. **Choose Window⇨Properties⇨Properties to open the Property inspector if it's not already open.**

7. **In the Property inspector, type in a name in the Instance Name text box.**

    Your instance now has a name — `snowflake`, for example.

8. **Create a new layer in your movie, and select the first frame in the new layer.**

9. **Choose Window⇨Actions to open the Actions panel if it's not already open.**

   If necessary, click the collapse arrow on the Actions panel's title bar to expand it.

10. **Click the Script Assist button to turn it off if it is selected.**

    Now you can type your code directly, without interference from Script Assist.

11. **Type the following code in the right pane of the Actions panel:**

```
import flash.events.EventDispatcher;
import flash.display.Sprite;
function dragMovie(event:MouseEvent):void {
        snowflake.startDrag();
}
snowflake.addEventListener(MouseEvent.MOUSE_DOWN,
        dragMovie);

function dropMovie(event:MouseEvent):void {
        snowflake.stopDrag();
}
snowflake.addEventListener(MouseEvent.MOUSE_UP,
        dropMovie);
```

    If your instance isn't named `snowflake`, substitute the name you gave to your instance instead.

    This code tells Flash to start dragging your movie clip instance when you click it, and to stop dragging it when you release the mouse button. You might have noticed that it's similar to the code in the "Using ActionScript with Buttons" section, earlier in this chapter.

12. **Choose Control⇨Test Movie and then click and drag your movie clip.**

    Your mouse drags the movie clip!

You can constrain the movement of the movie clip to certain areas. For example, on a slider bar, you don't want the movie clip going all over the page — only along the bar. You can constrain the movement by specifying a constraint rectangle for the movie clip. See `startDrag` in the ActionScript 2.0 Language Reference for more details. (In the Actions window, select `startDrag` and click the Help button next to the Script Assist button to view the discussion of `startDrag` in the Help section.)

Exploring ActionScript Further

Flash contains approximately one zillion more ActionScript methods and properties than the ones that we cover in this chapter. For more information, choose Help⇨Flash Help, and in the Help window that appears, browse through

Programming ActionScript 3.0 or *ActionScript 3.0 Language and Components Reference*. In the following sections, we briefly explain a few more aspects of ActionScript programming to give you an idea of some of the possibilities.

Programming constructs

If you're familiar with programming, you'll recognize many commands in ActionScript, such as For and While, which let you process certain ActionScript statements repeatedly while certain conditions that you specify are true. The If and Else statements create conditional expressions.

Making comments

To help make your ActionScript clear when you look back at it a few months from now, you should add comments that explain the purpose of the ActionScript. You can add comments when Script Assist is on by choosing Language Elements⇨Operators⇨Comment⇨// (or Language Elements⇨ Operators⇨Comment⇨/*..*/) and then typing your comments in the Comments text box, which is in the Parameters area in the upper-right pane of the Actions panel.

It is definitely easier, though, to type your comments with Script Assist off. Temporarily turn off Script Assist in the Actions panel by clicking the Script Assist button. Then in the Script pane, type two slashes (//) and then your comments. Anything on the line after the two slashes is ignored when running the animation. If you need more than one line for comments, type the two slashes at the beginning of each comment line.

If you're like we are, you love Script Assist and will want to turn it on again (by clicking the Script Assist button) after typing your comments.

External scripting

You can keep your ActionScript in separate text files that your Flash movie can load when needed. This makes it easier to reuse your beautiful ActionScript code in multiple movies. You can create your ActionScript files with any text editor that you like.

Adobe recommends that instead of adding ActionScript to frames all over the place, you put all of your ActionScript code in a single place, making it easier to find and debug all your code. To make your code easy to find and manage, it's probably best to put all your code in the first frame of the first layer of the Timeline or in a separate text file.

To create a separate new ActionScript file within Flash, choose File➪New and then choose ActionScript File from the General tab of the New Document dialog box. You can type your ActionScript code in this file and save it.

You can also create ActionScript files by using Dreamweaver or a separate text editor, such as Notepad (Windows) or TextEdit (Mac). (In TextEdit, choose TextEdit➪Preferences, and when the Preferences window appears, select Plain Text rather than Rich Text in the New Document Attributes section.) Be sure to save the file with the .as suffix, which stands for ActionScript, of course.

To include the code from a separate ActionScript file in any part of your movie, simply add this ActionScript into a frame:

```
include "your-filename-goes-here.as"
```

This specifies an ActionScript file in the same directory as your .fla or .swf file.

Discovering more about ActionScript

ActionScript gives you tremendous power over your Flash movies. If you enjoy using ActionScript, you might want to check out some of the great resources we list in Chapter 15.

Editing Sounds

After you place a sound, you can edit the sound to fine-tune its settings. You should delete unused or unwanted portions of a sound to reduce file size. You can also change the volume while the sound plays.

To edit a sound, follow these steps:

1. **Click a frame that contains a sound (or import a sound, as we describe in the preceding section, "Placing sounds into a movie").**

2. **Choose Window➪Properties➪Properties to open the Property inspector, if it isn't already open.**

   If necessary, expand the Property inspector to its full size.

3. **Click the Edit button to open the Edit Envelope dialog box (see Figure 11-2).**

Figure 11-2:
Use the Edit Envelope dialog box to edit your sounds.

Envelope line — left channel

Play

Stop

Envelope line — right channel

Zoom in

Zoom out

Frames

Seconds

To see a specific section of a sound in more detail, click the Zoom In button. Zoom in when you want to edit small details of a sound.

 To see more of a sound's time frame, click the Zoom Out button. Zoom out to edit the sound as a whole.

 You can display sounds in terms of seconds or frames. Click the Seconds button to show sounds in seconds. Click the Frames button to display sounds by frames.

Deleting parts of a sound

Between the left (top) and right (bottom) channel display is a narrow strip that controls the starting and ending points of a sound. By deleting the beginning and end of a sound, you can eliminate unused portions of the sound. Along this strip are two vertical bars: one at the beginning of the sound and another at the end. These bars control when the sound starts and ends. Use them to edit the sound as follows:

✔ **Time In control:** This bar, on the left edge of the sound, specifies the start of the sound. Drag the bar to the right to delete the beginning of the sound.

✔ **Time Out control:** This bar, on the right edge of the sound, specifies the end of the sound. Drag the bar to the left to delete the end of the sound.

Changing the volume

On both the left and right channel displays, Flash shows an envelope line to indicate the approximate direction of the sound's volume (refer to Figure 11-2). Where the volume changes, Flash places small squares, called *envelope handles.* To change the sound's volume, drag an envelope handle up (to increase the volume) or down (to decrease the volume). This is how you create sound fade ins and fade outs.

You can click an envelope line to add a new envelope handle. This new handle enables you to create a new direction for the sound's volume at the handle's location. To remove an envelope handle, click it and drag it out of the Edit Envelope window.

When you finish editing a sound, click OK to close the Edit Envelope dialog box.

Managing Sound

Sound can increase the size of your movie by such a great extent that you need to pay attention to how you use it. You should make every effort to compress the sound. You can also lower the sampling rate; however, your sound's quality is then reduced. Nevertheless, you should try out all the possibilities until you get the best results.

The *sampling rate* is the rate at which the computer measures sound and converts it into numerical data. The computer makes these sample measurements many thousands of times per second. A higher sampling rate provides more information about the sound and, therefore, better audio quality. But all those extra measurements make for a much bigger data file.

Flash offers two ways to control the properties of a sound:

- ✔ **Use the Publish Settings dialog box to specify properties for all the sounds in a movie.** If you have only one sound or a few similar sounds, specifying settings this way is easy.

- ✔ **Use the Sound Properties dialog box to specify properties of specific sounds.** As long as you don't specifically override these properties when you publish, these settings stick. Use the Sound Properties dialog box when you want to specify different properties for each sound.

Because you specify the publish settings when you publish a movie, we discuss those settings in Chapter 13. In this section, we explain how to fine-tune sound properties in the Sound Properties dialog box.

To open the Sound Properties dialog box, open the Library (choose Window⇨ Library) and double-click the icon of the sound that you want to work with. Figure 11-3 shows the Sound Properties dialog box.

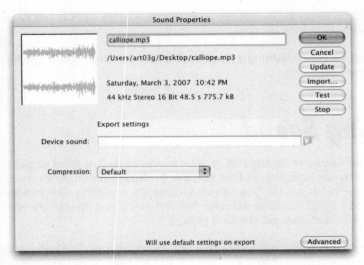

Figure 11-3:
Use the
Sound
Properties
dialog box
to set the
properties
of individual
sounds,
including
their
compres-
sion and
quality.

At the top of the dialog box, Flash displays statistics for the sound — its location, date, sample rate, channels, bit rate, duration, and file size. Use the Export Settings section to specify how you want to export the file. For each compression type, Flash displays the settings available for that type in the drop-down list. When you choose settings, look at the bottom of the dialog box, where Flash displays the new file size in kilobytes and in percentage of original size. The file size reduction can be pretty amazing. Here are the options available in the Compression drop-down list box:

✔ **Default:** This option uses the compression settings specified in the Flash tab of the Publish Settings dialog box when you publish your .swf file. (Chapter 13 gives you more information on publishing to .swf files.)

✔ **ADPCM:** You can convert stereo to mono to cut down file size. Available sampling rates are 5, 11, 22, and 44 kHz. You can choose from 2, 3, 4, or 5 bits. Choose 5 bits for the best sound; the default is 4 bits. ADPCM is short for *Adaptive Differential Pulse Code Modulation*. This compression method produces files that take up less storage space than CD-quality audio. In case you're wondering what the heck this compression is, it's used to store music on Sony Mini Discs.

✔ **MP3:** MP3 is a popular and efficient compression method. (To change the settings of an imported MP3 file, be sure to deselect the Use Imported MP3 Quality check box.) You can convert stereo to mono and choose a bit rate measured in kilobits per second. You can choose from 8 Kbps (poor quality) to 160 Kbps (near-CD quality). Generally, you want something between these two extremes. Try a bit rate between 20 and 84

Kbps for a good balance of file size and quality. You can also choose the quality — Fast, Medium, or Best. The Fast option optimizes the sound for faster download from your Web site but with some quality compromise. For music, MP3 provides the best compression, letting you keep your quality as high as possible.

✔ **Raw:** This option exports the sound with no sound compression. You can convert stereo to mono and select the same sampling rates as for ADPCM.

✔ **Speech:** This option exports the sound with compression techniques specially designed for speech. You can select the same sampling rates as for ADPCM. A good choice for speech is 11 kHz.

After you specify a group of settings, click the Test button. This handy button lets you hear how your sound file sounds with each setting.

The Sound Properties dialog box also lets you update the original sound after you modify it with sound-editing software — just click the Update button. You can also click Import to import a sound file. The Stop button stops playing a sound that you're previewing.

When you're finished, click OK to finalize your settings and close the dialog box.

Video Magic

The Flash Player has achieved more universal adoption than any other Web video technology, so Flash can be a great way to deliver video over the Web. Flash Player version 6 and later can play video, and (as of this writing) Adobe claims that more than 98 percent of U.S. Web surfers have Flash Player 6 or higher, compared with 83.2 percent for Windows Media Player, 66.9 percent for Apple's QuickTime Player, and 55.3 percent for Real Player. The Adobe Web site provides more details — you can check it out at www.adobe.com/products/player_census/flashplayer/.

Flash can use a variety of video formats. You can use Flash to create or import Flash Video (FLV) files. (*FLV* is a file format developed by the Flash team for video on the Web.) If you have QuickTime 7 installed on your Mac or QuickTime 6.5 for Windows on your PC, you can import files in the AVI, MPG/MPEG, MOV, and DV formats. If you have DirectX 9 or higher installed on your Windows PC, you can import files in the AVI, MPG/MPEG, and Windows Media File (WMV and ASF) formats.

Four ways to use video in Flash

You may include video in your Flash movie in various ways. For starters, you may embed video in your SWF file and play it in the Timeline. This lets you play your video from within your `.swf` file. This can work well for short video clips (perhaps ten seconds or less), but longer video clips might make your Flash file take a loooooooong time to download, and these clips might have problems with audio/video synchronization. For more information, see the next sections in this chapter, "Preparing to embed video in Flash" and "Embedding and editing a video."

And using Flash CS3, you may also

- ✔ **Stream video from your Web server.** You can connect to an `.flv` video file from within your `.swf` file and play the video while it downloads from a plain old Web server. This is a cool feature and definitely a good idea if you have a video longer than around ten seconds. Your audience can start to watch the video while it's still downloading, and the audio and video won't get out of sync. For more information, see the "Streaming a video" section, later in this chapter.

- ✔ **Stream video from a Flash video streaming service.** You can play your video from a Web hosting service provider that specializes in Flash video. This can give you good performance if you want to do fancy things like host video-on-demand applications, webcam chats, live-event broadcasts, and real-time collaboration applications. But it's not cheap, so if you're a new Flash user, you probably don't need to think about this option for now.

- ✔ **Stream video from a Flash Media Server.** You can play your video from a Flash Media Server that you host. This can give you good performance for heavy-duty deployment of multiple Web video streams, as if you are your own Flash video streaming service, but the Flash Communication Server software is complex, and again it's not cheap, with prices ranging from free for a developer version to $4500 and up. So unless your boss is investing zillions in a Flash video Web site, you again probably don't need to worry about this option.

Preparing to embed video in Flash

If you have a video file that you want to embed into your Flash file, you first need to find out the frame rate of your video and make sure that your Flash document has the same frame rate, to avoid erratic playback.

On the Mac, you can do this by following these steps:

1. **Click the Finder in the Dock. In a Finder window, open your Applications folder and double-click the QuickTime Player.**

   The QuickTime Player starts, and the QuickTime Player menus appear.

2. **In the QuickTime Player menus, choose File⇨Open File, and in the file dialog box that appears, locate and select your video, and then click the Open button.**

   Your video appears.

3. **Choose Window⇨Show Movie Info.**

   The Movie Info window appears.

4. **Make a note of the video's frame rate (shown in the Movie Info window as FPS — frames per second).**

   You might also want to note the normal size of the video. (A typical size is 720 x 480 pixels.)

5. **Choose File⇨Quit.**

   The QuickTime Player closes.

6. **Return to Flash (perhaps by clicking the Flash icon in the Dock), open or create a Flash movie if one isn't open, and choose Modify⇨ Document.**

   The Document Properties dialog box appears, showing the document's dimensions, frame rate, and other properties.

7. **To avoid unstable video playback, change the number in the Frame Rate text box to match your video's frame rate.**

In Windows, you can match your Flash movie's frame rate to your video's frame rate by following these steps:

1. **If your video is not an .avi file or a .wmv file, skip to Step 2. If your video is an .avi or a .wmv file, right-click the file and choose Properties. In the Summaries or Details tab, note the number of fps (frames per second) for your movie. Close the Properties window, and skip to Step 8.**

   You might also want to note the normal size of the video. (A typical size is 720 x 480 pixels.)

2. **From Windows, choose Start⇨Programs⇨QuickTime⇨QuickTime Player.**

   If you don't have the QuickTime Player in your Start menu, point your Web browser to www.apple.com/quicktime/download, follow the instructions there to download and install QuickTime, and then choose Start⇨QuickTime⇨QuickTime Player.

3. **In the QuickTime Player, choose File⇨Open Movie in New Player.**

   The Open dialog box appears.

4. **Locate and select your video, and then click the Open button.**

   Your video appears.

5. **Choose Window⇨Show Movie Info.**

   The Movie Info window appears.

6. **If necessary, click the More Info disclosure triangle to see the detailed information about the movie. Make a note of the video's frame rate (shown in the Movie Info window as Movie FPS — frames per second).**

   You might also want to note the normal size of the video. (A typical size is 720 x 480 pixels.)

7. **In the video window, choose File⇨Exit.**

   The QuickTime Player closes.

8. **In Flash, open (or create) a Flash movie if one isn't open, and choose Modify⇨Document.**

   The Document Properties dialog box appears, showing the document's dimensions, frame rate, and other properties.

9. **To avoid unstable video playback, change the number in the Frame Rate text box to match your video's frame rate.**

   If you downloaded QuickTime while Flash was running, you have to quit Flash and restart Flash if you want to import a `.mov` file.

Embedding and editing a video

You can easily import video directly into your Flash animations. Flash's Import Video wizard walks you through the complexities of compressing and embedding your video. The wizard even lets you split up your video clips before importing them so that after they're in Flash, it's easy to rearrange different sections of them.

Embedding video in your Flash movie is convenient if your video is short — perhaps ten seconds or less. If the video is longer, downloading your video while the Flash movie plays is probably a better approach.

Before you embed video into Flash, first you should make sure that the frame rate of your video and your Flash movie match, which we show you how to do in the preceding section, "Preparing to embed video in Flash." After you've done that, you can make video clips part of your Flash movie by following these steps:

1. **Click a keyframe where you want to put your video (or create a keyframe by clicking a frame and choosing Insert⇨Timeline⇨ Keyframe).**

2. **Choose File⇨Import⇨Import Video.**

   The Video Import Wizard appears.

3. **Select the On Your Computer option to import a video from your computer.**

4. **Click the Choose button.**

   The Open File dialog box appears.

5. **Find and choose a video file in the Open File dialog box and then click the Open button. Then in the Import Video dialog box, click the Next (Windows) or Continue (Mac) button.**

   The Import Video dialog box now gives you choices for deploying your video, including Embed Video in SWF and Play in Timeline.

6. **Select the Embed Video in SWF and Play in Timeline option, and then click Next (Windows) or Continue (Mac).**

7. **You probably want to select Movie Clip from the Symbol Type drop-down list, and you probably want to select Integrated from the Audio Track drop-down list.**

   The Video Import Wizard gives you a choice of symbol type for your embedded video. You can also decide whether to import your audio track integrated with the video or as a separate track. Embedding your video as a movie clip symbol and with the audio track integrated are usually good choices. When you embed your video in a movie clip symbol, the video's Timeline is within the movie clip and plays independently of the main Timeline. This gives you a lot of flexibility, and lets you move your video around easily within your Flash movie. However, if your Flash movie is mostly just going to play back the video on the main Timeline without doing much else, Embedded Video in the Symbol Type drop-down menu is an appropriate choice.

8. **If you want to edit the video first, select the Edit the Video First option. Otherwise, select the Embed the Entire Video option and skip to Step 18.**

   You have a choice of importing the entire video or editing it first. If your movie's codec doesn't support editing, the edit option is not available. (The *codec* is the software that encodes the movie's images and sound into a computer file and then decodes it for playback. Many codecs exist, and they use different techniques with varying advantages and disadvantages.)

9. **Click Next (Windows) or Continue (Mac).**

   The Split Video pane in the Video Import Wizard appears, as shown in Figure 11-4.

Figure 11-4: In the Video Import Wizard, you can split your video clip into sections while bringing them into Flash.

To view your video in the preview pane, click the Play button or drag the playhead (the triangle above the scrubber bar). Click the Stop button to stop playing the video. To zero in on a particular frame of video, you might want to move backward or forward a frame at a time by clicking the Backward or Forward button.

10. **To change the beginning frame of a video clip, drag the leftmost triangle below the scrubber bar, or move the playhead to the desired frame and click the In button to set the new beginning frame. To change the ending frame of a video clip, drag the rightmost triangle below the scrubber bar, or move the playhead to the desired frame and click the Out button, to set the new ending frame.**

    The beginning and ending frames are *In* and *Out* points, respectively.

11. **To see your video with the new In and Out points, click the Preview Clip button.**

    The video plays in the preview pane, starting at the new In point and ending at the new Out point.

12. **When you're happy with the In and Out points that you've set, click the + (Plus) button to create a video clip with the current In and Out points.**

    The name of the clip appears in the scroll pane on the left side of the Video Import Wizard. (The pane with the list of clip names is called a *scroll pane* because if you fill it up with enough clip names, scroll bars will appear so that you can scroll the list up and down.)

13. **To rename the clip, click the name in the scroll pane and type a new name.**

    The new name appears in the scroll pane.

14. **Repeat Steps 10 through 13 to extract additional clips with new In and Out points from the same file.**

15. **To change the In and Out points in one of the new clips in the scroll pane, click the clip's name in the scroll pane, move the In and Out points as we describe in Step 10, and then click the Update Clip button.**

16. **To delete a clip from the scroll pane, click the name of the clip in the scroll pane, and then click the – (minus) button at the top of the scroll pane.**

    The selected clip disappears from the list.

17. **Click Next (Windows) or Continue (Mac).**

    The Encoding pane in the Video Import Wizard appears, as shown in Figure 11-5. This pane lets you select an encoding profile and advanced settings.

Figure 11-5:
In the Encoding pane of the Import Video dialog box, you can select how much compression to apply to your video clip.

18. **Click the Flash Video encoding profile drop-down list and select a suitable profile.**

    You can select profiles for users with modems or with the different speeds (40–700 Kbps) of modems, local area networks, digital subscriber lines (DSLs), or cable modems.

    Higher-speed connections make it practical to use higher-quality video that requires less compression.

19. **Click Next (Windows) or Continue (Mac).**

    The Finish Video Import pane appears in the Video Import Wizard, summarizing your choices.

20. **If you want to change any of your choices, click Go Back. Otherwise, click Finish.**

    The Flash Video Encoding Progress window appears. Encoding your video may take quite a while. When Flash finishes encoding your video, the window disappears, and the movie clip or clips (or embedded video symbol or symbols) containing your video appear on your Stage and in your library (which you can view by choosing Window➪Library, if it isn't visible).

Now your video segments are inside movie clips (if you choose that in Step 7), and as with any other movie clips, you can drag them around on the Timeline, rearrange them, rotate them, motion tween them, paint on top of them in other layers, and tween their brightness and transparency — you can mangle them, destroy them, and bring them to life in all the usual Flash ways. This is pretty amazing. (See Chapter 9 for lots more animation ideas.)

Streaming a video

You can set your Flash movie up to stream a video while the video appears inside your Flash movie. That means that viewers can see the video play fairly smoothly even while it's still downloading from the Web — without having to wait until the entire video has downloaded. This is a fantastic feature. You'll certainly want to do this rather than embed your video in Flash if your video is more than a few seconds long.

These streaming video files are in the .flv Flash video format. This is the format of all the videos you see at www.youtube.com and video.google.com.

To make an .flv video file to put online and then stream, follow these steps:

1. **Click a keyframe (or create one by clicking a frame and choosing Insert➪Timeline➪Keyframe).**

    Your video will start on this keyframe.

2. **Choose File⇨Import⇨Import Video.**

   The Video Import Wizard appears.

   You're about to import a video file into your Flash movie. Ultimately you will put the file on a Web server, but first you need to create and publish the .flv file.

3. **Select the On Your Computer option if you want to import a video from your computer. If you want to import an .flv video file from the Web, select the Already Deployed to a Web Server, Flash Video Streaming Service, or Flash Media Server option, type the Web address of the video file into the URL text box, and skip to Step 11.**

   Importing a video file from the Web works only for video files that are already in the .flv format.

4. **Click the Choose button.**

   The Open File dialog box appears.

5. **Find and choose a movie file in the file dialog box, and then click the Open button.**

6. **In the Import Video dialog box, click the Next (Windows) or Continue (Mac) button.**

   The Import Video dialog box now gives you choices for deploying your video.

7. **Select one of these options: Progressive Download from a Web Server, Stream from Flash Video Streaming Service, or Stream from Flash Communication Server.**

   You're choosing the method that you'll ultimately be using to stream the video. Using a Flash Video Streaming Service or the Flash Communication Server isn't cheap, so if you're just getting started, you undoubtedly want to choose Progressively Download from a Web Server. This lets you upload the .flv file to any Web server for streaming, which is really cool.

8. **Click Next (Windows) or Continue (Mac).**

   The Encoding pane in the Video Import Wizard appears. This pane lets you select an encoding profile and advanced settings.

9. **Click the Flash Video encoding profile drop-down list and select a suitable profile.**

   You may choose between profiles for users with modems or with the different speeds (40–700 Kbps) of modems, local area networks, digital subscriber lines (DSLs), or cable modems.

   Higher quality video is less compressed and therefore requires a larger file size and higher bandwidth for speedy delivery.

10. **You may grab and drag the In point and Out point markers (the triangles below the scrubber bar, below your video image in the Video**

Import Wizard) to give the video clip displayed there a new starting and ending point, if you want.

This is convenient because sometimes you want to import only part of a video clip. To facilitate this, you can grab and drag the playhead pointer (the triangle above the scrubber bar) to preview different locations in your video clip.

11. Click Next (Windows) or Continue (Mac).

The Skinning pane of the Import Video dialog box appears.

12. In the Skin drop-down list, select the style of play controls you want for your video.

The *skin* is the graphic design of the video play controls. You can infer the characteristics of some skins from their names. For example, the skin named `SkinOverPlaySeekMute.swf` has the play controls placed over the video and include Play, Seek, and Mute buttons. You are probably going to love fooling around choosing your skin — it's so easy. The skin you select in the drop-down list appears as a preview in the pane above the drop-down list.

13. Click Next (Windows) or Continue (Mac).

The Finish Video Import pane appears in the Import Video dialog box, summarizing what happens next, and you may want to make notes on that, because unfortunately this information disappears when you click Finish in Step 14. Among other things, this pane tells you where your new `.flv` file will be located relative to your `.swf` file.

14. If you want to change any of your choices, click Go Back. Otherwise, click Finish.

When you click Finish, the Flash Video Encoding Progress window appears. When Flash finishes encoding your video, the window disappears, and the encoded video and the player controls appear on the Stage. You may find it interesting to compare the file size of your new `.flv` file to the original video file size. (You can find the new `.flv` file in the location shown in Step 13.)

15. Choose Window➪Component Inspector.

The Component inspector appears. If necessary, expand the inspector to its full size.

16. Click the Parameters tab in the Component inspector, and click the row labeled source.

The name of the `.flv` file is highlighted.

17. **Click the magnifying glass next to the contentPath text box, and the Content Path dialog box appears. Here you can enter the Web address of the final location for your `.flv` file on your Web server or Flash Media Server.**

    For example, you might type **`http://www.helpexamples.com/ flash/video/clouds.flv`**.

18. **Upload your new `.flv` file to your Web server, your Flash Media Server, or your Flash Video Streaming Service. Also, upload the video skin you chose in Step 12 — you can find a copy of it on your computer in the same folder as your `.fla` file.**

    For instance, if you choose `SkinOverPlaySeekMute` in Step 12, you see a file there called `SkinOverPlaySeekMute.swf`, which you need to upload to your Web server in the same directory as your `.fla` file. (If you don't upload the skin, the video will still play, but it will have no video playback controls.)

19. **Choose Control⇨Test Movie.**

    A new window appears showing your Flash movie, and your video appears with the play controls in the style of the skin you chose in Step 12.

20. **Use the play controls to play your streaming video.**

    Your video `.flv` file plays from within your Flash movie while it downloads from your Web server, your Flash Media Server, or your Flash Video Streaming Service. It probably looks great. This is pretty amazing.

21. **Add more elements to your Flash movie if you like.**

22. **Choose File⇨Publish Settings to choose the settings for your HTML file and `.swf` file in the Publish Settings dialog box, click Publish, and then click OK.**

    Flash creates an HTML file and an `.swf` file that contains your Flash movie. (See Chapter 13 to find out how to set your publish settings and publish your files.)

23. **Upload your HTML file and your `.swf` file to a Web server.**

    For others to see your video, you must upload four elements to the Web: the HTML file and the `.swf` file that you upload in this step, plus the `.flv` file and the skin file that you upload in Step 18. The `.flv` file doesn't need to be hosted at the same site as the other elements, as long as you entered the Web address of the `.flv` file in Step 17.

Part V
The Movie and the Web

"Evidently he died of natural causes following a marathon session animating everything on his personal Web site. And no, Morganstern — the irony isn't lost on me."

In this part . . .

The not-so-secret desire of every Flash movie animation is to appear in bright lights on the Web. In this part, we show you how to make that happen. We explain how to put all the pieces together to create a way-cool Flash-only site. You see how to build a Web site that contains a complete navigational system so that viewers can quickly get the information they need. We cover three techniques for creating a complete site.

We also discuss the nitty-gritty details of publishing your Flash movie so a Web browser can display it. Besides the Flash Player file, Flash can create the HTML code you need and the alternative images you might want to use in case a viewer doesn't have the Flash Player. Flash makes it easy: Just specify your settings and click Publish.

Chapter 12

Putting It All Together

*W*hen creating your Flash animation, you need to consider how you will integrate it with your entire Web site. Are you creating a small animation to insert into an existing HyperText Markup Language (HTML) site, or do you want your entire site to be *Flashed?* In this chapter, we cover techniques for creating entire presentations, Web pages, and sites using Flash.

Adding the Power of Components

Components in Flash are built-in, precoded wonders that simplify the creation of interactive Flash movies. Components can be used to add interaction and navigation elements to your Flash movies, allowing you to create surveys, forms, interactive art galleries, or even complete graphical user interfaces for your Flash movies. Among other things, you can also use components (with the help of some fairly sophisticated ActionScript) to access and manipulate data from the Web and other sources.

Flash CS3 ships with more than two dozen ActionScript 2.0 components and more than three dozen ActionScript 3.0 components. You can download more components built by Flash community members by choosing Help⇨ Flash Exchange.

When you create a Flash document or open an existing one, Flash will display either ActionScript version 2.0 components or version 3.0 components in the Components window depending on the document's ActionScript version. In this book, we focus on ActionScript 3.0 because of its performance improvements and features.

Some of the components that ship with Flash CS3 are

- **RadioButtons:** These let you make one choice from several buttons.
- **CheckBoxes:** You can mark or clear each CheckBox.
- **Buttons:** Clicking one of these makes something happen in your movie. (Button components have more features than button symbols.)
- **ComboBoxes:** These are drop-down lists.
- **Lists:** These are scrolling lists of choices.
- **Video playback controllers:** With these, your audience can start, stop, and adjust the volume of video and audio in your Flash documents.

To add a component to your Flash movie, drag it from the Components panel (see Figure 12-1) onto the Stage.

Figure 12-1: The Components panel contains prebuilt user-interface elements that you can use in your Flash movies.

Components can add significantly to the size of your Flash Player movie, so consider the benefits of including them versus their cost in download time.

In the following sections, we look at how to use several types of components. We skip Button components because button symbols that you make yourself (as described in Chapter 8) are easier to use and usually do everything you need.

Getting ready to work with components

Before you work with any of Flash's components as described in the following sections of this chapter, you need to bring up the Components panel and the Parameters tab of the Property inspector. Follow these steps:

1. **You'll be typing some ActionScript, so create a layer, perhaps called** Actions, **where you can place the ActionScript.**

2. **If the Components panel is not already visible, choose Window⇨ Components.**

3. **If the Components panel is not expanded, click the expand button in the window's title bar.**

4. **If all the components in the category are not displayed, click the plus sign (Windows) or the disclosure triangle (Mac) to the left of the User Interface category in the Components panel.**

5. **If the Property inspector is not already open, choose Window⇨ Properties⇨Parameters.**

6. **If necessary, expand the inspector to its full size.**

7. **Click the Parameters tab.**

    The Property inspector appears with the Parameters tab on top.

Now you're ready to work with components.

Before you start to work on a component, make sure the Components panel and the Parameters tab of the Property inspector are set up as described in the preceding steps.

Using RadioButtons in a Flash movie

RadioButtons are groups of buttons that permit you to choose one (and only one) item from the group, like the buttons on a car radio. The following example describes how to create two RadioButtons that display specified text in a dynamic text box.

To use a set of RadioButtons in your Flash movie, follow these steps:

1. **Decide which elements of your Flash movie will change when a RadioButton is selected; then add those elements to the Flash movie if you haven't already done so.**

   For example, if you decide that the contents of a dynamic text box will change when a RadioButton is selected, create a dynamic text box on the Stage and give it an instance name, such as *myInfo*. (See Chapter 5 to discover how to create dynamic text.)

2. **Drag two or more RadioButtons from the Components panel onto the Stage.**

   You need at least two RadioButtons in every set of RadioButtons for them to work as they're intended. In a Flash movie, when you enable a RadioButton in a set, that button is turned on and all others in the set are turned off.

3. **Select one of the RadioButtons and type a name in the Instance Name field of the Property inspector.**

4. **Repeat Step 3 for each RadioButton, giving each a unique instance name.**

   For example, you might give the instance name *option1* to one RadioButton, and the instance name *option2* to another RadioButton.

5. **Select one of the RadioButtons.**

   You're going to set its parameters in the next steps.

6. **To change the RadioButton's label, click in the label field in the Parameters tab of the Property inspector, type a new name for the RadioButton, and press Enter (Windows) or Return (Mac).**

   The RadioButton's label changes on the Stage. For example, you could type *FedEx Air* as the label.

   In Steps 3 and 4, you give each instance of the RadioButton a name. Here in Step 6 you can change the label near the RadioButton on the Stage. It's helpful to understand that the RadioButton's instance name and the RadioButton's label on the Stage are separate items of information and don't need to be the same.

7. **To change the RadioButton's initial state, click the Selected drop-down list in the Property inspector and select True or False.**

   The Selected drop-down list is next to Selected in the Property inspector — it will probably say False by default, but when you click it, a drop-down list of two choices appears.

If you select True, the RadioButton is initially selected (the RadioButton's circle is filled in). If you select False, the RadioButton is initially clear.

8. **To change the group to which the RadioButton belongs, type a new name in the Group Name box in the Property inspector.**

   For example, you might type *myRadioGroup*. All the RadioButtons with the same group name act as one group. Selecting one RadioButton in the group deselects all the other RadioButtons with the same group name.

9. **To change the position of the RadioButton's label, click in the box to the right of LabelPlacement in the Property inspector so that the Label Placement drop-down list appears, and make a selection.**

   If you choose top or bottom, you undoubtedly want to type a larger value in the Height box to increase the height of the RadioButton box. The Height (H) box is at the bottom right of the Parameters tab of the Property inspector.

10. **To associate additional information with the RadioButton, enter the information in the Value box in the Property inspector.**

    For example, in the preceding Step 6 you might label your RadioButtons FedEx Air and FedEx Ground. Then here in Step 10, in the Value box in the Property inspector for each RadioButton, you could enter the shipping cost for each RadioButton.

11. **Repeat Steps 5 through 10 for each RadioButton.**

12. **Choose Window⇨Actions to open the Actions panel if it isn't open already, and in the Actions panel click the Script Assist button to deselect it (if it's selected).**

    This allows you to type code directly.

13. **Select Frame 1 of your Actions layer in the Timeline and enter the following code in the Script pane of the Actions panel:**

```
import fl.controls.RadioButton;
import flash.text.TextField;
import flash.events.EventDispatcher;
option1.addEventListener(MouseEvent.CLICK,
        myClickHandler);
option2.addEventListener(MouseEvent.CLICK,
        myClickHandler);
function myClickHandler(event:MouseEvent):void {
    myInfo.text = event.target.value;
}
```

You can replace `myClickHandler` with any name that you like. `option1` and `option2` are the instance names of the RadioButtons we use as an example in Step 4, and `myInfo` is the name of the dynamic text field we mention in Step 1.

When the user clicks the FedEx Air RadioButton, the dynamic text box displays the cost for FedEx Air. Likewise, clicking the FedEx Ground radio button displays the cost for FedEx Ground.

Each instruction in ActionScript is called a *statement* and is written with a semicolon at the end. *Function definitions*, by contrast, start with the keyword `function`, followed by the name you give to the function, followed by parentheses that contain the names of any parameters you want to pass to the function, followed by curly brackets that contain one or more statements.

In the first three statements in the preceding code, we import three files to make the application programming interfaces for RadioButtons, text fields, and event listeners available to our Flash movie. Basically that means we tell our Flash file where to find lots of useful software code that we can call on to easily make our RadioButtons, text fields, and events perform commonly needed tasks.

Statements 4 and 5 in the code connect *event listeners* to the RadioButtons. These event listeners are software instructions that wait for a mouse to click one of the buttons, and notify Flash when that happens. The code after Statement 5 defines a function that is a click handler so that when you click one of the RadioButtons in `myRadioGroup`, Flash sets the text of the dynamic text field to whatever is in the value parameter of the RadioButton that you click.

The following code is an example of how to change the contents of the dynamic text box that we describe in Step 1:

```
myInfo.text = event.target.value;
```

As you learn more ActionScript, you can use RadioButtons to perform entirely different actions, and you can replace this code with other ActionScript code to do something else. For example, the value of the RadioButton could be the name of a frame that the movie would go to when the RadioButton is selected.

Or, for example, if you want to set the text of the dynamic text field to be the label of the RadioButton that you click, replace this statement:

```
myInfo.text = event.target.value;
```

with this statement:

```
myInfo.text = event.target.label;
```

The Property inspector has three tabs in the upper-left corner — one tab for properties, one tab for filters, and one tab for parameters. If you have a RadioButton selected but its parameters don't appear on the Property inspector, you probably clicked the Properties tab by accident. Click to select the Parameters tab in the upper-left corner of the Property inspector; now it should display the RadioButton parameters.

When you look at the preceding code, you may be thinking, "Huh?" But it's possible to do a lot of coding in Flash without getting a PhD in ActionScriptology first. You can accomplish a lot by copying existing code, playing with it, and observing the effect.

Using CheckBoxes in a Flash movie

CheckBoxes are square boxes that you can check or uncheck to indicate that an option is selected or deselected. Unlike RadioButtons, more than one CheckBox can be selected at a time.

The following steps describe an example of using CheckBoxes that display a movie clip for each checked box:

1. **Decide which elements of your Flash movie will change when a CheckBox is selected; then add those elements to the Flash movie if you haven't already done so.**

   For example, perhaps you made movie clips of a cat, a tree, and a field, and you want to use CheckBoxes so that users can choose as many or as few as they like. And let's say that you named the instances *cat, tree,* and *field* and the CheckBoxes *catBox, treeBox,* and *fieldBox.*

2. **Drag a CheckBox from the Components panel onto the Stage.**

3. **To change the CheckBox's label, click the Label field in the Property inspector, type a new name for the CheckBox, and press Enter (Windows) or Return (Mac).**

   The CheckBox's label changes on the Stage.

4. **To change the CheckBox's initial state, click the word to the right of Selected in the Property inspector and select True or False in the drop-down list that appears.**

   If you choose True, the CheckBox is initially marked. If you choose False, the CheckBox is initially cleared.

5. **To change the CheckBox's label placement, click the word to the right of LabelPlacement in the Property inspector and make a selection in the drop-down list that appears.**

6. **To give the CheckBox an instance name, type a name in the Instance Name field in the Property inspector.**

   For instance, you can enter *myCheckBox* (or *treeBox* or *catBox* or *fieldBox).*

7. **Repeat Steps 2 through 6 for each CheckBox that you want to make.**

8. **Choose Window⇨Actions to open the Actions panel if it isn't open already. In the Actions panel, click the Script Assist button to deselect it (if it's selected).**

   This allows you to type code directly.

9. **Select Frame 1 of your Actions layer in the Timeline and enter the following code in the Script pane of the Actions panel:**

```
import fl.controls.CheckBox;
import flash.display.DisplayObject;
import flash.events.EventDispatcher;
tree.visible = false;
cat.visible = false;
field.visible = false;
treeBox.addEventListener(MouseEvent.CLICK, seeTree);
catBox.addEventListener(MouseEvent.CLICK, seeCat);
fieldBox.addEventListener(MouseEvent.CLICK, seeField);
function seeTree(event:MouseEvent):void {
    tree.visible = event.target.selected;
    }
function seeCat(event:MouseEvent):void {
    cat.visible = event.target.selected;
    }
function seeField(event:MouseEvent):void {
    field.visible = event.target.selected;
    }
```

You can replace `seeTree`, `seeCat`, and `seeField` with any names you like. In this example `tree`, `cat`, and `field` are the instance names of your movie clips and `treeBox`, `catBox`, and `fieldBox` are the instance names of the CheckBoxes.

Statements 1, 2, and 3 in the code import three files to make the application programming interfaces for CheckBoxes, object visibility, and event listeners available to our Flash movie. Statements 4, 5, and 6 make the CheckBoxes for the tree, cat, and field invisible. Statements 7, 8, and 9 add an event listener to each of the three CheckBoxes so that when you select one of the CheckBoxes, Flash executes the corresponding function `seeTree`, `seeCat`, or `seeField`. These three functions are defined in the last lines of the code. As a result, when the user checks the `tree` CheckBox, for example, the `Tree` movie clip appears.

An *event listener* is a little bit of code that checks for events that may be connected to a particular object in your Flash movie (such as our CheckBoxes here) and performs a specified function when they occur. Picture an event listener as a tiny dedicated spy or ear always waiting to hear one particular click.

Using ComboBoxes in a Flash movie

A *ComboBox* is text box that shows the current selection, combined with a drop-down list of alternate selections. The following example describes how to create a ComboBox that displays the item chosen from a list in a dynamic text box:

1. **Decide what elements of your Flash movie will change when a menu item in the ComboBox is selected. Add those elements to the Flash movie if you haven't already done so.**

   For example, if you decide that the contents of a dynamic text box will change when a menu item in the ComboBox is selected, create a dynamic text box on the Stage and give it an instance name, such as *myInfo2*. (See Chapter 5 to discover how to create dynamic text.)

2. **Drag a ComboBox from the Components panel onto the Stage.**

3. **In the Instance Name box in the upper-left corner of the Property inspector, type a name.**

   For example, type the name *myComboBox*.

4. **To control whether the user can edit the items in the ComboBox's menu list, select True or False from the drop-down list for the Editable parameter of the Property inspector.**

   Selecting True allows the user to rename each item on the menu list. Selecting False prevents that from happening.

5. **To create items in the menu list:**

   a. **Double-click the text box to the right of dataProvider in the Property inspector.**

      A dialog box appears.

   b. **In the dialog box, click the plus sign to add a menu item or click the minus sign to delete a menu item.**

   c. **Click the upward-pointing triangle to move an item up the list and click the downward-pointing triangle to move a menu item down on the list.**

      When you add an item to the list, it is excitingly named `label0`, `label1`, `label2`, and so on

6. **To change a menu item's name from `label0` (or `label1` or `label2` and so on) to something more interesting and meaningful, click the menu item's Value input box in the menu item's label column and type a more useful name there.**

   For example, you might change the name of each menu item to the name of a different kind of dance maneuver, such as Charleston, Fox Trot, Twist, or Mashed Potato.

7. **Click OK.**

   The dialog box closes.

8. **To change the number of items that can be displayed in the ComboBox without a scroll bar, click the Row Count field in the Property inspector and type a new number.**

   The default number is 5.

9. **If you want to make the ComboBox wider so that longer menu items are more readable, choose Modify➪Transform➪Scale and pull the handles that appear on the ComboBox's borders.**

10. **Choose Window➪Actions to open the Actions panel if it isn't open already. In the Actions panel, click the Script Assist button to deselect it (if it's selected).**

    When Script Assist is turned off, you can type ActionScript code directly.

11. **Select Frame 1 of your Actions layer in the Timeline and enter the following code in the Script pane of the Actions panel:**

```
import fl.controls.ComboBox;
import flash.display.DisplayObject;
import flash.events.EventDispatcher;
myComboBox.addEventListener(Event.CHANGE,
        danceChosen);
function danceChosen(e:Event):void {
        myInfo2.text = "You chose: ";

        myInfo2.appendText(myComboBox.selectedItem.lab
        el);
        }
```

    You can replace danceChosen in the preceding code with any name you like. myComboBox in this example is the instance name of your ComboBox that we mention in Step 3, and myInfo2 is the name of the dynamic text field described in Step 1.

In the preceding code in the definition of the function danceChosen, the two statements that change the text in myInfo2 make the label of the ComboBox appear in the text box.

You could replace these statements with different statements in this function for a different result. For example, you might instead use some ActionScript code that sets the Flash playhead to move to different frame labels in different sections of the Flash movie that correspond to the selected label in the ComboBox.

The first three statements in the preceding code import three files so that the application programming interfaces for ComboBoxes, object visibility, and event listeners are available to our Flash movie. The fourth statement adds an event listener to `myComboBox` so that when you select a menu item in `myComboBox`, the statements in the function `danceChosen` set the text of the dynamic text field to the label of the ComboBox menu item that the viewer selects.

When the user chooses a dance from the list, that dance appears in the dynamic text box. Because the function inserts, *You chose* before the text, the result might be *You chose Mashed Potato*.

If things aren't working when you test your ComboBox, the ActionScript code you typed may contain typos or other errors. Flash often reports these errors in the Output panel when you choose Control➪Test Movie. The error messages in the Output window may seem obscure, but they can give you an idea of where your problem may be.

Using Lists in a Flash movie

A *List* component in Flash is a scrollable list of selectable items. In the following example, we show you how to create a list that displays the chosen value in a dynamic text box. To use list components in your Flash movie, follow these steps:

1. **Decide which elements of your Flash movie will change when a viewer selects a menu item in the list. Add those elements to the Flash movie if you haven't already done so.**

   For example, if you decide that the contents of a dynamic text box will change when a list item is selected, create a dynamic text box on the Stage and give it an instance name, such as *myInfo3*. (See Chapter 5 to discover how to create dynamic text.)

2. **Drag a list from the Components panel onto the Stage.**

3. **In the Instance Name text field in the left corner of the Property inspector, type a name.**

   For example, name the instance *myList*.

4. **In the Selection Width field (labeled W) in the Property inspector, type a number to change the List box's width, if desired.**

   The width should be wide enough to show the desired text. For example, you might want a width of 300 pixels.

5. **Choose Window➪Actions to open the Actions panel if it isn't open already. In the Actions panel click the Script Assist button to deselect it (if it's selected).**

6. **Select Frame 1 of your Actions layer in the Timeline and enter this code in the Script pane of the Actions panel:**

```
import fl.controls.List;
import flash.text.TextField;
import flash.events.EventDispatcher;
myList.addItem({label:"iAXE", data:99});
myList.addItem({label:"Switch Stealth", data: 199});
myList.addItem({label:"Fender Telecaster", data:399});
myList.addEventListener(Event.CHANGE, showPrice);
function showPrice(event:Event) {
    myInfo3.text = "This guitar is priced at: $" +
        event.target.selectedItem.data;
}
```

The labels and data in the `myList.addItem` statements are inside curly brackets that are inside parentheses.

You can replace `showPrice` with any name you like. `myList` in this example is the instance name of your list, described in Step 3, and `myInfo3` is the name of the dynamic text field that we mention in Step 1.

In this example we use ActionScript to create three list items. However, if you prefer you can instead manually create the list items in the Property inspector. In that case you don't need to type the fourth, fifth, and sixth statements in the preceding code. To manually create the list items, fill out the list in the way described in Steps 5 through 9 in the preceding section "Using ComboBoxes in a Flash movie."

The first three statements in the preceding code import three files so that the application programming interfaces for List boxes, text fields, and event listeners are available to our Flash movie.

In the next three statements, we use ActionScript to add three guitars to the list. The seventh statement adds an event listener to `myList` that "listens" for a viewer selecting a menu items in `myList`. When the viewer selects one of the menu items, the event listener performs the `showPrice` function, which is defined in the next lines of code. `showPrice` sets the text of the dynamic text field to "This guitar is priced at $" and whatever is the dollar value stored in the data field of the list menu item that the viewer selects. You can replace the statement in the `showPrice` function with other ActionScript code to do other things with the selected values.

Creating a Preloader

If you're ambitious and create a huge Flash file, downloading it to a viewer's browser might take a long time. Your audience won't wait forever. To solve this problem, you can create a *preloader,* which is a tiny movie that loads quickly and tells your viewers to wait.

Creating a nice preloader with ActionScript 3.0 may require more lines of fancy ActionScript code than you may want to deal with if you're new to Flash. For now, you might want to start out with a simple preloader that you can create by following these steps:

1. **Assuming that you've already created your main movie, add a scene for your preloader by choosing Window⇨Other Panels⇨ Scene. In the Scene panel, check the plus box at the bottom of the Scene panel. Drag it above the scene of your main movie. Rename it "preloader."**

   See Chapter 9 for the lowdown on creating and changing the order of scenes.

2. **In the first scene (the preloader), create a movie clip, and put into the movie clip whatever you want your audience to see while the rest of your movie loads. Keep this movie clip simple so that it loads quickly.**

   You might, for example, create a simple, attractive animation that informs the audience that the movie is loading.

3. **Choose Window⇨Library to open the Library if it isn't already open, and drag an instance of the movie clip from the Library onto the Stage.**

4. **Choose Control⇨Test Movie to view your movie.**

   Flash loops the movie clip in your preloader scene so that it plays over and over until your main movie is loaded.

When you test your preloader by choosing Control⇨Test Movie, your main movie might load so quickly that you don't even see the preloader. Choose View⇨Simulate Download to see how your preloader works while your main movie loads. (See Chapter 13 for more information on testing a movie and analyzing its download performance.) You can also upload your file to a test page on your Web site to see how the preloader works. Make sure that your preloader is long enough for the human eye to see. Remember that one frame is displayed for only a fraction of a second.

Creating an Entire Web Site with Flash

You can use Flash to create your site's complete user interface, along with all the graphics and text. Some Web sites are almost 100 percent Flash (for example, www.funonmars.com, the Web site of this book's technical editor,

Sally Cruikshank). But most Web sites with Flash (including www.adobe.com) are a hybrid of Flash and HTML. So, a Flash Web site may have the following structure:

- ✔ An HTML home page that contains the following:
  - • A user interface (and perhaps other graphics) built in Flash
  - • Tests that detect the Flash Player and Player version (provided by default when you publish your Flash movie — see the "Testing for the Flash Player" section, later in this chapter)
  - • Alternate HTML content for viewers who don't have Flash, and a button that viewers can use to get the Flash Player if they want, as described in the section "Creating alternative sites," later in this chapter

- ✔ Additional HTML pages that, like the home page, utilize a user interface (and other graphics) built in Flash, for all the remaining pages in the Web site. You might want each of these pages to also test for Flash in case your viewers don't enter the site through your home page.

- ✔ HTML pages that contain a non-Flash version of the Web site, if you want the site to be available to those who don't have and don't want to install the required version of Flash.

If you create your entire Web site out of one big Flash file, your users can't use their browser's Back button to navigate back and forth through your Flash movie. An advantage of creating multiple HTML pages with Flash on each page is that the browser's Back button still works.

Your opening HTML page is usually the first thing your viewers see and may be the most important page on your site, so be sure to think carefully about your goals for this page. You may want to put lots of useful information or other important material on your home page so that your viewers quickly see that your site is worth exploring.

To match the color of a Flash movie in a Web page to the rest of the page, match the background colors of the movie (by choosing Modify⇨Document) and the HTML page. (This technique doesn't work if your Web page uses an image for a background.)

Your site probably contains buttons that people can use to navigate through your site, get more information, or contact you. You can create the navigation structure in many ways. Here are three:

- ✔ Attach event listeners to buttons to trigger the display of movie clips or Flash Player movies (.swf files). See Chapter 10 for an example of a button that plays a movie clip.

✔ Use buttons to trigger the navigateToURL function, to link to other HTML pages on your site. You can, of course, create the HTML pages with Flash. We explain how to do this in the next section.

✔ Use buttons to display information or graphics located on other parts of your Timeline by using the gotoAndPlay or gotoAndStop function. We discuss this option in the upcoming "Using the Timeline to store Web content" section.

You can use combinations of these techniques. For example, you can use an event listener to display information when the mouse cursor is over a button, and you can use an event listener and the navigateToURL function to link to another page when the user clicks the button.

Creating navigation with navigateToURL

You can use an event listener to trigger a navigateToURL function from a button so that the button links to another HTML page. See Chapter 8 to find out how to add an event listener to a button to trigger the navigateToURL function.

Using the Timeline to store Web content

In most cases, you use the Timeline to display frames in sequence — in other words, animation. But the Timeline can also store static frames. You can create anything on the Stage in those frames, and you can display what is in those frames whenever you want. You can use ActionScript to jump to a frame based on a user interaction and to stop there until the next user interaction. So different frames on the Timeline can become the equivalent of separate Web pages.

Suppose that you have several buttons on the left side of your page. You want viewers to see different graphics and animation on the right side of the page when they roll the mouse over each button. Perhaps rolling over one button displays a product description and rolling over another button displays a description of a second product.

To create a set of buttons that move the playhead to different sections of the Timeline, follow these steps:

1. **Place instances of your buttons on one side of the Stage (for example, the left side), in separate layers on the first frame of the Timeline of your movie.**

2. **Open the Property inspector if it isn't already open (choose Window⇨Properties⇨Properties). If necessary, expand the inspector to its full size.**

3. **Create a new layer and give it a name, such as Product Views.**

4. **A few frames out (on Frame 10, for example) on the Product Views layer, create a keyframe.**

5. **In the Frame Label text box on the left side of the Property inspector, type a label name.**

   In this example, name the frame labels *myFrameLabel1*, *myFrameLabel2*, and so on.

6. **On the Stage, create the graphics and words for the product description or whatever that you want displayed when a user rolls the mouse over the first button.**

   If you want to display animation when a user rolls over the first button, drag a movie clip from the Library. (Check out Chapter 7 for the scoop on creating movie clips.)

   Place the graphics so that they don't cover the buttons when the graphics appear.

7. **Repeat Steps 4 through 6 to create a label and a product description on the Product Views layer for each button, on a new keyframe that is later on the Timeline each time.**

   At each new keyframe, delete the previous content, and then add what you want to display for the new product description.

8. **Select a button.**

9. **In the Instance Name text box on the left side of the Property inspector, type a unique instance name for the button.**

   In this example, name the buttons *myButton1, myButton2,* and so on.

10. **Repeat Steps 8 and 9 for each button.**

11. **On each layer that contains a button, add a keyframe at the same time on the Timeline as the keyframe for the last product description.**

    Now your buttons will stay visible when each product description is displayed.

12. **Create a new layer and give it a name, such as *myCode*.**

13. **Open the Actions panel (choose Window⇨Actions). In the Actions panel, click the Script Assist button to deselect it (if it's selected).**

14. **Select Frame 1 in the myCode layer in the Timeline and enter the following code in the Script pane of the Actions panel:**

```
this.stop();
```

If you don't do this, your movie simply plays through all the frames, displaying your product descriptions one after another. But you want viewers to see a particular product description only when they roll over a particular button.

15. **Select Frame 1 in the myCode layer in the Timeline, and enter this additional code in the Script pane of the Actions panel:**

```
function menuChoice1(event:MouseEvent):void
{
    this.gotoAndStop("myFrameLabel1");
}

myButton1.addEventListener(MouseEvent.ROLL_OVER,
    menuChoice1);
```

myButton1 is the instance name of the first button that you created in Step 4, and myFrameLabel1 is the name of the first frame label you created in Step 9.

In the preceding code, menuChoice is defined as a function that moves the playhead of the Timeline of the current movie to the myFrameLabel1 frame and stops. After the function definition is the statement that connects an event listener that "listens" for a rollover to the button that has the instance name myButton1. When the mouse rolls over the button, the event listener calls the function menuChoice1.

16. **Select Frame 1 in the myCode layer in the Timeline, and enter this additional code in the Script pane of the Actions panel:**

```
function menuChoice2(event:MouseEvent):void
{
    this.gotoAndStop("myFrameLabel2");
}
myButton2.addEventListener(MouseEvent.ROLL_OVER,
    menuChoice2);
```

This code connects the second button that you made to an event listener and an event handler.

17. **For each additional button that you made, repeat Step 16 to add more code to Frame 1 in the myCode layer in the Timeline. Substitute the new button's instance name for myButton2. Substitute the new**

destination frame's label for `myFrameLabel2`. And substitute a new function name for `menuChoice2`.

18. **Choose Control⇨Test Movie to try it out!**

    When you roll over a button, the graphics, text, and movie clip animation on the appropriate frame appear.

Figure 12-2 shows a Timeline with frames that are displayed when the mouse cursor passes over buttons. If you use `CLICK` rather than `ROLL_OVER` in Step 15 and 16, you can display different information when the mouse clicks each button.

Figure 12-2: You can use the Timeline to display different graphics and text when the mouse cursor passes over each button.

You can build on this further by, for example, sending the user back to the first frame when the mouse rolls off the button — like this.

```
function menuChoice1A(event:MouseEvent):void
{
     this.gotoAndStop(1);
}
myButton1.addEventListener(MouseEvent.ROLL_OUT,
        menuChoice1A);
```

Notice that the new function is named `menuChoice1A` (not `menuChoice1`). It's important that the new function has a new name. For each state of each button, you can add a different function and a different `EventListener`.

Testing for the Flash Player

Although more than 98 percent of the world's Web surfing population reportedly have the Flash Player installed, that's still not everyone, and some have fairly old versions of the Flash Player. For viewers who don't have the Flash Player, it often downloads automatically (as a result of the code that Flash places in the HTML file when you publish your .swf and HTML files, as we describe in Chapter 13). If Flash doesn't download automatically, those users might not be able to view your site.

You can test for the presence of the Flash Player and, perhaps more important, you can test to see which version of the Flash Player they have. If you're using features that exist only in Flash CS3, make sure that viewers have Flash Player 9, because many people might still have Flash Player 8 (or an even earlier version) installed.

Detecting the Flash Player version

You may detect a particular Flash Player version by simply selecting the Detect Flash Version check box in the HTML tab in Flash's Publish Settings before you publish your movie. (See Chapter 13 for the scoop on specifying Publish Settings.) This does a great job of detecting a particular Flash Player version.

Then when your Web page comes up in a Web browser, if the Flash Player of the specified version can't be found or if the Web browser doesn't have scripting enabled, the resulting HTML code displays the sentence Alternate HTML content should be placed here on your Web page. You can edit the HTML to replace that sentence with whatever alternative content you want to display.

Creating alternative sites

This alternative HTML content could consist of HTML code for a page in a series of HTML-only, non-Flash pages, if you feel that your audience needs it. Some Flash sites include a complete set of non-Flash (HTML) pages for viewers who don't have the Flash Player and don't want to download it.

If you use features unique to Flash Player 9, you can also create, for example, a Flash 6 site that uses only features available in Flash 6. The overwhelming majority of Web surfers have Flash Player 6 or later. But don't forget how much time you spend updating your Web site now. Imagine updating two or three sites! Make sure you think carefully about who your audience is and the consequences of having so many alternatives.

For detailed information on how many computer users have which versions of the Flash player, check out the latest statistics at www.adobe.com/products/ player_census/flashplayer/version_penetration.html. You may be surprised by the statistics.

Using the Movie Explorer

The Movie Explorer is a great tool for analyzing an entire movie. When you start creating complex relationships among several Timelines, you might have trouble remembering what you've done. The Movie Explorer lays out the entire structure of your movie for you to see. The Movie Explorer is also a great tool for troubleshooting problems. By visually displaying your movie's components, you can more easily find where the trouble lies.

Another use for the Movie Explorer is to analyze other people's .fla files. When you open someone else's Flash file, you might wonder where all the action is. It might all be hidden in movie clips and ActionScript that calls other movies and movie clips. The Movie Explorer can help you ferret out the magic behind the animation.

To open the Movie Explorer, choose Window⇨Movie Explorer. The Movie Explorer is shown in Figure 12-3.

Figure 12-3: Go exploring with the Movie Explorer to discover the many nooks and crannies in a movie.

You usually know what you're looking for when you open the Movie Explorer. For example, you might be looking for ActionScript or movie clips. Use the buttons at the top of the Movie Explorer to specify which movie elements are shown in the main window:

✔ **Show Text:** Displays all text objects in the movie.

✔ **Show Buttons, Movie Clips, and Graphics:** Displays a list of those objects.

✔ **Show Action Scripts:** Lists all ActionScript in the movie.

 ✔ **Show Video, Sounds, and Bitmaps:** Lists those objects.

 ✔ **Show Frames and Layers:** Shows each frame and each layer that contains objects.

 ✔ **Customize Which Items to Show:** Opens the Movie Explorer Settings dialog box, where you can indicate which items you want to display by selecting or deselecting them in a list of check boxes. You can also choose to display Movie Elements (scenes), Symbol Definitions (a separate listing by symbol), or both. Click OK to close this dialog box.

Movie elements are shown in a hierarchical manner in the Movie Explorer. For example, if a frame has an action attached to it, you see a plus sign (Windows) or a disclosure triangle (Mac) next to the button. Click any plus sign or right-pointing triangle to expand the display — in this case, to reveal the ActionScript attached to that frame. Click any minus sign (Windows) or downward-pointing triangle (Mac) to collapse the display.

In the Find text box, you can type any expression to search the entire movie. Suppose that you want to know whether a movie contains the `navigateToURL` action. Just type **navigateToURL** in the Find text box, and the Movie Explorer displays every instance containing that word.

 The Find feature is not case sensitive, which is handy if you can't remember how things are capitalized. But the Find feature is sensitive to spaces, so if the movie contains *navigateToURL* and you type **navigate To URL**, you don't get any results.

You can use the Movie Explorer to select objects on the Stage or frames. Just click the item in the Movie Explorer, and Flash selects the object or frame. (If you select a frame, Flash also includes the frames up to the next keyframe.) If you select a scene, Flash selects the first frame of the scene.

The Movie Explorer contains an extensive menu that you can access by clicking in the upper-right corner of the Movie Explorer panel, or right-clicking (Windows) or Control+clicking (Mac) inside the Movie Explorer panel.

Some of the more useful features of this menu follow:

✔ **Find in Library:** Opens the Library (if it isn't already open) and highlights the object that you previously selected in the Movie Explorer.

✔ **Rename:** Lets you rename the selected object, such as a button instance.

- ✔ **Copy All Text to Clipboard:** Copies all the text in the Movie Explorer to the Clipboard so you can paste it into another application.

- ✔ **Print:** Prints the entire contents of the Movie Explorer. All items, whether collapsed or expanded, are printed.

If you have difficulty understanding one of the more advanced Flash files from the resource Web sites that we recommend in Chapter 15, try opening the Movie Explorer. Look for actions and movie clips. You might be surprised at what you can discover by using this tool.

Making Your Site More Accessible

Flash includes capabilities that make it possible for you to make Flash more accessible to people with disabilities. Most of the components in Flash CS3 are designed to be accessible to the visually impaired through the use of screen readers, which generate a spoken description of the contents of your Flash screen. Screen reader software is widely available from a variety of companies.

Users can also navigate around most of Flash's components by using the keyboard rather than the mouse — this is automatically built into the components. And ActionScript has features that can enhance the accessibility of Flash documents.

One of the easiest ways to make your Flash movie more accessible to people with disabilities is to use the Accessibility panel. When you add buttons, movie clips, text fields, input text fields, or components to your movie, you can use the Accessibility panel to make them accessible to screen readers. (Not all components can be made accessible, but most can.) To make a button, movie clip, text, Input Text field, or component accessible, follow these steps:

1. **Open the Accessibility panel (choose Window⇨Other Panels⇨ Accessibility).**

   If the panel isn't expanded, click the collapse arrow on the panel title bar.

2. **Select the button, movie clip, text, Input Text field, or component on the Stage.**

3. **In the Accessibility panel, select Make Object Accessible.**

4. **If you selected a movie clip in Step 2 and you want objects embedded in the movie clip to also be accessible, select the Make Child Objects Accessible check box.**

   For example, select the Make Child Objects Accessible check box if you want to allow text objects in the movie clip to be read by the screen reader software.

5. **In the Name box, type a name for the symbol or component.**

   The screen reader can read this name aloud.

6. **In the Description box, type a description of the symbol or component.**

   The screen reader can read this description aloud.

7. **In the Shortcut box, type a keyboard shortcut that viewers can use to select the object, if appropriate.**

   For instance, if the object is a RadioButton that needs to be selected to receive input, follow this step.

   The screen reader can then use this information to read aloud something like, "The shortcut for this text field is Ctrl+K." (Not all screen readers support this feature.) Typing information in the Shortcut box doesn't actually implement keyboard shortcut functionality. You need to use ActionScript to detect and respond to any shortcut key presses.

8. **In the Tab Index box, you may enter the number corresponding to the object's tab index value, if appropriate.**

   The *tab index* determines how users can use the Tab key to navigate through and select one of the buttons, check boxes, and other controls in your movie. For example, suppose that you have three buttons with a tab index of 1, 2, and 3, respectively. When the movie starts, if the user presses the Tab key three times, the button with the tab index of 3 would be selected for input.

If you have the Accessibility panel open when nothing in your movie is selected, the panel offers you the option to Make Movie Accessible, which is selected by default. This allows screen readers to read the different objects in the Flash movie. You definitely want this option selected if you want to make your movie accessible to screen readers and other hardware and software for people with disabilities. Of course, you also have to use the Accessibility panel to name each object, as we describe in the preceding steps, for this to be useful.

Chapter 13

Publishing Your Flash Files

*Y*our Flash movie is completed. Now you need to publish it in its final form — most likely an .swf file that you can post on your Web site. In this chapter, we explain how to prepare a Flash movie for publishing and help you determine the ideal publish settings for your needs. We also discuss how to publish to other graphic file formats such as PNG, in case you want to create a non-Flash site or use your material in another program. We cover all the bases so that you can get your animation up and running.

The filenames of Flash-published movies end with the .swf suffix. The letters *SWF* originally stood for *Shockwave Flash*, but nobody uses that term for Flash movies anymore, even though the letters remain the same. So we refer to SWF files as Flash Player files, not Shockwave Flash files. Flash converts your movie data into a highly compact and efficient form in an SWF file; the SWF file contains only the information needed for playback of your movies. In contrast, when you save your movies by choosing File➪Save (or File➪ Save As), they are saved with the .fla suffix. They are saved in a format that can be read by the Flash CS3 application, but not the Flash Player. The .fla file contains lots of information about layers, Library items, your video source files, and so on, which you need when you are creating your movies and which the Flash Player doesn't need.

Optimizing Movies for Fast Download

Throughout this book, we offer suggestions for designing a Flash movie with speedy downloading in mind. In this section, we put the suggestions together so that you can review your movie as a whole before you publish it.

Reducing your Flash Player file sizes is no longer so important because many people now have high-speed Internet connections. But not everyone does. So it still isn't a bad idea to spend a little time thinking about shrinking the size of your Flash movies.

Simplifying artwork

By simplifying the artwork in your movie, you can greatly reduce the size of a Flash movie, thereby increasing its speed. Here are the most important techniques:

- **Use symbols for every object that appears more than once.** You can turn any object or group of objects into a symbol. Nest your symbols — for example, turn an object into a symbol and then use it in a movie clip or button. Remember that you can change the color of symbol instances — you don't need to create a new symbol. (Chapter 7 covers symbols in detail.)

- **Group objects whenever possible.** Groups are almost as efficient as symbols. (Chapter 4 explains how to create groups.)

- **Use vector graphics rather than bitmaps when you can.** When you do use bitmaps, don't animate them unless you need to. Bitmaps and bitmap animation can increase your Flash Player file size and thus the download time. However, with the rising adoption of broadband Internet access, bitmaps are an increasingly important part of Flash projects, including the sites referred to in this book, and now Photoshop files can easily be imported into Flash. (Chapter 3 explains how to import a bitmap.)

- **Optimize curves (choose Modify⇨Shape⇨Optimize).** You can optimize curves to reduce the number of lines used to create a shape. This can be tiresome on a large project, but if you really need to reduce the size of your Flash movie, this may help. (Check out Chapter 4 for further explanation.)

- **Use solid lines rather than dashed, dotted, and other line types when possible.** Try to avoid custom line widths. (We explain line types in Chapter 3.)

- **Use the Pencil tool rather than the Brush tool whenever possible.** The Pencil tool uses fewer bytes in your movie.

✔ **Use the Web-safe color palette.** Avoid custom colors. (Check out Chapter 3 for the lowdown on colors.) Custom color definitions are kept with the Flash Player file.

✔ **Avoid using transparency when you don't need it.** Using transparency doesn't make your Flash file bigger, but it can slow down playback because of the extra calculation required. (On the other hand, sometimes transparency effects make your movie look really great.) See Chapter 7 to find out about changing the transparency of the elements in your movie.

✔ **Use solid fills rather than gradients.** Gradients are more complex and make the Flash Player file bigger. However, gradients are also key to the Flash look that is so popular. They help to make vector graphics look less flat.

Optimizing text

Text can consume lots of bytes. Here's what you can do to reduce the byte bite:

✔ **Reduce the number of fonts and font styles (bold, italic) as much as possible.** Use simpler sans serif fonts if you can. You get the best results file-size-wise with the device fonts (sans, serif, and typewriter), although you might find these device fonts boring. Flash doesn't need to store the outlines of device fonts in the .swf file, so these take up fewer bytes. And usually your Flash projects will look better if you don't use too many fonts — a useful rule in the graphic design world is to avoid using more than three fonts in a design. (See Chapter 5 for more information on fonts.)

✔ **If you create text fields, limit the text and specify any restrictions that you can in the Character Options dialog box.** (Choose Window⇨Property⇨Properties to open the Property inspector if it's not already open, and then click Character in the Property inspector to open the Character Options dialog box.) For example, exclude unnecessary character outlines, such as numbers.

Compressing sound

You can compress sounds to reduce the file size. When you compress individual sounds in the Sound Properties dialog box, you can fine-tune settings for each individual sound in your movie. Later in this chapter, we review how to compress sound when you publish a Flash movie. Use the MP3 format whenever possible because it compresses well. If you need more information on compressing sounds, check out Chapter 11.

Here are some other ways that you can reduce the size of your sound files:

- ✔ Adjust the sound's Time In and Time Out points to prevent silent areas from being stored in your .swf file.
- ✔ Reuse sounds by using different In and Out points and by looping different parts of the same sound.
- ✔ Don't loop streaming sound.

See Chapter 11 for more information on editing, looping, and streaming sound.

Animating efficiently

One of the most effective ways to reduce file size is to use tweens (see Chapter 9). Frame-by-frame animation creates larger files. Keeping animation localized in one area also helps. Small animations (animations where the objects don't move much) produce smaller file sizes than wide-area animations.

Testing Movies

Before publishing your movie, you should test it. The first step is to simply play your animation, as we explain in Chapter 9. But playing the animation on the Stage doesn't provide you with enough information to determine problems caused by file size. To find those kinds of bugs, you have to use the Test Movie command or test your movie in a browser. The following sections tell you how to test both ways.

Flash CS3 is optimized for the tasks that you perform when creating a Flash movie (such as drawing, adding keyframes, showing and hiding layers, and typing ActionScript code). It's not optimized for playing back your animation — the Flash Player is optimized for that. Your .fla file contains lots of information that you need when you're creating your movies but the Flash Player doesn't need. The Flash Player plays only .swf files, which you can create when you choose File⇨Publish.

Using the Test Movie command

After playing your animation, you should use the Test Movie or Test Scene command. Then you can use the Bandwidth Profiler (and other tools described in the following steps) to provide estimates of downloading speed so you can find bottlenecks that pause your animation. You can also see the results of movie clips and all ActionScript code.

If you're using movie clips, they won't play when you choose Control⇨Play. To see them play you must choose Control⇨Test Movie or Control⇨Test Scene.

To test a movie or scene, follow these steps:

1. **Choose Control⇨Test Movie (or Test Scene).**

   Flash publishes your movie to an .swf file by using the current settings in the Publish Settings dialog box (see the section "Publishing Flash Movies," later in this chapter) and opens a new window. You see your animation run. You can change the settings in the Publish Settings dialog box (choose File⇨Publish Settings) before using this command.

2. **Choose View⇨Download Settings and choose a downloading speed between that of a 14.4 modem (1.2 Kbps) to a T1 line (131.2 Kbps).**

   If you repeatedly change the download settings, you get a better sense of their effect. To specify your own settings, choose Customize, and in the Custom Modem Settings dialog box, enter the menu text that you want to appear on the menu and the bit rate in bytes per second. Click OK. Then open the Download Settings menu again and choose your customized setting, which now appears on the menu.

3. **Choose View⇨Bandwidth Profiler to see the graph that shows the downloading performance.**

   The bandwidth profiler (as shown in Figure 13-1) displays the byte size of each individual frame. Frames whose bars rise above the lower red horizontal line cause loading delays.

4. **To see settings for any one frame, stop the movie by clicking the frame's bar.**

   To the left of the bandwidth profiler, Flash displays the movie's statistics: dimensions, frame rate, file size, movie duration, and the amount of animation to preload in frames and seconds. You also see the size of each individual frame.

Figure 13-1:
When you test a movie, Flash helps you analyze the downloading performance of your movie.

Frames with bars above this line cause loading delays.

5. **Choose View⇨Streaming Graph to see how the Flash movie streams into a browser.**

6. **Choose View⇨Frame by Frame Graph to see which frames contribute to delays.**

   A frame whose bar extends above the red line may cause a bottleneck when the movie downloads at the connection speed you choose in Step 2. By default, Flash opens the SWF window in Streaming Graph mode.

7. **Choose View⇨Simulate Download if you want to see the Flash movie play as if loading at the speed you choose in Download Settings in Step 2.**

8. **To close the SWF window, click its Close button.**

After you analyze your movie, you can go back and optimize it to eliminate delays. A short delay in the first frame is usually acceptable, but significant delays during the movie result in jerky animation or pauses.

If you have a long movie divided into scenes, you can save time by using the Test Scene command instead of the Test Movie command.

Testing a movie in a Web browser

The final steps of testing a movie are publishing it and viewing it in a Web browser. For a quick view, you can use the Publish Preview command. Flash publishes your movie to an .swf file, creates the appropriate HTML file, and opens the HTML file in your default browser. Viewing your Flash Player file in a browser reveals how the browser will display the movie when you upload it to a Web site.

Flash uses the current settings in the Publish Settings dialog box to create the preview, including the types of file formats that you have selected.

To preview your movie in a browser, follow these steps:

1. **Choose File⇨Publish Settings to open the Publish Settings dialog box. Choose the desired file formats and publish settings, and then click OK.**

   See the "Publishing Flash Movies" section, later in this chapter, for more information on the Publish Settings dialog box.

2. **Choose File⇨Publish Preview and choose the desired format from the submenu.**

   Flash opens your browser and runs your movie.

3. **Close your browser to end the preview.**

As with any Web page material, you need to consider the following when testing a Flash Player file:

- ✔ **The browser that your audience is using:** Preview your Flash Player file in the current version of both Internet Explorer (IE) and Mozilla Firefox, if possible. You should probably try out at least one earlier version of Internet Explorer, too. And you should test it in Safari on a Mac. Okay, so you probably won't do all this, but don't say that we didn't tell you.

- ✔ **The resolution of viewers' screens:** Test at least the following common settings: 800 x 600 and 1024 x 768. Remember that the amount of material that appears on the screen changes with the resolution. If you preview at 640 x 480, you can be sure that people with higher resolutions can see your entire movie, but then again, a Flash movie that fits in a 640 x 480 screen may look pretty humble on a 1280 x 1024 screen.

- ✔ **The color settings of viewers' screens:** Color settings might range from 256 colors to 16 million. If you aren't using Web-safe colors, some viewers might not see them accurately. But the vast majority of viewers now have thousands or millions of colors, which means that it's not so important to test that your movie looks good with fewer colors.

Professional Web site developers take this testing phase seriously. No matter how good an animation looks on your screen, it's not a good animation if it doesn't translate well to your target number of viewers' screens.

Saving Your Work in Flash 8 Format

If you're collaborating on a Flash project with a group of friends or co-workers and they're still using Flash 8 (the predecessor of Flash CS3), there is still hope for them. You can save your work in Flash 8 format.

To save your work in Flash 8 format, follow these steps:

1. **Choose File⇨Save As.**

   The Save As dialog box appears.

2. **Choose where you want to save your file and then type the filename you want to use.**

3. **Click the Format drop-down list and select Flash 8.**

4. **Click Save.**

   If you're using features new to Flash CS3, a window appears, listing the new features that won't be saved in the Flash 8 file and asking whether you want to continue. Click the Save as Flash 8 button if you want to continue. If you do so, some of the data in your file will not be available in this saved version. So be sure to save a CS3 version as well to keep all your data intact.

Publishing Flash Movies

So you're finally ready to publish your Flash masterpiece. It's time to choose File⇨Publish Settings. This brings you to the Publish Settings dialog box. Don't be overwhelmed by all the options. Usually, you use only a few of them. Start by specifying the settings. Then publish the movie to create the .swf file viewed on a Web page.

After you specify the settings, you can click OK rather than Publish if you want to go back to your Flash movie file and choose Control⇨Test Movie to see the results of your settings. You can try various settings until you're satisfied. Then click Publish to create the final SWF (Flash Player) file. Published files are in the same folder as your FLA movie file by default; you can specify another location if you want. Of course, you can also move the files afterward.

The Publish Settings dialog box lets you easily specify all your settings in one place. Then you click the Publish button, and Flash creates the SWF (Flash Player) file according to your settings. Choose File⇨Publish Settings to open the Publish Settings dialog box with the Formats tab on top, as shown in Figure 13-2.

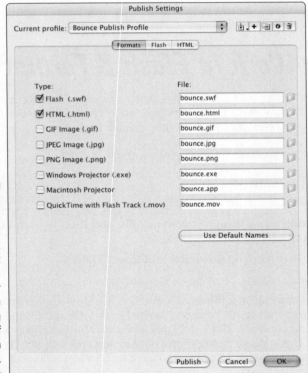

Figure 13-2:
The Publish Settings dialog box is your one-stop place for starting the publishing process of your Flash movie.

Flash automatically names the files that it creates for you, using the Flash movie's name and adding the appropriate file extension, such as `.html` and `.swf`. You can see the names in the Formats tab of the Publish Settings dialog box. To specify your own name for a file, click the File text box and type the new name. To revert to the default filenames, click the Use Default Names button.

Most of the time, you need only the Flash (`.swf`) and HTML formats. But if you want other formats, select them on the Formats tab. When you mark an additional format, the dialog box adds a new tab for that format (except for the projector formats, which don't need one).

After you mark the formats you want, click each tab to specify the settings for that format. The next few sections of this chapter explain each format, why you might want to use it, and how to specify the settings.

After you finish specifying all your settings, click the Publish button, and Flash does your bidding, creating the files that you need to put your great creation on the Web.

Publishing to SWF

The second tab in the Publish Settings dialog box (choose File⇨Publish Settings) is the Flash tab, which creates the Flash Player file, also called an `.swf` file. On this tab, shown in Figure 13-3, you specify settings that affect the `.swf` file.

Flash gives you the following options:

- **Version:** Allows you to save in previous version formats for backward compatibility (or in the Flash Lite format for playing Flash movies on mobile phones, but that's a subject for another book). If you use new features but choose an old Flash Player version, Flash warns you of potential problems when you publish your movie.

- **Load Order:** Specifies how Flash displays the first frame of the Flash movie. Bottom Up (the default) loads layers from the lowest layer upward. Top Down loads layers starting from the top layer and moving downward. Your viewers will see the difference between these two settings only if the Flash movie is loading slowly (because of a slow Internet connection, for example). Because faster Internet access speeds are becoming increasingly common, you may not need to worry about this.

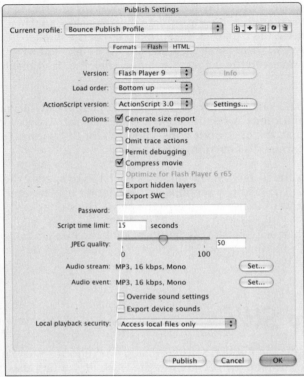

Figure 13-3:
Specify how
Flash
creates the
SWF (Flash
Player) file.

✔ **ActionScript Version (for Flash Player 6, 7, 8, and 9, and Flash Lite 2.0 and 2.1 only):** Specifies whether your movie is using ActionScript 1.0, 2.0, or 3.0. ActionScript 2.0, which was introduced in 2003, added new commands to ActionScript that are mostly of interest to intermediate or advanced programmers who are building applications in Flash that implement new classes and subclasses of objects. ActionScript 3.0 is new in Flash CS3. Fundamental changes in the underpinnings of ActionScript in version 3.0 make it possible for ActionScript 3.0 code to execute up to ten times faster than code from earlier versions.

In this book, we use the new methods for handling events and other new methods of ActionScript 3.0, so generally you will want to choose ActionScript version 3.0 in the ActionScript Version drop-down list. You can try choosing ActionScript 1.0 in the ActionScript Version drop-down list and an earlier version of the Flash Player (such as Flash 5 or Flash 6) in the Version drop-down list, and then see whether you get a warning when you publish your movie. If you don't get a warning, your published movie will safely play on older versions of Flash, and thus may reach a larger audience.

✔ **Generate Size Report:** Creates a `.txt` file that you can use to trouble-shoot problem areas. The report relates the various parts of your movie to the number of bytes that they require in the `.swf` file.

The size report can be more useful than the bandwidth profiler in pinpointing the location of the giant-size parts of a movie. It's worth reviewing, and it's interesting (and often surprising) to see the size of the various elements of the `.swf` file.

✔ **Protect from Import:** Prevents the `.swf` files from being downloaded from the Web site and imported back into Flash. This feature doesn't provide 100-percent-guaranteed protection, but it helps keep your work from being "borrowed."

✔ **Omit Trace Actions:** Omits special codes used by programmers. *Trace actions* insert into Flash movies the codes used to record and display technical information about a Flash movie's progress in a special window, named the Flash Debugger. Programmers use this information to *debug* (remove errors from) their ActionScript programming. If you added Trace actions to your Flash movie, select the Omit Trace Actions check box to omit these codes from the `.swf` file, and your file will be smaller.

✔ **Permit Debugging:** Lets you use the Debugger to debug a Flash movie from another computer. If you permit debugging, you can add a password to protect the movie file. Although this option is useful for ActionScript programmers, discussing it is beyond the scope of this book.

✔ **Compress Movie:** Compresses your Flash Player file, especially text and ActionScript, so that it can download faster. This option is great except that your compressed file does not play in Flash Player versions earlier than Flash Player 6.

Your Flash movie probably uses some feature that's been added to Flash after Flash Player 5 anyway, so you might as well go for it and compress your movie.

✔ **Optimize for Flash Player 6 r65:** This option appears if you choose Flash Player 6 when you choose the Flash Player version at the top of the dialog box. Flash Player 6 r65 was an updated version of Flash Player with significant bug fixes and performance enhancements.

✔ **Export Hidden Layers:** This option is set by default. If you deselect this option, Flash will not publish layers (including layers inside movie clips) that are marked as hidden. Deselecting this option can be useful because then you can test different versions of your document simply by hiding layers.

✔ **Export SWC:** If you're new to Flash, you can safely leave this option disabled. SWC files are packages of precompiled components. Components in Flash can be implemented either in an `.fla` file or an `.swc` file. The User Interface components (such as CheckBoxes, ComboBoxes and RadioButtons) are implemented as FLA-based components, and the FLVPlayback and FLVPlaybackCaptioning components are SWC-based. You can use ActionScript to add SWC-based components while a Flash Player movie is running so that they can be kept in `.swc` files that are separate from your Flash Player file. Because `.swc` files contain precompiled components, the components appear faster than ordinary movie clips. If you enable this option, when you publish your file, Flash creates an `.swc` file that contains your SWC components and an `.swf` file that uses the `.swc` file.

✔ **Password:** Allows you to select a password for debugging, if you enable the Debugging Permitted (or Protect from Import) check box. This option prevents viewers from debugging (or importing) the movie unless they have the password.

✔ **Script Time Limit:** If a Flash movie seems to be stuck in an endless loop, after 15 seconds the Flash Player will present the user with dialog box asking whether to continue or quit. Here you can set the limit to a time other than the default of 15 seconds.

✔ **JPEG Quality:** Sets the compression (size) versus quality of bitmaps, if you have any in your movie. You can set the quality anywhere from 0 (the lowest quality and highest compression) to 100 (the highest quality and lowest compression).

✔ **Audio Stream:** Displays and sets the audio compression for *stream sounds* (sounds that use the Stream Sync setting in the Property inspector when a frame with the sound is selected). This setting applies if you haven't set the compression for individual sounds in the Sound Properties dialog box. Also, if you enable the Override Sound Settings check box in the Publish Settings dialog box, this setting overrides the setting in the Sound Properties dialog box. To change the current setting, click Set. The options are the same as in the Sound Properties dialog box. (Turn to Chapter 11 for details on setting sound properties.)

✔ **Audio Event:** Displays and sets the audio compression for event sounds (as set in the Property inspector when a frame with the sound is selected). Otherwise, the compression setting is the same as Audio Stream.

✔ **Override Sound Settings:** Select this option to override settings in the Sound Properties dialog box. Then the settings here apply to all sounds in your movie.

✔ **Export Device Sounds:** This gives you the option of exporting sounds in formats suitable for playback on mobile devices, such as certain mobile phones and personal digital assistants (PDAs). To do this, you use proxy sound files, a discussion of which is beyond the scope of this book.

✔ **Local Playback Security:** If you select Local Access Only, your Flash movie can interact only with files and resources on the computer that it's playing on. If you select Access Network Only, your movie can interact only with files and resources on the network, and not with those on the computer it's playing on. (This separation of local and network access helps make it more difficult for a malicious programmer to create a Flash file that collects data from your computer and transmits it over a network such as the Internet.)

If all these settings seem like a bit much, you can always just use the default settings, go with the flow, and check the results.

Publishing to HTML

HTML is the basic language of Web pages. If you work on a Web site, you can write the HTML code from scratch or use an HTML editor. However, many people use a Web authoring program, such as Dreamweaver.

To place a Flash Player file on a Web page, you need the proper HTML code. You probably also want some sophisticated JavaScript code in the Web page that takes care of recent changes in Internet Explorer so that your Flash movies will activate automatically, without first requiring that the user respond to a prompt for a click. (*JavaScript* is a programming language that is designed to give Web pages capabilities far beyond what HTML can do.) Luckily, Flash can create all this code for you, in formats suitable for most browsers.

As the result of a patent lawsuit, in 2006 Microsoft released an updated version of Internet Explorer that prompts the user with a request for a confirmation click for each Flash file, QuickTime movie, and other Active X control in each Web page, to confirm that the user wants to activate it. Yikes!

Understanding the HTML code for a movie

Figure 13-4 shows the type of HTML code and JavaScript code that Flash generates when you publish your Flash file by using default settings, as displayed in TextEdit on a Mac. (In TextEdit, before opening your HTML file, be sure to choose TextEdit➪Preferences and then select the Plain Text option in the New Document Attributes section of the Preferences dialog box.) Windows users can use Notepad to view HTML code created by the Publish command.

Figure 13-4:
Flash by
default
creates
HTML and
JavaScript
code that
looks like
this when
you publish
a movie to a
player file.

```
● ● ●                    ≣ Movie of the Year.html
<html xmlns="http://www.w3.org/1999/xhtml" xml:lang="en" lang="en">
<head>
<meta http-equiv="Content-Type" content="text/html; charset=iso-8859-1" />
<title>Movie of the Year</title>
<script language="javascript">AC_FL_RunContent = 0;</script>
<script src="AC_RunActiveContent.js" language="javascript"></script>
</head>
<body bgcolor="#ffffff">
<!--url's used in the movie-->
<!--text used in the movie-->
<!-- saved from url=(0013)about:internet -->
<script language="javascript">
        if (AC_FL_RunContent == 0) {
            alert("This page requires AC_RunActiveContent.js.");
        } else {
            AC_FL_RunContent(
                'codebase', 'http://download.macromedia.com/pub/shockwave/cabs/flash/swflash.cab#version=9,0,0,0',
                'width', '550',
                'height', '400',
                'src', 'Movie of the Year',
                'quality', 'high',
                'pluginspage', 'http://www.macromedia.com/go/getflashplayer',
                'align', 'middle',
                'play', 'true',
                'loop', 'false',
                'scale', 'showall',
                'wmode', 'window',
                'devicefont', 'false',
                'id', 'Movie of the Year',
                'bgcolor', '#ffffff',
                'name', 'Movie of the Year',
                'menu', 'true',
                'allowScriptAccess','sameDomain',
                'movie', 'Movie of the Year',
                'salign', ''
                ); //end AC code
        }
</script>
<noscript>
        <object classid="clsid:d27cdb6e-ae6d-11cf-96b8-444553540000" codebase="http://download.macromedia.com/pub/
shockwave/cabs/flash/swflash.cab#version=9,0,0,0" width="550" height="400" id="Movie of the Year" align="middle">
        <param name="allowScriptAccess" value="sameDomain" />
        <param name="movie" value="Movie of the Year.swf" /><param name="loop" value="false" /><param name="quality"
value="high" /><param name="bgcolor" value="#ffffff" /><embed src="Movie of the Year.swf" loop="false" quality="high"
bgcolor="#ffffff" width="550" height="400" name="Movie of the Year" align="middle" allowScriptAccess="sameDomain"
type="application/x-shockwave-flash" pluginspage="http://www.macromedia.com/go/getflashplayer" />
        </object>
</noscript>
</body>
</html>
```

If you know some HTML, some parts of this page will look fairly familiar. (And if you don't, you might want to check out *HTML 4 For Dummies,* 5th Edition, by Ed Tittel and Mary Burmeister, from Wiley Publishing, Inc.) The page starts with the *tags* (codes) that all HTML documents contain, namely `<html>`, `<head>`, `<title>`, and `<body>`. Here's how to understand the code in Figure 13-4:

✔ After `<body`, you see `bgcolor="#ffffff">`. This is the background color of the entire HTML page.

By default, Flash makes the background color of the HTML page the same color as the background of your Flash movie, but you might prefer to change it to a different color to help visually define the Flash movie.

✔ After the comments (which start with `<!`) is JavaScript code between the `<script language="javascript">` tag and the `</script>` tag. This code is used by another JavaScript file (named `AC_RunActiveContent.js`) created by Flash when you publish your Flash movie. The JavaScript code writes HTML code that your Web browser will display. So the JavaScript code creates the HTML code that creates the Web page that you end up seeing.

✔ After the `</script>` tag, you see a `<noscript>` tag. All the code after the `<noscript>` tag is the HTML for the Web page that will appear if users have JavaScript turned off in their browser.

✔ Next you see the `object` tag. Microsoft Internet Explorer requires this tag to display your Flash Player files. The `object` code includes the following:

- Detailed codes (which are required to tell Internet Explorer how to display your player file).

- The specification of the version of the Flash viewer to look for and where to download it if necessary.

- The width and height of the Flash movie in the browser.

- The name of the file (`value="Movie of the Year.swf"`).

- Parameter settings for local or network access, looping, quality, and background color. You set the background color by choosing Modify⇨Document in Flash and choosing a background color in the Document Properties dialog box. (See Chapter 2 for details on using this dialog box.)

- The `embed` code is for Netscape Navigator, Mozilla, and Mozilla Firefox browsers, and accomplishes the same thing as the `object` code.

✔ Finally, you see the closing `</object>` tag, the closing `</noscript>` tag, and the tags that end every HTML document: `</body>` and `</html>`.

If you want to use the HTML document as is, you can. But if you want to combine your Flash Player file with the elements in another HTML file (as you would for a Flash button, for example), you need to combine the code in the two documents.

One way you can do this is to treat as one unit all the code in the first document (the HTML document created in Flash when you choose File⇨Publish), starting with `<script language="javascript">` and ending with `</script>`, which is the tag immediately before the `<noscript>` tag. Think of this unit as your Flash movie code. Then copy HTML from your second HTML document and paste it before or after your unit of Flash movie code, to display HTML elements before or after your Flash movie.

If you didn't change your default folder locations in the Formats section of the Publish Settings dialog box, your `.swf` file will be in the same folder as the HTML file that Flash creates when you publish your movie. In that case, the HTML `<object>` and `<embed>` tags created by the Flash publishing process reference the `.swf` file by simply mentioning the filename. For that to work, the `.swf` file must be in the same folder on your Web site's server as your Web page's HTML file.

If you usually keep image files in a subfolder and want to also place your `.swf` file in that subfolder, you can specify that location in the Formats tab of the Publish Settings dialog box. Click the small folder icon to the right of the name of the `.swf` file, and navigate to the subfolder where you want it to be placed.

Specifying Flash Player detection and other HTML settings

To create the HTML file, you need to specify the HTML settings on the HTML tab of the Publish Settings dialog box, as shown in Figure 13-5.

Figure 13-5:
Specify
how Flash
creates
HTML code
to display
your movie.

Template

The first setting, Template, lets you select a template. The *template* determines the format and contents of the HTML file. To keep matters simple, select the default, Flash Only. Table 13-1 explains the other template options, although it's very possible that you may never need to use anything other than the default, Flash Only.

Table 13-1	HTML Template Options
Option	*What It Does*
Flash for Pocket PC 2003	Creates an HTML file with `<object>` and `<embed>` tags and with Pocket PC–specific alignment. Can be used with Pocket IE and with desktop Internet Explorer and Netscape browsers.
Flash HTTPS	Creates an HTML file with JavaScript code that displays your Flash movie without requiring a user to first respond to a prompt. Uses the HTTPS protocol to specify where to go to download the Flash Player if necessary. *HTTPS* is designed to send data over the Web more securely than the standard method (HTTP). Also creates a JavaScript file in your HTML output folder, and this must be uploaded along with the HTML file.
Flash Only (Default)	Creates an HTML file with JavaScript code that displays your Flash movie without requiring a user to first respond to a prompt. Also creates a JavaScript file in your HTML output folder, and this must be uploaded along with the HTML file.
Flash with AICC Tracking	Includes support for AICC-HACP tracking when using Macromedia Learning Interactions. (AICC is Aviation Industry Computer-Based-Training Committee, and HACP is HTTP AICC Communications Protocol.)
Flash with FSCommand	Used when you have added an `FSCommand` action to your movie to interface with JavaScript. The HTML file also includes the `<object>` and `<embed>` commands.
Flash with Full Screen Support	Creates an HTML file with JavaScript code that displays your Flash movie without requiring a user to first respond to a prompt. Includes support for playing your Flash movie full screen. Also creates a JavaScript file in your HTML output folder, and this must be uploaded along with the HTML file.
Flash with Named Anchors	Creates an HTML file with `<object>` and `<embed>` tags. Adds browser scripting and HTML anchors so that viewers can bookmark Flash content in Flash Player 6 and later, and thus use the Web browser's Back button effectively while navigating within a Flash movie. This could be a great feature, but many browsers don't support it, so it's fairly useless.

(continued)

Table 13-1 *(continued)*

Option	What It Does
Flash with SCORM 1.2 Tracking	Includes support for SCORM (Sharable Content Object Reference Model) version 1.2 tracking when using Macromedia Learning Interactions.
Flash with SCORM 2004 Tracking	Includes support for SCORM 2004 tracking when using Macromedia Learning Interactions.
Image Map	(If you don't know what an image map is, don't worry about this option.) Instead of displaying an SWF player file, uses a GIF, JPEG, or PNG image (which you need to choose in the Formats tab) as a client-side image map coded in your HTML page.
QuickTime	Creates `<embed>` and `<object>` tags in an HTML page to display a QuickTime Flash movie based on your Flash movie. You need to select the QuickTime check box on the Formats tab. A QuickTime Flash movie plays with only QuickTime 4 or later. QuickTime 4 can recognize only Flash 3 features. QuickTime 5 can recognize Flash 4 features. (QuickTime 4 and 5 are old, so this isn't an interesting way to publish your Flash movies.)

Below the Template drop-down list is the Detect Flash Version check box. (This option is available only if you choose Flash Player 4 or later in the Flash tab of the Publish Settings dialog box and the Flash HTTPS or Flash Only template.) Select this check box to add browser scripting to detect the Flash Player for the version of Flash you specify on the Flash tab. When this check box is enabled, the Version number text boxes below it are also enabled. If you want to more exactly specify the minimum version required, type revision numbers in the Minor Revision and Incremental Revision text fields there. (*Minor Revision* and *Incremental Revision* appear in tooltips when you move the mouse cursor over the text boxes.)

If you select the Detect Flash Version check box, when you publish your Flash file, the resulting HTML code prints "Alternate HTML content should be placed here" in your Web page if the Flash Player of the specified version can't be found or if the Web browser doesn't have scripting enabled. (Scripting must be enabled by the Web browser for the Flash Player version detection to work.) You can edit the HTML to replace the sentence "Alternate HTML content should be placed here" with whatever alternative content you want to display when the Flash Player version can't be found.

Dimensions

The Dimensions options control the size allotted to your Flash Player movie on your Web page. You have three options:

- **Match Movie** matches the width and height that you set in the Movie Properties dialog box (choose Modify⇨Document).

- **Pixels** lets you specify the Width and Height in pixels. Type the desired values in the text boxes.

- **Percent** lets you specify the area used by the Flash Player movie as a percentage of the browser window size. The 100% setting is ideal for pages designed to take up the entire page. Type the desired percentage values in the text boxes labeled Width and Height.

Playback

The Playback section determines the values of parameters in the HTML code. You have four options:

- **Paused at Start** creates a PLAY parameter whose value is FALSE. The person must start the movie by clicking a button in the movie — the button's instance needs to have a Play action in it. Alternatively, viewers can right-click (Windows) or Control+click (Mac) the movie and choose Play in the shortcut menu, but they might not be aware of this. By default, this check box is deselected, so movies start to play automatically.

- **Loop** creates a LOOP parameter whose value is TRUE. The movie repeats over and over. By default, this check box is selected, so make sure to clear it if you don't want to loop your movie!

- **Display Menu** creates a MENU parameter set to TRUE. This option enables viewers to right-click (Windows) or Control+click (Mac) the movie and choose from a menu. The menu options in Flash Player 9 are Zoom In/Out, Show All, Quality (High, Medium, or Low), Play, Loop, Rewind/Forward/Back, Settings, Print, Show Redraw Regions, Debugger, and About Adobe Flash Player 9. Without this option, Settings, Show Redraw Regions, Debugger, and About Adobe Flash Player 9 are the only items on the shortcut menu. By default, Display Menu is selected.

  Show Redraw Regions shows you the outlines of the regions of your movie that Flash is currently refreshing.

- **Device Font** applies to Windows playback only. When this check box is selected, the HTML file includes a DEVICE FONT parameter set to TRUE, and Flash substitutes *anti-aliased* (smoothly curved) system fonts for fonts not available on the viewer's system. This applies only to static text you create in Flash. By default, this item is not selected.

Quality

The Quality section determines the `quality` parameter in the `<object>` and `<embed>` tags of the HTML code. Quality refers to the level of anti-aliasing, which means the smoothing of the artwork so that it doesn't have jagged edges. The lower the quality, the faster the playback. Usually, you want to find a middle ground between quality and speed. You have six options:

✔ **Low** doesn't use any anti-aliasing (and looks awful).

✔ **Auto Low** starts at a low quality but switches to a high quality if the viewer's computer, as detected by the Flash Player, can handle it.

✔ **Auto High** starts at a high quality but switches to a low quality if the viewer's computer can't handle the playback demand. This option should provide good results on all computers.

✔ **Medium** applies some anti-aliasing but doesn't smooth bitmaps. This option is a good middle ground between low and high. This setting is the default.

✔ **High** always uses anti-aliasing for vector art. Bitmaps are smoothed only if the file doesn't contain tweens. (See Chapter 9 for the scoop on tweens.)

✔ **Best** always uses anti-aliasing, including for bitmaps.

Window Mode

Window Mode specifies how the player movie's window interacts with the rest of the page. Here are your options:

✔ **Window** plays your movie as an opaque rectangle within your Web page and does not allow your HTML to render other content in that rectangle. This is the default mode.

✔ **Opaque Windowless** creates an opaque background for the movie so that other elements in the Web page don't show through when they're behind the movie. This setting does allow your HTML to render content in front of the movie.

✔ **Transparent Windowless** makes the Flash background color transparent so that other elements on your Web page show through (or can appear on top of) your Flash content. This setting might slow down playback.

The code for the Transparent and Windowless modes has an effect only in more recent browsers running on Windows or Mac OS X — Internet Explorer version 5 and later, Netscape version 7 and later, Mozilla 1 and later, Firefox 1 and later, and Opera 6 and later.

HTML Alignment

The HTML Alignment setting specifies the ALIGN attribute and specifies how the Flash Player movie is aligned within the browser window. You have five options:

- ✔ **Default** theoretically centers the Flash movie. If the browser window is smaller than the movie, this option theoretically crops the edges of the movie. But in our tests, the default is always left even though it should be center.

- ✔ **Left** aligns the movie along the left side of the browser window. If the window is too small, this option crops the other sides of the movie.

- ✔ **Right** aligns the movie along the right side of the browser window. If the window is too small, this option crops the other sides of the movie.

- ✔ **Top** aligns the movie along the top of the browser window. If the window is too small, this option crops the other sides of the movie.

- ✔ **Bottom** aligns the movie along the bottom of the browser window. If the window is too small, this option crops the other sides of the movie.

Scale

The Scale setting defines how the movie is placed within the boundaries specified by code in the HTML page when (and only when) you set a width and height different from the movie's original size, using the Pixels or Percent options in the Dimensions section of the Publish Settings dialog box. You have four options:

- ✔ **Default (Show All)** displays the entire movie without distortion but might create borders on two sides of the movie.

  The Show All setting shows all the elements in your Flash movie, even those that you move to the sides, off the Stage.

- ✔ **No Border** scales the movie to fill the dimensions without distortion but might crop portions of the movie.

- ✔ **Exact Fit** fits the movie to the dimensions, distorting the movie if necessary.

- ✔ **No Scale** stops the movie from changing its scale if the viewer resizes the Flash Player window.

Flash Alignment

Flash Alignment determines how the movie fits within the movie window (as opposed to the browser window). It works together with the Scale and Dimensions settings. In other words, it determines how the Flash movie fits within the dimensions you specify. For the Horizontal setting, you can choose Left, Center, or Right. For the Vertical setting, you can choose Top, Center, or Bottom.

Show Warning Messages

At the bottom of the Publish Settings dialog box is the Show Warning Messages check box. When it's selected, you see warning messages during the publishing process. The publishing process continues, but you know that you might have made an error. For example, if you've chosen a template that requires a GIF or JPEG image but you haven't selected either format on the Formats tab, you see a warning message.

After you choose your settings, click OK to return to your movie or click Publish to publish it.

Publishing to Other Formats

You can use Flash's Publish Settings to generate files in a variety of other formats besides HTML pages and Flash Player movies. These other formats are GIF images, animated GIFs, JPEG images, PNG images, QuickTime movies, and self-playing Windows and Mac projectors.

Even if you use Flash all day, every day, you might never need to generate GIF images, JPEG images, or QuickTime images from your Flash movies, so we won't clog up your life by describing the Publish Settings for those formats here.

Creating PNG graphic files

PNG files can display millions more colors than GIF files and support transparency. They offer some of the advantages of both GIFs and JPEGs. To create a PNG image, choose PNG Image on the Formats tab of the Publish Settings dialog box (refer to Figure 13-2). Flash creates a PNG tab in the dialog box, as shown in Figure 13-6.

Flash publishes the first frame of your movie unless you label a different frame with the #Static label. (To create a label, click the frame and choose Window➪Properties➪Properties to open the Property inspector. If necessary, expand the Property inspector to its full size. Type a label name in the Frame text box on the left side of the Property inspector.)

Figure 13-6:
Use the
PNG tab to
create PNG
images.

You have the following options:

- **Dimensions** lets you specify your own Width and Height settings if you deselect the Match Movie check box. This could be useful if you want to create a thumbnail image to use on a Web page to link to your movie. By default, Flash matches the dimensions of the movie.

- **Bit Depth** controls the number of bits per pixel, which in turn means how many colors the image contains. You can select 8-bit for 256 colors (like a GIF), 24-bit for 16.7 million colors, or 24-bit with Alpha, which allows for transparency. When you choose 24-bit with Alpha, the image's background becomes transparent. This is one of the things that designers love about PNG files.

- **Options** specifies how the PNG file appears:

  - **Optimize Colors** removes unused colors from the file's color table to reduce the size of the file.

- **Interlace** causes a static PNG image to load in incremental resolutions, so the image appears first fuzzy and then successively sharper. Some people like this option because viewers may be able to click the image before it fully downloads, thus reducing their waiting time.

- **Smooth** anti-aliases (smoothes) the artwork. Text usually looks better (and the file size is larger), but occasionally you may get an undesirable halo effect around your art. In that case, turn off smoothing.

- **Dither Solids** does just that — it dithers solid colors as well as gradients and images. *Dithering* is a way to approximate colors not available on the color palette by using a range of similar colors. This applies only to files with 8-bit color. See the Dither option, which we describe a few paragraphs from now.

- **Remove Gradients** turns gradients into solids. Gradients may not look good in a Web-safe color table. Nevertheless, Flash uses the first color in the gradient, which may not be the color you want.

✔ **Dither** enables dithering for files with 8-bit color, as we define in the Dither Solids bullet in the Options descriptions. Dithering helps to create more accurate looking colors but increases file size. Choose one of the three options:

- **None** disables dithering.

- **Ordered** provides a medium amount of dithering and a corresponding medium increase in file size.

- **Diffusion** provides the best-quality dithering and increases file size the most. It works only with the Web 216-color palette. (Refer to Chapter 3 for a description of color palettes.)

✔ **Palette Type** determines the color palette for the PNG image. This applies only to PNG files with 8-bit color. (Refer to Chapter 3 for a discussion of colors in Flash.) You have four options:

- **Web 216** uses the standard 216-color palette that includes only Web-safe colors (those that look good on all Web browsers). You can usually get good results for Flash artwork without increasing file size.

- **Adaptive** creates a unique color table for your file, based on the actual colors present. You get more accurate color (although these colors may not be Web safe), but the file size may be larger. Use this option if an accurate representation of the colors is most important, as in a photographic bitmap image. You can use the Max Colors text box to specify how many colors you want in the table. The default is 255. Use fewer colors to reduce the file size.

- **Web Snap Adaptive** works like the Adaptive option but optimizes the color palette for the Web. Colors close to the 216 Web-safe colors are turned into one of the colors on that palette. Other colors function like the Adaptive option. As with the Adaptive option, you can specify the number of colors on the palette in the Max Colors text box.

- **Custom** lets you specify a palette in the ACT format. Click the file folder icon near the Palette text field to browse for a color palette file. (Read the section in Chapter 3 on solid colors for an explanation of how to create a color palette and save it in ACT format.)

- The **Max Colors** option is enabled only when you choose Adaptive or Web Snap Adaptive, and the **Palette** option is enabled only when you choose Custom.

✔ **Filter Options** controls how an image is analyzed line by line to compress it. You have these options:

- **None** applies no filtering. The resulting file is larger than with the other options.

- **Sub** filters adjoining pixel bytes (working horizontally). This works best when the image has repeated horizontal information.

- **Up** filters in a vertical direction. This works best when the image has repeated vertical information.

- **Average** uses a mixture of horizontal and vertical comparison; this is a good first-try option.

- **Path** employs a more complex method that uses the three nearest pixels to predict the next one.

- **Adaptive** creates a unique color table for your PNG file based on the actual colors present. You get more accurate color, although these colors might not be Web safe. The file size might also be larger. Use this option if accurate representation of colors is most important, as in a photographic bitmap image.

After you specify your settings, click OK to return to your movie or click Publish to publish your PNG image and create the other files you've chosen.

Creating self-playing movies

You can also create projectors in the Publish Settings dialog box. A *projector* is a self-playing Flash movie that doesn't require the Flash Player. All the interactive and animated features of your Flash movie work in a projector. You can use a projector for a Flash movie that you want to burn on a CD-R or DVD-R computer disc (The projector format is not compatible with the format of a DVD movie disc, though.) Projector files tend to have much larger sizes than their corresponding .swf files.

You can create a Windows or Mac version from either platform. But if you create a Mac version in Windows, you need to use a file translator, such as BinHex so that the Mac Finder recognizes it as an application.

To create a projector, follow these steps:

1. **Choose File➪Publish Settings.**

    The Publish Settings dialog box opens.

2. **On the Formats tab, select the Windows Projector check box or the Macintosh Projector check box, or both.**

3. **Click Publish.**

4. **Click OK or Cancel to close the Publish Settings dialog box.**

For Windows, Flash creates an EXE file. For the Mac, Flash creates a Macintosh Projector application. If you create the Macintosh Projector file in Flash while using a Windows computer, the Macintosh Projector file is stored inside a compressed BinHex file (HQX), which can then be uncompressed on a Mac.

Don't forget to test your movie after you copy it to a CD-ROM or another computer. Try it out with a variety of processor speeds if possible.

Using Publish Profiles

You can save all the settings that you configure in the Publish Settings dialog box as a *publish profile*. You can then duplicate, modify, export, import, and delete your publish profiles and trade them with your collaborators. You can create standard publish profiles, which you use to make sure that all your files are published uniformly, and you can create specialized publish profiles specific to a single project. The following sections tell you how.

Creating a publish profile

To create a publish profile, follow these steps:

1. **Choose File➪Publish Settings.**

    The Publish Settings dialog box appears.

2. **Click the Create New Profile button (the + symbol) in the upper-right part of the dialog box.**

    The Create New Profile dialog box appears.

3. **Type a name for your profile and then click OK.**

   The Create New Profile dialog box disappears, and the name of your new profile appears in the Current Profile drop-down list of the Publish Settings dialog box.

4. **Specify the publish settings for your document in the Publish Settings dialog box, as we describe in earlier sections of this chapter, and then click OK.**

Duplicating or renaming a publish profile

You might want to duplicate a publish profile to use it as a springboard for new variations. To duplicate a publish profile, do the following steps:

1. **Choose File⇨Publish Settings.**

   The Publish Settings dialog box appears.

2. **In the Current Profile drop-down list (near the top of the dialog box), select the publish profile that you want to rename (or copy).**

3. **Click the Rename Profile button (or the Duplicate Profile button — the horizontal arrow button), in the upper-right part of the dialog box.**

   The Profile Properties dialog box (or the Duplicate Profile dialog box) appears.

4. **Type a new name for your profile (or the name for your duplicate profile) and then click OK.**

   The dialog box disappears. The name of your renamed profile (or your duplicate profile) appears in the Current Profile drop-down list of the Publish Settings dialog box.

Modifying a publish profile

You might use a particular publish profile as, for example, a standard for your co-workers. As circumstances change, you might want to modify the publish profile, and that's easy to do. To modify a publish profile, follow these steps:

1. **Choose File⇨Publish Settings.**

   The Publish Settings dialog box appears.

2. **In the Current Profile drop-down list (near the top of the dialog box), select the publish profile that you want to modify.**

3. **Select the publish settings that you want for your document in the Publish Settings dialog box, as we describe in the earlier sections of this chapter, and then click OK.**

Deleting a publish profile

To delete a publish profile, follow these steps:

1. **Choose File⇨Publish Settings.**

   The Publish Settings dialog box appears.

2. **In the Current Profile drop-down list (near the top of the dialog box), select the publish profile that you want to delete.**

3. **Click the Delete Profile button (the trash can) in the upper-right part of the dialog box.**

   A dialog box appears asking you to confirm that you want to delete the profile.

4. **Click OK.**

Exporting and importing publish profiles

To use a publish profile in documents other than the document in which you created it, first you export it from the document in which you created it. Then you import it into the new document.

This makes your work easier if, for example, you're working on a Flash project with a team and need to publish your Flash documents according to a single standard. The entire team can easily share the same publish profile.

To export a publish profile, follow these steps:

1. **Choose File⇨Publish Settings.**

   The Publish Settings dialog box appears.

2. **In the Current Profile drop-down list (near the top of the dialog box), select the publish profile that you want to export.**

3. **Click the Import/Export Profile button (the vertical arrow button in the upper-left part of the dialog box) and select Export in the drop-down list.**

   The Export Profile dialog box appears.

4. **In the dialog box, select a location where you want to save the file and then click Save.**

   The default location is a folder named Publish Profiles, which is located in the Flash CS3 application folder. The file is saved as an .xml file.

To import a publish profile, follow these steps:

1. **Choose File⇨Publish Settings.**

   The Publish Settings dialog box appears.

2. **Click the Import/Export Profile button (the vertical arrow button in the upper-left part of the dialog box) and then select Import in the drop-down list.**

   The Import Profile dialog box appears.

3. **In the dialog box, browse to find the publish profile that you want to import and then click Open.**

   The name of the imported publish profile appears in the Current Profile drop-down list of the Publish Settings dialog box.

Using Publish Preview

If you want to specify publish settings, see the results, and then go back to tweak your settings, you can use Publish Preview rather than Publish. Publish Preview creates the files specified in the Publish Settings dialog box, just as the Publish command does. The only difference is that Publish Preview automatically displays the requested file, usually the .swf file. The value is in simply saving the steps of manually opening your files in your browser — helpful when you're doing lots of tweaking and going back and forth between your publish settings and your browser to see what works best.

To use Publish Preview, follow these steps:

1. **Specify your settings by using the Publish Settings dialog box (as we explain earlier in this chapter) and then click OK.**

2. **Choose File⇨Publish Preview.**

3. **In the Publish Preview submenu, choose the file format that you want to preview.**

4. **When you're finished, close the window or browser.**

Posting Your Movie to Your Web Site

After you finish publishing your movie, you probably want to post your .swf file on your Web site or place it on a CD-R or other media.

You can make Mac and Windows projectors and copy them onto a CD-R by using CD-burner software. Then you can view your Flash movie independently of a Web browser. Or copy your published HTML and .swf files onto a CD-R along with any external scripts, image files, or text files used by your HTML and .swf files.

Refer to the "Understanding the HTML code for a movie" section, earlier in this chapter, for instructions on modifying the HTML code if you want to place your .swf file on an existing Web page or place your .swf file in a subfolder.

To post your movie to a Web site, upload the HTML, the .swf file, and the JavaScript file.

The default HTML file that Flash generates when you publish a Flash movie depends on an external JavaScript file that Flash generates along with it.

If your HTML or .swf files load data from any image files, text files, or external scripts (such as JavaScript or ActionScript files), you need to upload those, too.

Open your browser and load the Web page that contains your Flash movie. We hope it works perfectly and looks great! If not, check out the HTML code, check your publish settings, and make sure that the necessary files are in the proper location on your Web site's server.

Exporting Movies and Images

In addition to publishing, Flash lets you export image files and QuickTime movies. Export a Flash file when you want to use it in another application. For example, you may want to export a frame as a PNG file and insert it into a word processing document. You can use Export Movie to export to a QuickTime movie or to create a still image of every frame.

After you export a movie or image, you can then import it into the desired application for further editing or display.

Note that when you choose File➪Export➪Export Movie to export a movie to a format such as GIF, JPG, or PNG, you export a sequence of individually numbered images. That might give you some interesting raw material to import into other graphics applications. In fact, exporting a Flash movie as a PNG sequence is how many professional animation jobs are now done. The sequence of PNG files is then imported into Adobe After Effects to be converted to Cineon files, which are used to put the animation onto movie film.

To export a movie or image, follow these steps:

1. **Open the Flash document from which you want to export.**

   See Chapter 1 for information about opening an existing Flash movie.

2. **To export to an image, select the frame that you want to export. Otherwise, skip to Step 3.**

3. **Choose File⇨Export⇨Export Image or File⇨Export⇨Export Movie.**

4. **In the dialog box, navigate to the desired location and type a name for your image or movie.**

5. **In the Save as Type (Format on a Mac) drop-down list, select the type of file.**

6. **Click Save.**

7. **Depending on the format that you selected, a dialog box might appear. If so, specify the settings and then click OK.**

   These settings are similar to the kind of settings that we describe earlier in this chapter, in the "Creating PNG graphic files" section.

Table 13-2 lists the types of files that you can export.

Table 13-2			Export File Types
File Type	*Windows*	*Mac*	*Comments*
Adobe Illustrator (AI)	X	X	A vector format.
Drawing Exchange Format (DXF)	X	X	A format that you can import into AutoCAD, although you lose fills.
Encapsulated PostScript (EPS)	X	X	A vector format used in Adobe Illustrator and recognized by many other applications.
Graphics Interchange File (GIF)	X	X	A bitmap format, limited to 256 colors.
Joint Photographic Experts Group (JPEG/JPG)	X	X	A bitmap format that supports 24-bit color.
Flash Video (FLV)	X	X	A video format designed for use with video conferencing and other communications applications.

(continued)

Table 13-2 *(continued)*

File Type	Windows	Mac	Comments
PICT (PCT)		X	A bitmap format that can be used with most Mac and many PC applications. The PICT format supports transparency and variable bit depths.
Portable Network Graphic (PNG)	X	X	A bitmap format that supports variable bit depths and transparency.
QuickTime (MOV)	X	X	A QuickTime 4 format movie.
QuickTime Video (MOV)		X	On Macs only, uses the Video QuickTime 3 format, bitmapping all content.
Video for Windows (AVI)	X		A bitmap video format. Files can get large.
Windows Audio (WAV)	X		Exports just the sound.
Windows Bitmap (BMP)	X		A bitmap format. Many applications recognize it. Offers variable bit depths and transparency support. File size is large.
Windows Metafile and Enhanced	X		A vector format supported by many Metafile (WMF/EMF) applications. Creates smaller files than EPS.

Creating Printable Movies

Suppose that you want your Web site viewers to be able to print a form on your Web site that you created in Flash. Or perhaps you want them to print your contact information so that your Web page can become your business card. The Flash Player printing features enable your viewers to print receipts, information sheets, coupons, or whatever else helps you do business on the Web. You can specify certain frames in a movie — including frames in the main Timeline, a button, or a movie clip — to be printable from the Flash Player shortcut menu. Viewers right-click (Windows) or Control+click (Mac) to access the Print command.

Your viewers need instructions on how to print, so place some text some-where telling them what to do.

Of course, viewers can use their browser's Print command to print, but the result isn't nearly as controllable. When we tried it, our browser printed only the first frame, which was useless in our example. The browser also added the Uniform Resource Locator (URL), the name of the movie, the date, and the page number.

By default, the Flash Player shortcut menu lets viewers print the entire movie, frame by frame. This feature is useless for most purposes. But by specifying which frames are printed and the print area, you can use the Player's Print command to make specific information or forms available to your viewers.

Preparing your movie for printing

If you want a nice, clean result, you need a nice, clean frame. The Flash Player prints all objects on all layers of the movie. If you want to create a form, for example, put it in its own frame and make sure that objects on other layers don't continue into that frame.

Alternatively, you can specify the print area so that you include only the area that you want printed, excluding other objects on the Stage in the frame. But if you specify a small area, this area becomes the entire page size when printing, so the objects in that small area are enlarged to take up the entire printed page. You can control the layout by changing the dimension, scale, and align-ment HTML settings (on the HTML tab of the Publish Settings dialog box).

Make sure that everything you want to print is on the Stage. For example, if you want to print from a movie clip, it must be on the Stage and have an instance name.

You can make a movie clip invisible by setting its `_visible` property to `false`. (Use the Actions panel.) This capability enables you to instruct view-ers to print an item that they don't see on the screen — for example, a form that's formatted differently on paper and on the computer screen.

If your movie displays text instructing users how to print from the printable area, you might want to exclude this text from the printable area. They prob-ably don't want to print the instructions on how to print, right?

Specifying printable frames

To specify which frame or frames you want to print when your viewers choose Print in the Flash Player shortcut menu, follow these steps:

1. **With the movie open, choose Window⇨Properties⇨Properties to open the Property inspector.**

   The shortcut is Ctrl+F3 (Windows) or ⌘+F3 (Mac). If necessary, expand the Property inspector to its full size.

2. **Select from the Timeline the frame you want printed.**

3. **If the frame you selected is not a keyframe, make it a keyframe by choosing Insert⇨Timeline⇨Keyframe.**

   Turn to Chapter 9 for the lowdown on keyframes.

4. **In the Property inspector, type #p in the Frame text box, as shown in Figure 13-7. Below the Frame text box, set the Label Type drop-down list to Name (the default).**

Figure 13-7:
Use the
Property
inspector to
label frames
for printing.

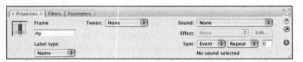

For each additional keyframe that you want to specify for printing, select the frame and then label it #p in the Property Inspector Frame text box.

Specifying the print area

Unless you specify the print area, the Flash Player prints the entire Stage. If you have loaded other movies, the Flash Player uses their Stage size. You might, however, want to specify a different area. As we mention earlier in this chapter, you might want to include instructions on how to print, but you may not want the instructions to be printed. You can exclude other objects on the Stage as well.

Choosing a very small print area results in an output of very big objects. The Flash Player sizes your objects to take up the entire printed page.

You create an object, usually a rectangle, to specify the print area. To specify the print area, follow these steps:

1. **Click a frame that you have labeled #p (as we describe in the preceding section).**

2. **Create a rectangle around the area that you want to be printed.**

   You might have to experiment with different sizes of rectangles. See the instructions in the section "Printing movies from the Flash Player," a little later in this chapter, to test the printing of your movie.

   Use the No Fill feature for the rectangle so that you can see the material that you want to print.

3. **Select the rectangle and choose Edit⇨Cut to cut it to the Clipboard.**

4. **Click a frame without a #p label but on the same layer.**

   Using the next frame might be a good choice to keep the printing area rectangle conveniently close to the frame you've specified for printing.

5. **Choose Edit⇨Paste in Place.**

   You now have a rectangle of the right size, but in its own frame — a frame without a #p label.

6. **Select the frame containing the rectangle and choose Window⇨Properties⇨Properties to open the Property inspector.**

   If necessary, expand the Property inspector to its full size.

7. **In the Frame text box on the left side of the Property inspector, type #b to signify that the shape in this frame will be used as the boundary for the print area.**

   You can have only one #b label in a Timeline. Also note that if you use a #b label, it must be on the same layer as the #p label.

Printing movies from the Flash Player

Before uploading your printable movie to your Web site, you should test the printing function. To do so, use the Publish Settings dialog box to specify the publish settings that you want, as we explain throughout this chapter. Then choose File⇨Publish Preview⇨Default. Your browser opens, and you see your movie play.

To test-print your movie, right-click (Windows) or Control+click (Mac) in the browser. In the Flash Player shortcut menu, choose Print.

On the Mac, the Page Setup dialog box appears; choose the printer, paper size, orientation, and scale, and then click OK.

Then for both Mac and Windows, the Print dialog box appears. Choose the print range to select which frames to print or choose All. In Windows, you can also choose Selection to print the current frame. If only one frame has been made printable, the Pages option appears dimmed. Any option that you choose prints the frame you've specified for printing. Click OK (Windows) or Print (Mac) to print.

After you upload your movie onto your Web site, viewers use the same procedure to print your movie.

Place on your page some text that explains to your viewers how to print your movie. Many viewers don't even know that the shortcut menu exists.

Part VI
The Part of Tens

The 5th Wave   By Rich Tennant

"See? I created a little felon figure that runs around our Web site hiding behind banner ads. On the last page, our logo puts him in a non lethal choke hold and brings him back to the home page."

In this part . . .

In the famous *For Dummies* Part of Tens, we answer the ten most-asked questions — or at least the ten questions we most wanted to answer. In the chapter on the ten best Flash resources, we manage to give you dozens of Flash resources, such as the many Flash resource Web sites (while convincing our publisher that only ten exist). Finally, to top off the book, we give you our votes for ten great Flash designers. Surf to see the work of all ten and be amazed and inspired by the possibilities!

Chapter 14

Ten Frequently Asked Questions

In this chapter, we answer some frequently asked questions about Flash while explaining how to create some cool effects and streamline the process of creating Flash movies.

How Do I Combine Two Flash Movies?

It's not difficult to merge two Flash movies. You simply copy all the frames in each scene in your first movie to new scenes that you create in your second movie. To merge two Flash movies into one, follow these steps:

1. **Choose File⇨Open. In the Open dialog box that appears, navigate to and select the Flash movie you want to copy from.**

   The Flash movie you select appears on the Stage.

2. **Click the Edit Scene button near the top right of the Stage. In the drop-down list that appears, choose the scene you want to copy.**

   The scene you select appears on the Stage.

3. **Unlock all the layers in the scene.**

   See Chapter 6 for information on unlocking layers.

4. **Choose Edit➪Timeline➪Select All Frames.**

   This selects all keyframes and tweens in all layers in the scene.

5. **Choose Edit➪Timeline➪Copy Frames.**

   This copies all the keyframes and tweens in your scene.

6. **Choose File➪Open. In the Open dialog box that appears, navigate to and select the Flash movie you want to copy to.**

   The Flash movie you select appears on the Stage.

7. **Choose Insert➪Scene.**

   An empty scene appears on the Stage.

8. **Click the first frame in the Timeline and choose Edit➪Timeline➪ Paste Frames.**

   This pastes the scene you copied from your first movie into your new scene in your second movie.

9. **Repeat Steps 1 through 8 for each scene you want to copy from your first movie.**

10. **Choose Control➪Test Movie.**

    Your second movie now includes all the scenes you copied from your first movie.

Why Is Motion Tweening Not Working?

When you create a tween correctly, Flash draws an arrow on the Timeline between the two keyframes. If there's a broken line between the two keyframes instead, something is wrong and the tween won't work. Here are some possible solutions:

- **Tween the right stuff.** Make sure that you've created a group, some text, or an instance of a symbol. Motion tweening requires this.

- **Add an ending keyframe.** If you have a dashed line instead of a solid line indicating your motion tween on the Timeline, you didn't properly create an ending keyframe. Undo the steps that created the tween, create an ending keyframe, and try again. And make sure the ending keyframe is also a group, some text, or an instance of a symbol, and nothing else. If you accidentally paste something extra in either keyframe, the tween won't work.

✔ **Isolate the problem.** If you can't figure out why your motion tweening isn't working, you might have some action or setting that you don't even remember. Movies can get complex, and comprehending all the relationships and interconnections can be difficult. Try copying to the Clipboard the object that you're animating and then pasting it into a new, "clean" movie. You can copy and paste frames as well. In the new movie, you should be able to analyze the situation more clearly.

✔ **Undo or revert.** If the animation worked previously, try undoing your last several actions. You can also try removing any recently created objects or ActionScript. If you can revert to the time your animation worked, you can start again from there.

✔ **Put each object on its own layer.** If you have more than one object on a layer, place each object on its own layer. (Refer to Chapter 6 for a discussion of working with layers.) Animate only one object on a layer. This solves many, many tweening problems.

How Can I Sync Sound with Motion?

Suppose that you want certain parts of your animation synchronized with specific sounds. For example, you want a bouncing ball to synchronize with the beat of some music you imported into Flash. Without specifically synchronizing the sounds, the sound and the animation might play at different speeds. A faster computer might play the animation faster but doesn't adjust the length of the sound. Or a slow computer might take its time displaying a transparent ball bouncing, and the synchronization with sound will drift. (For basic information on adding sound to Flash, refer to Chapter 11.)

To synchronize the animation with the sound, you need to use a stream sound. When you add the sound file to a frame, choose Stream in the Sync drop-down list in the Property inspector. Then adjust the keyframes so that the animation and the sound end at the same time.

To be more precise, you can synchronize your animation with specific parts of the sound. To accomplish this task, choose Modify➪Timeline➪Layer Properties and choose 200% or 300% in the Layer Height drop-down list. You can also click the little button in the upper-right corner of the Timeline and choose Medium or Large for the size of the frames in the option menu that appears. Now you can see the shape of your sound wave more clearly so that you can adjust the keyframes of your animation to match certain parts of the sound.

One way to pinpoint which frame to use for placing an animation event is to drag the playhead (the red rectangle) just above the Timeline. This technique lets you control the speed of the animation. You can drag left or right until you find the exact frame that you want to work with. You can then move a keyframe to that frame, for example, to move an animation event to a frame that contains a specific portion of your sound.

What Is the Best Way to Import Bitmaps?

Maybe you're working on an animation, and you need to include your boss's photograph or a photo of the product that you sell. Or maybe you want an effect in your Flash movie that you can create only in Photoshop. So you need to use a bitmap image. What bitmap format do you use?

You might not have a choice of format. If your information systems department hands you a logo with a solid white background in JPEG format, you probably have to use it.

At other times, you can choose your format. For example, when you scan a photo, most scanner software lets you choose from among several formats. A digital camera may also let you choose the format. Of course, if you create the bitmap in an image-editing program, you can choose from any format that the program supports. (Turn to Chapter 3 for instructions on importing bitmap images. ***Hint:*** Choose File⇨Import⇨Import to Stage or File⇨Import⇨ Import to Library.)

Here are some commonly used bitmap formats:

- ✔ The **GIF** file format can't have more than 256 colors. You can use the GIF format for simple drawings that have a limited color palette, but for that you may be better off with the PNG format, described later in this list.

- ✔ **JPEG** files can display many more colors than GIF files and therefore produce more realistic photos and other complex drawings. Although JPEG graphics can be highly compressed to reduce file size, they may lose some detail or color fidelity as a result, depending on how much you choose to compress them.

- ✔ **BMP** doesn't lose quality when compressed, but the BMP format results in larger file sizes than GIF or JPEG.

- ✔ **PNG** is a nice compromise between file size and image quality. The PNG format doesn't lose quality when compressed and allows many more colors than the GIF format. And it provides the capability for transparency. If you want the smallest file size but don't want to compromise quality, the PNG format is a good choice. The Flash image compressor works best and most efficiently with images that have not been compressed by using techniques that may lose some image quality.

Your final result is the .swf file that you publish. Flash compresses bitmaps (as well as the entire movie) when the movie is exported to an .swf Flash Player file. Therefore, you need to think about the entire round-trip journey that your bitmap will make. You might have to test varying bitmap formats and publish the movie for each one to see the exact results.

When you export, you can set the JPEG quality on the Flash tab of the Publish Settings dialog box. You also set the overall quality on the HTML tab. For that quality setting, only the High and Best settings *smooth* (anti-alias) the bitmaps in the movie. (Refer to Chapter 13 for more information about publishing your Flash movie.)

When you import a bitmap image into Flash, you can take the following steps to ensure good-looking results:

- ✔ **Save your graphics in the highest quality possible.** If you have a photograph, don't import it as a GIF file.

- ✔ **Don't overcompress your original bitmaps.** Find a happy medium. Try saving an image at several compression levels to see the difference in quality and size.

- ✔ **Set the compression type and quality in the Bitmap Properties dialog box.** After you import the image, open the Library (choose Window⇨ Library) and right-click (Windows) or Control+click (Mac) the image and choose Properties to open the Bitmap Properties dialog box, as shown in Figure 14-1.

Figure 14-1: Use the Bitmap Properties dialog box to fiddle with your bitmaps.

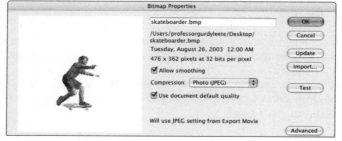

How Do I Rescale My Movie's Size?

You create a beautiful Flash movie that takes up the entire page. But then your boss says that you need to fit it into an existing HTML page, which translates into reducing the size of the whole thing by 25 percent. What do you do? Get a new boss, if possible. Barring that, you can rescale the size of the movie by following these steps:

1. **Decide the amount of the reduction you need to achieve, such as 25 percent.**

2. **If you have any hidden layers, right-click (Windows) or Control+click (Mac) any layer and choose Show All.**

   This step ensures that all layers are considered in the reduction.

3. **Click the Edit Multiple Frames button (just below the Timeline).**

4. **Drag the onion-skin markers to the beginning and ending frames of your animation.**

   See Chapter 9 if you need more information on how to use the onion-skin markers.

5. **Choose Edit⇨Select All.**

6. **Choose Window⇨Transform to open the Transform panel.**

7. **In the Transform panel, select the Constrain check box.**

8. **In the Width or Height input box, type the new number for your reduction percentage, and press Enter (Windows) or Return (Mac).**

   Flash scales your animations by the reduction percentage.

9. **Choose Modify⇨Document.**

   The Document Properties dialog box appears.

10. **In the Width and Height boxes, type new numbers reflecting the reduction percentage size.**

    Here you'll have to first do a little math, multiplying the old Width and Height by the reduction percentage to come up with the new numbers you type in.

You're done! Flash scales your entire movie as you specified. You may have to drag everything so that it fits appropriately within your smaller-sized movie.

Size requirements are key pieces of information that you need to nail down before building a Flash movie so that you can avoid any need to rescale your movie's size.

What Are the Best Tips for Creating Movies?

Every Flash user collects a number of techniques that make creating a Flash movie easier. Following are a few ideas to help you get started:

✔ Save multiple versions of your movie by choosing File⇨Save As. If a problem arises, you can always go back to a previous version and start again.

✔ As soon as you have an overall structure, test your movie in a variety of browsers (for example, Internet Explorer, Mozilla Firefox, and on a Macintosh, Apple's Safari) at various resolutions, if possible. It's easier to correct problems early, before your project becomes too complex. Choose Control⇨Test Movie as soon as you develop your animation and continue to test it in this way for each new significant change. It's also a good idea to keep testing your movie with Publish Preview (by pressing F12) to see how it will work in a browser.

✔ Add comments (see Chapter 10) to your ActionScript so that you can figure out what you did when you go back to your movie after your vacation.

✔ Use consistent names for symbols. Many Flash users add the type of symbol after the name, so a button could be called *Contact_btn* and a movie clip could be called *Intro_mc.* When you start creating movie clips inside buttons, you might get confused if you don't name your symbols intelligently.

✔ Use meaningful names for your instances. If you have three instances of a button symbol, you need to be able to distinguish which is which. You can name them by their purpose, such as *Email, Services,* and *Clients.*

✔ When you complete work on a layer, lock the layer to avoid making unwanted changes.

You're sure to discover other techniques as you become more experienced in Flash.

Can Flash Do 3-D?

You can't really create 3-D in Flash. Flash is decidedly a 2-D program. But, not to be deterred, Flash users have created many tricks to make you think you're seeing 3-D.

One simple approach is to rotate a 2-D object in what appears to be 3-D space. For example, you can draw a circle, turn it into a symbol instance, and in a motion tween scale it in one dimension so that it becomes progressively more of an oval until all you see is a straight line. Continue to expand it from the line through fatter and fatter ovals until you have a circle again. You've apparently rotated the circle 180 degrees. Continue until you're finished. You can select a group of frames and copy them or reverse them. (Turn to Chapter 9 for more details.) You can see a simple example in Figure 14-2.

Figure 14-2:
The circle is
2-D, but it
looks like it's
rotating in
3-D; here,
you see the
first quarter
revolution.

You can also use shape tweening to create this 3-D effect. You can shape tween a circle into a line and back again to make it look like it's rotating.

For fancier results, you can use software packages designed for creating 3-D animation for Flash, such as Swift 3D. Also, some high-end 3-D animation packages, such as Maya, have Flash export capabilities built in. Another technique for simulating 3-D is to import an object from a 3-D program, such as 3D Studio Max, AutoCAD, or Maya.

In the following steps, we use AutoCAD as an example. To import an object from AutoCAD, follow these steps:

1. **In AutoCAD, create the 3-D object and display the view you want to start with.**

2. **Choose File⇨Export.**

   The Export Data dialog box opens. The Files of Type drop-down list should read `Metafile (*.wmf)`.

3. **In the File Name box, enter a name for the file. Add a 1 after the filename. Click Save and select the object when prompted.**

4. **Rotate the 3-D model slightly.**

   In AutoCAD 2000 and later, you can use the 3DORBIT command for this step.

5. **Save this new view as a `.wmf` file as we explain in Step 2, consecutively numbered from the first file.**

   For example, if the first file is 3d1.wmf, name the second file 3d2.wmf.

6. **Repeat Steps 2 through 5 until you've rotated the model 360 degrees.**

7. **In Flash, choose File⇨Import⇨Import to Stage.**

8. **In the Files of Type drop-down list, select Windows Metafile (*.wmf), select the first WMF file that you created, and then click Open.**

9. **When Flash asks whether you want to import all the files in the sequence, click Yes.**

   Flash imports all the files, placing them in consecutive keyframes. The WMF file may be imported with a border as well as the lines that make up the object.

10. **For each keyframe, do the following:**

    a. **If your graphic has a border:** Click anywhere outside the objects, select just the border, and press Delete.

    b. **If your graphic is imported as one object:** Select all the objects and then choose Modify⇨Break Apart.

    c. **Select the objects and then choose Modify⇨Convert to Symbol.**

You can now play your animation. Note that you lose any shading or materials that you created in AutoCAD, so your model has a wire-frame look. You can use fills to modify your 3-D object in Flash to create the appearance of solidity.

For an example of creating a simple 3-D animation by using this technique, go to the companion Web site at www.dummies.com/go/flashcs3 and look for the 3d rotation.fla file.

What if you don't have a 3-D program? Well, do you have Microsoft Word? Yes, folks, you can create 3-D objects in your lowly word processing program. To create a 3-D object with Word, follow these steps:

1. **Open Microsoft Word and, in a new document, open the Drawing toolbar if it isn't already open by choosing View⇨Toolbars⇨Drawing.**

2. **On the Drawing toolbar, click the AutoShapes drop-down arrow and select a shape.**

   You can even draw your own shape by using the Scribble tool (one of the options on the Lines submenu, under AutoShapes).

3. **Click in your blank document to place the shape.**

   If you want, use the Fill Color tool to change the fill. Select the shape and then, in the Fill Color drop-down list, select Fill Effects and create a cool gradient on the Gradient tab.

4. **Click the 3-D button at the right end of the Drawing toolbar and select a 3-D perspective from the box that opens.**

   You might need to try out a few choices until you get the best effect.

5. **Click the 3-D button again and click the 3-D Settings button at the bottom of the box to open the 3-D Settings toolbar.**

   Use the Tilt Left, Right, Up, or Down button to tilt the object until it looks perfectly flat so that you don't see any of the 3-D effect. Keep the 3-D Settings toolbar open.

6. **Choose Edit➪Copy to copy the shape to the Clipboard.**

7. **Return to Flash and choose Insert➪New Symbol; specify a movie clip behavior for the symbol and then name it.**

8. **Click OK.**

9. **Choose Edit➪Paste to paste the shape into the first frame.**

10. **Go back to Word and decide which way you want your shape to rotate.**

    You can choose up, down, left, or right.

11. **Select your 3-D shape in the Word document and click twice on Tilt Left (or Right, Up, or Down) on the 3-D Settings toolbar.**

12. **Copy the shape to the Clipboard.**

13. **Go to Flash and create a keyframe in the next frame.**

14. **Paste the shape from the Clipboard.**

15. **Repeat Steps 11 through 14 until you're looking at your shape on edge.**

16. **Select all the frames except the first and the last, and then choose Edit➪Timeline➪Copy Frames.**

17. **Click the first empty frame (the one after your last frame) and then choose Edit➪Timeline➪Paste Frames.**

    You now have the quarter revolution twice, and you need to modify the second set so that it becomes the second quarter revolution.

18. **Select all the frames that you've pasted and choose Modify⇨ Timeline⇨Reverse Frames.**

   If you play the animation now, it looks as though the shape is revolving one quarter and then back again.

19. **Select the first of the frames that you pasted and choose Modify⇨ Transform⇨Flip Horizontal (if you used Tilt Left or Right in Word) or Flip Vertical (if you chose Tilt Up or Down in Word).**

20. **Repeat Step 19 with the remaining frames that you've pasted.**

   You now have a half revolution.

21. **Select all but the first and last frames and then choose Edit⇨ Timeline⇨Copy Frames.**

22. **Click the first empty frame after the last frame and choose Edit⇨ Timeline⇨Paste Frames.**

23. **Select all the frames that you've pasted and choose Modify⇨ Timeline⇨Reverse Frames.**

You're done! Play your animation and watch your shape roll.

This method does have some disadvantages. First, all of your images from Word are imported as bitmaps, not vector images. Second, you're animating frame by frame. As a result, your file is larger and downloads more slowly. If you use this method for just a small animation, however, it beats finding out how to use a fancy 3-D program (and paying for it, too). Test the results and see whether it works for you.

Look on our companion Web site (`www.dummies.com/go/flashcs3`) for `rotating star.fla`, which is an example of using Word to create 3-D objects. The animation is in a movie clip, so choose Control⇨Test Movie to see the results (or open the `.swf` file directly).

How Do I Center a Flash Movie in a Web Page?

As we discuss in Chapter 13, you can make your Flash movie appear in a Web page by choosing both the Flash and HTML formats in your Publish Settings and then publishing your movie. Flash then generates the HTML code (like the code in Figure 13-4) for a Web page. This Web page appears to contain your Flash movie when you view the Web page in a browser. To make the Flash movie centered in that Web page, you just need to add a little bit of extra code to the HTML page, which you can do with a text editor.

To add the code for centering your Flash movie in the Web page, follow these steps:

1. **After choosing the Publish Settings for Flash and HTML (using the Flash Only or Flash HTTPS template in the HTML tab of the Publish Settings dialog box, as we describe in Chapter 13), choose File⇨ Publish.**

   Flash creates a Flash Player (.swf) file and a Web page (HTML) file.

2. **Start a text editor or an HTML editor, and open the HTML page within the editor.**

   You can use an HTML editor such as Dreamweaver or a text editor such as Notepad (Windows) or TextEdit (Mac). In TextEdit, choose TextEdit⇨ Preferences, and when the Preferences window appears, in the New Document Attributes section (or in the New Document tab, if you have a newer version of TextEdit), select Plain Text rather than Rich Text.

3. **Find `</head>` in the file and insert this code before it:**

   ```
   <style type="text/css" media="screen">
       body {text-align: center; }
       div#container {width: 550px; margin: 0px auto;
       text-align: left; }
   </style>
   ```

   Be sure you find `</head>`, not `<head>`.

   This code defines some Cascading Style Sheet (or CSS) styles that your Web browser will use to dynamically create margins on the left and right of a Flash movie that is 550 pixels wide so that the movie is automatically centered on the page. If your Flash movie is, say, 200 pixels wide, change 550px in the preceding code to 200px.

4. **Find the third occurrence of `<script` in the file (after `about: internet`) and insert `<div id="container">` before it.**

   Be sure not to put anything between the `<script>` and `</script>` tags.

5. **Find `</noscript>` in the file and insert `</div>` after it.**

   Be sure you find `</noscript>`, not `<noscript>`.

   In HTML lingo `<div>` and `<style>` and any other words starting with a bracket (`<`) are called *tags*. The `<div>` tag defines the beginning of a division or section of a Web page, and the `</div>` tag defines the end of it. By giving the `<div>` an `id` equal to `"container"`, the Web browser will use the style that you defined for `"container"` in Step 3 and apply it to everything between the `<div>` and `</div>` tags.

   Figure 14-3 shows an example of an HTML file with all the code added.

6. **In the editor, save the file with the changes you made.**

Now when you view the HTML page in a Web browser (assuming it's a fairly recent version of a Web browser), your Flash movie appears centered in the Web page.

Figure 14-3: Here's the code previously shown in Figure 13-4, revised with `<style>`, `</style>`, `<div>`, and `</div>` tags, which center the movie in the Web page.

```
                                        ● movie of the year.html
○ ○ ○
<html xmlns="http://www.w3.org/1999/xhtml" xml:lang="en" lang="en">
<head>
<meta http-equiv="Content-Type" content="text/html; charset=iso-8859-1" />
<title>movie of the year</title>
<script language="javascript">AC_FL_RunContent = 0;</script>
<script src="AC_RunActiveContent.js" language="javascript"></script>
<style type="text/css" media="screen">
        body { text-align: center; }
        div#container { width: 550px; margin: 0px auto; text-align: left; }
</style>
</head>
<body bgcolor="#ffffff">
<!--url's used in the movie-->
<!--text used in the movie-->
<!-- saved from url=(0013)about:internet -->
<div id="container">
<script language="javascript">
        if (AC_FL_RunContent == 0) {
            alert("This page requires AC_RunActiveContent.js.");
        } else {
            AC_FL_RunContent(
                'codebase', 'http://download.macromedia.com/pub/shockwave/cabs/flash/
swflash.cab#version=9,0,0,0',
                'width', '550',
                'height', '400',
                'src', 'movie of the year',
                'quality', 'high',
                'pluginspage', 'http://www.macromedia.com/go/getflashplayer',
                'align', 'middle',
                'play', 'true',
                'loop', 'false',
                'scale', 'showall',
                'wmode', 'window',
                'devicefont', 'false',
                'id', 'movie of the year',
                'bgcolor', '#ffffff',
                'name', 'movie of the year',
                'menu', 'true',
                'allowScriptAccess','sameDomain',
                'movie', 'movie of the year',
                'salign', ''
                ); //end AC code
        }
</script>
<noscript>
        <object classid="clsid:d27cdb6e-ae6d-11cf-96b8-444553540000" codebase="http://download.macromedia.com/pub/
shockwave/cabs/flash/swflash.cab#version=9,0,0,0" width="550" height="400" id="movie of the year" align="middle">
        <param name="allowScriptAccess" value="sameDomain" />
        <param name="movie" value="movie of the year.swf" /><param name="loop" value="false" /><param name="quality"
value="high" /><param name="bgcolor" value="#ffffff" /> <embed src="movie of the year.swf" loop="false" quality="high"
bgcolor="#ffffff" width="550" height="400" name="movie of the year" align="middle" allowScriptAccess="sameDomain"
type="application/x-shockwave-flash" pluginspage="http://www.macromedia.com/go/getflashplayer" />
        </object>
</noscript>
</div>
</body>
</html>
```

What Are the Size Limits for a Flash Movie?

Usually you won't be too concerned about how big a movie you can create with Flash, because one of the reasons to use Flash is that it employs vector graphics, tweening, and other methods to create small files that download quickly over the Web. If you're using Flash to create gigantic projects, that can be great fun and even workable in some cases, but keep in mind that Flash wasn't primarily designed to do that. On the other hand, more and more studios are using Flash for production animation (including broadcast TV shows), and video is now an important feature of Flash.

In any case, it's interesting to know that, other than limits imposed by your computer's RAM, CPU, hard drive, video card, browser, and operating system, there are few limits to the size and complexity of a Flash movie. However, there are at least two limits: the minimum size of your Stage is 1 pixel wide and 1 pixel high, and the maximum Stage size is 2880 pixels wide by 2880 pixels wide.

How Do I Dynamically Load Music from the Web?

You can use ActionScript to load music into your movie live from the Web by using the ActionScript `load()` and `play()` methods. (Turn to Chapter 10 to find out more about ActionScript.) To load an MP3 file on the Web into your movie while your movie is playing, follow these steps:

1. **Create a new layer.**

   Chapter 6 explains how to add a new layer.

2. **Click a keyframe.**

   If the frame you want to use is not a keyframe, right-click (Windows) or Control+click (Mac) it and choose Insert Keyframe.

3. **Choose Window⇨Actions to open the Actions panel if it isn't open already. In the Actions panel, click the Script Assist button to deselect it (if it's selected).**

   If necessary, click the Actions panel title bar to expand the panel.

4. **In the Script pane of the Actions panel, enter the following code:**

   ```
   var mySound:Sound = new Sound();
   var
         myChoice="http://www.hotjazzcaravan.com/Music/
         Im_an_Old_Cowhand_clip.mp3";
   var myRequest:URLRequest = new URLRequest(myChoice);
   var myContext:SoundLoaderContext = new
         SoundLoaderContext(8000, true);
   mySound.load(myRequest, myContext);
   mySound.play();
   ```

   Replace `http://www.hotjazzcaravan.com/Music/Im_an_Old_Cowhand_clip.mp3` in the code with the Web address of the audio you want to play. Or if the audio is going to remain in the same folder as your Flash Player file, you can simply replace it with, for example, `Im_an_Old_Cowhand_clip.mp3`. You can replace `mySound`, `myChoice`, `myRequest`, and `myContext` with any names you like.

The first ActionScript statement of the preceding code creates an instance of a new sound object with the name mySound. (ActionScript statements end with a semicolon.) The second ActionScript statement creates a variable and sets it equal to a Web address (a URL). The third ActionScript statement creates an instance of a request for an item that has that Web address. The fourth ActionScript statement specifies how many milliseconds of buffering (in this case, 8000 milliseconds, which equals 8 seconds) to use when loading the sound. The fifth ActionScript statement loads the sound specified in the third statement as a streaming sound by using the buffer size specified in the fourth statement. Then the sixth ActionScript statement plays the sound.

The preceding code loads your file as *streaming audio.* You hear streaming audio as it's being sent over the Web to you. You don't have to download the entire audio file before you can start hearing it.

 5. **Choose Control⇨Test Movie and enjoy the music.**

Chapter 15

Ten Best Flash Resources

*F*lash is such a flexible program that you'll never stop discovering what it can do. And just when you think you've got it, out comes a new version. In this chapter, we point you to the many resources you can turn to when you want to increase your knowledge about Flash.

Of course, we think that this book is a great resource on Flash. But you're already using this book, and much more about Flash is out there, readily available to help you become a truly great Flash designer and animator.

Check Out Award-Winning Movies

It's always wise to pattern yourself after the best, and you can find the best Flash movies on a couple of sites. For example, the Flash Forward Conference Web site lists winners in many categories at `www.flashforwardconference.com/past_winners`. These movies are winners in the conference's annual contest.

Best Flash Animation Site (at www.bestflashanimationsite.com, of course), showcases Flash sites that have been voted the best each week by viewers. This is a good place to find top-notch examples of Flash in a variety of categories, including Applications, Corporate, Experimental, Technical Merit, and Video.

Look on the Flash Web Pages

Adobe maintains large resources for Flash users on its Web site. Go to www. adobe.com/support/flash and www.adobe.com/devnet/flash, where you can find tips, tutorials, support, technical notes, news, and updates.

Visit Our Site

Check out the *Adobe Flash CS3 Professional For Dummies* page on the Wiley Web site. You can find the site by surfing to www.dummies.com/go/flashcs3. It contains sample files from the book, tips, and updates. We hope that you find the site helpful!

Take a Course

Many colleges and universities offer courses in Flash. Sometimes these courses are part of a Web design or graphic arts course, or they might stand alone. To find these courses, call local educational institutions and ask.

The advantage of a course led by a teacher is that you have a chance to ask questions — and receive answers. A teacher also guides the learning process and possibly even gives you lots of tips and hints!

You might also consider taking self-paced courses in Flash offered by Adobe or instructor-led courses at an Adobe Authorized Training Center. Visit www. adobe.com/training for more information, including free sample lessons.

Join a Flash Discussion Group

Adobe maintains active Flash support forums, where anyone can ask questions and get answers from other members of the Flash community. To read messages from and send messages to these discussion forums, point your Web browser to `www.adobe.com/cfusion/webforums/forum/index.cfm?forumid=15`.

Also available are several popular Internet newsgroups for discussing Flash — including one for general technical discussions of Flash and one for discussions of designing entire Web sites by using Flash. You can view messages on these newsgroups by visiting `http://groups.google.com/group/macromedia.flash` and `http://groups.google.com/group/macromedia.flash.sitedesign`.

If you have software for reading newsgroups on your computer, you can alternatively go to `news://forums.macromedia.com/macromedia.flash` and `news://forums.macromedia.com/macromedia.flash.sitedesign` to read messages from and send messages to these two groups.

Several other excellent active discussion groups reside on Web sites. The best way to tell whether a discussion group is active is to see how many messages have been posted in the past one or two days. You can also check out how many different people are participating. See the following section in this chapter.

You can also subscribe to electronic mailing lists for ongoing discussions sent by e-mail. With more than 3000 members, the Yahoo! FLASHmacromedia list is one of the largest lists specifically for users who want to discuss Flash techniques. You can ask questions and get answers from the community of Flash users. To sign up or to view the Web archive of messages, go to `http://tech.groups.yahoo.com/group/FLASHmacromedia`.

You can find more than 600 other Flash e-mail discussion groups at Yahoo! alone. Find them by surfing to `http://tech.dir.groups.yahoo.com/dir/Computers___Internet/Software/Multimedia/Macromedia_Flash` (that's three underscores between *Computers* and *Internet*).

Check Out Flash Resource Sites

A huge Flash community is on the Internet — so vast, in fact, that you'll probably never be able to participate in all its offerings. These Web sites offer news, tutorials, discussion groups, tips, and links to other Flash resources.

Some of these sites are more up-to-date, lively, and complete than others. The quality of the tips and tutorials varies widely. Some specialize in tips for beginners; others are geared toward advanced users. The following list briefly reviews the ones that we find most useful, in alphabetical order:

- www.actionscript.org: This site is a well-designed, comprehensive resource on ActionScript. It includes extremely active discussion forums (with tens of thousands of messages); more than 200 tutorials on ActionScript at beginning, intermediate, and advanced levels; a library with more than 600 ActionScripts, more than 900 Flash movies, and more than 40 components; links; and an employment section.

- www.flashkit.com: Flash Kit is probably the largest Flash site, and it's up-to-date. (We define *up-to-date* as having Flash CS3 material within days after it has shipped.) You can find thousands of .fla files to download and study, hundreds of tutorials, dozens of active discussion forums (some with hundreds of thousands of posts), links, thousands of sounds, more than a thousand downloadable fonts — if you can think of it, you can find it here.

- www.flashgoddess.com: Flashgoddess is an informative site showcasing women who do brilliant work with Flash. It includes profiles of and articles on terrific Flash designers, a gallery of work by featured artists, a listing of women speakers, links, job listings, and more.

- www.flashmagazine.com: This site includes news and reviews of Flash and Flash-related products. You also find links, articles, and a list of hundreds of applications that can output Flash Player files.

- www.gotoandlearn.com: This is a site containing dozens of terrific, free Flash tutorials on video, developed by Lee Brimelow, a Senior Design Technologist at frog design.

- www.kirupa.com: This is MIT student Karupa Chinnathamei's site about Flash and other Web technologies. It contains more than 100 tutorials (many of them on video) and discussion forums with thousands of posts.

- www.ultrashock.com: Ultrashock is a multifaceted site that includes tutorials, downloads of more than 200 .fla files, and discussion forums with more than half a million posts.

Check Out Sites That Use Flash

You can get ideas by looking at what others do. (It's interesting, for instance, that simple Flash sites are sometimes the most beautiful and practical.) In Chapter 16, we list sites by ten great designers that use Flash. And many resource sites have showcases of great Flash sites, as Adobe does at www. adobe.com/products/flash/flashpro/productinfo/customers.

Attend a Flash Conference

Attending a conference on Flash is an exciting way to find out much more about Flash from an array of experts, see award-winning Flash movies, partic-ipate in workshops and seminars, hear the latest news from Adobe, make contacts with others interested in Flash, and generally immerse yourself in the world of Flash. Even just visiting the Web sites of some of these confer-ences can be instructive. Conferences you might consider attending include the following:

- **Flashforward (including the Flash Film Festival):** A two- or three-day conference, held two or three times per year in a changing roster of cities that has included San Francisco, Boston, New York, Seattle, and Austin. For information, visit www.flashforwardconference.com.

- **Flash in the Can Conference:** A three-day conference in the spring in Toronto, Ontario, Canada. For information, visit www.fitc.ca.

- **FlashBelt Conference:** A two-day conference in Minneapolis in June. For information, visit www.flashbelt.com.

Collect Flash Movies

Many Flash resource Web sites let you download .fla files. You can also trade .fla files with others who you know use Flash. Analyzing .fla files is one of the best ways to see how effects are created. In Chapter 12, we explain how to use the Movie Explorer to ferret out all the hidden details of an .fla file.

Be sure to check out the Library of an .fla file — many of the secrets lie there. And you can use the Movie Explorer to find and study all the actions in an .fla file. You'll soon be on your way to adapting the techniques that you see to your own projects.

Reuse Your Best Stuff

After you've created some great Flash movies, you can reuse your best stuff. *Fadeouts* (changing transparency), *glows* (soft edges), and masks are simple effects that you can use again and again. You can also reuse ActionScript on new objects. After you get a technique down, you don't need to reinvent the wheel. If you've created an animated logo, you can have an entirely new animation by merely swapping a symbol.

You can import items from the Library of any movie into your current movie. Choose File⇨Import⇨Open External Library and then choose the Flash file that contains the Library you want to use. Then drag the items that you want from the imported movie Library onto the Stage or into the Library of your current movie. This is a really nifty Flash feature.

Chapter 16

Ten Flash Designers to Watch

Trying to choose ten of the best designers who use Flash is almost absurd — so many brilliant designers are out there. Nevertheless, in this chapter we give you a shortcut to finding some of the most innovative and skilled Flash designers so that you can check out their work, get ideas, and see the possibilities.

Note that some of the sites they've designed can take a really long time to load if you don't have a broadband connection to the Web.

Hillman Curtis

Hillman Curtis's studio is one of the most well-known Flash design firms in the world. His clients include MTV, Yahoo!, Apple Computer, OgilvyOne Worldwide, British Airways, and RollingStone.com. His studio has won dozens of design awards. His motto is "making the invisible visible," and his work combines simplicity, freshness, and sophistication. You can check out the work of Hillman and his crew at www.hillmancurtis.com. View some terrific Flash Web page design by clicking on his Site Design link, and see what he's doing with Flash video by clicking his Film & Video link.

Anthony Eden

Australian designer Anthony Eden showcases a fascinating group of Flash experiments at his site, www.arseiam.com.

Chris Georgenes

Chris Georgenes is a freelance artist and animator whose clients include Adobe, Yahoo!, Gillette, Hasbro, Digitas, Pileated Pictures, and AOL. Check out his online portfolio of many charming animations at www.mudbubble. com and his blog at www.keyframer.com.

Ben Hantoot

Young Ben Hantoot is already one of the most, as he says, "over-the-top" animators on the planet. Other Flash sites look positively motionless compared to the site of his studio, www.webfeatsdesign.com. The incessant inventiveness of his work is outrageously delightful.

Seb Lee-Delisle

Seb Lee-Delisle is a Flash 3-D innovator who has pushed Flash's boundaries in games, physics simulations, and interactive 3-D animation. You can see some of his handiwork at his company's site at www.pluginmedia.net (be sure to check out the lab there). His blog (www.sebleedelisle.com) presents lots of interesting and useful material on 3-D techniques in Flash.

Eric Natzke

Interactive designer Eric Natzke presents some truly spectacular animation at www.natzke.com. Eric's online journal at http://lessordinary.natzke.com is also worth visiting.

Keith Peters

The BIT-101 Lab at the Web site of Keith Peters, www.bit-101.com, is a personal online laboratory. There, you can find the results of his more than 500 explorations with Flash, in which he uses various principles of math and physics to take Flash into interesting new artistic realms. He says, "It was my original intention, possibly now achieved, to have the largest repository of single-author experimental Flash files on the Web." We think you'll agree it's an outstanding achievement.

Micaël Reynaud

At www.dunun.com, the young, French, award-winning Flash designer Micaël Reynaud has created a site full of surprises that, like several of the sites in this chapter, is difficult to describe but charming to experience. His work at www.dunun.com/2002/, for example, combines music, imagery, and unusual user-interface techniques to showcase a panoramic view of this artist's multiple skills.

Grant Skinner

Canadian Grant Skinner is a Flash whiz with many ingenious ideas. You can enjoy some of them at his gallery of Flash experimentations at www.incomplet.org.

Jared Tarbell

Jared Tarbell uses ActionScript to generate beautiful imagery. Interestingly, his mathematical explorations in Flash often end up in commercial projects. You can see his work (and download his ActionScript code) at www.levitated.net.

Part VII
Appendixes

The 5th Wave   By Rich Tennant

SCREEEEEK

"Is this really the best use of Flash animation on our e-commerce Web site? A bad wheel on the shopping cart icon that squeaks, wobbles, and pulls to the left?"

In this part . . .

In the appendixes, we put everything that we couldn't fit elsewhere but thought too useful to forget. We explain how to install Flash (it's a snap), customize your preferences, and create your own keyboard shortcuts. One appendix shows you all the Flash CS3 panels, and labels them carefully so that you know what they do. And we tell you what's on the companion Web site (lots of stuff!).

Appendix A

Installing Flash and Setting Your Preferences

Installing Flash is simple. Nevertheless, sometimes a few pointers can help. And after you're up and running, you might want to customize how Flash works. You can set quite a number of preferences. You can also create your own keyboard shortcuts.

Now, time to stop stalling and start installing.

Installing Flash

Installing Flash is a cinch, although you have a few options. Here's the low-down on getting started. You can install Flash in four different ways:

- Install it from a DVD (onto a PC).
- Download it to a PC.
- Install it from a DVD (onto a Mac).
- Download it to a Mac.

We discuss these methods separately in the next four sections.

Installing Flash onto a PC from a DVD

So you went out and bought Flash in the box, and you have a DVD drive on your PC. To install Flash from the box, follow these steps:

1. **Exit all Windows programs.**

2. **Insert the DVD.**

   In most cases, the setup program starts automatically. If it doesn't, choose Start⇨Run and click Browse. Then find and double-click `Setup.exe` on your DVD drive. Click Run.

3. **Follow the instructions on the various screens that appear.**

   Unless you want to save space by not installing the lessons and samples, choose the typical installation. Other than that, the most significant choice that you have is where you install Flash. You can browse to change the location or accept the default, which is `C:\Program Files\Adobe\Adobe Flash CS3`.

4. **When the setup program has finished copying files, click Finish.**

5. **Read the ReadMe file offered on the last screen.**

   Although we guarantee that most of the stuff in the file is irrelevant to you, sometimes this file has just the weird detail that applies to your situation, so take the two minutes to read it.

Installing Flash by downloading it to your PC

If you like, you can download the Flash trial directly from the Adobe Web site. You can then pay for it within 30 days or it stops working. Follow these steps:

1. **Go to `www.adobe.com/downloads`.**

2. **From the list of Adobe products, select Flash CS3 Professional.**

3. **Follow the instructions on the screen for downloading the installation file.**

   When you download the file, you select a location on your hard drive. If you have a Downloads folder, you can use that. Another good option is the Desktop. Remember the location you choose.

4. **When the download is complete, double-click the installation file.**

   Here's where you need to remember where you saved the file. The installation program guides you through the process of installing Flash.

5. **If you're given a choice of installation types, you probably want to choose the typical installation.**

   The only other significant choice you have is where you install Flash. You can browse to change the location or accept the default, which is `C:\Program Files\Adobe\Adobe Flash CS3`.

After you install Flash, you can play with it! You can buy it at any time by clicking Buy Now on the first screen you see when you open Flash.

Installing Flash onto a Mac from a DVD

If you bought Flash in a box, use your DVD drive to install the program. To install Flash on your Mac from a DVD, follow these steps:

1. **Insert the DVD.**

   An installer icon appears on your desktop.

2. **Double-click the Flash CS3 Installer icon.**

3. **When a window appears, displaying a software license agreement, click the Accept button so that you can continue the installation.**

   Of course, being the responsible people we are, we recommend reading the license agreement.

4. **Unless you want to save space by not installing the lessons and samples, choose the Easy Install option, which is the default.**

   Other than that, the most significant choice you have is where you install Flash. You can browse to change the location or accept the default location, which is in the Applications folder on the startup disc drive.

5. **Click Install.**

   The installer program starts copying files. When it's finished, you see the Adobe Flash CS3 folder displayed on your computer screen, containing the Flash CS3 program, a few documents, and a bunch of other folders. One of the documents is the `ReadMe.htm` file. You can view the contents of this file by double-clicking it. Although most of the stuff in the file is irrelevant to you, sometimes the file has a detail that applies to your situation, so reading it can be worthwhile.

Installing Flash by downloading it to your Mac

In this ultramodern day and age, you can install Flash on your computer without ever leaving your Web browser. To download Flash, follow these steps (or something like them, assuming that the Adobe Web site doesn't change too much):

1. **Go to www.adobe.com/downloads.**

2. **From the list of Adobe products, select Flash CS3 Professional.**

   You need to choose a geographic location, complete or create a password, and answer a few questions.

3. **Follow the instructions on the screen for downloading the installation file.**

4. **When the download is complete, find and double-click the installation file.**

5. **Follow the instructions on the various screens that appear.**

   The installation program guides you through the process of installing Flash. The most significant choice you have is where you install Flash. You can browse to change the location or accept the default, which is the Applications folder on the startup disk drive.

After you install Flash, you can play with it for 30 days before it stops working. If you download the trial version, you can buy it at any time by clicking Buy Now on the first screen you see when you open Flash.

Setting Your Preferences

Flash offers numerous ways to customize how you work. Why not make Flash suit you? The main location for setting preferences is the Preferences dialog box, shown in Figure A-1, with the General category displayed by default. To open the Preferences dialog box, choose Edit➪Preferences (Windows) or Adobe Flash CS3➪Preferences (Mac). The following sections describe how to use this dialog box.

Figure A-1:
Use the Preferences dialog box to bend Flash to your will.

General category

Click the General category to set the following options:

- ✔ **On Launch:** When Flash opens, it can show a welcome screen that gives you options of opening an existing document or starting a new one. This is the default, but if you find the welcome screen useless, you can choose to always start a new document, open the documents that you were using the last time you used Flash, or start with no document and decide where to go from there.

- ✔ **Undo:** Here you choose whether you want to use object-level or document-level undo (as we explain in Chapter 4). Then choose the number of actions you want to keep. The text box is set to 100 by default; you can enter any value from 2 to 300. The higher the value, the more RAM Flash uses to remember all those steps. You might be surprised by how many commands you give in a short period of time, so 100 or more is probably a good setting. However, if you want to save commands from steps in the History panel, set the number of actions higher.

- ✔ **Workspace — Open Documents in Tabs:** (For Mac only.) This option is marked by default so that new documents open in a single window with tabs. Deselect this check box if you want each new document to open in a separate window.

- ✔ **Workspace — Open Test Movie in Tabs:** By default, Flash opens a new window to play your movie when you test it. Select this check box to instead open a new document tab (like the ones Flash creates for each open document).

- ✔ **Workspace — Auto-Collapse Icon Panels:** In the Flash workspace, you can collapse a panel to an icon by clicking the grey header bar at the top of a palette dock. Then clicking the icon makes the palette appear. The panel disappears automatically when you click anywhere outside the panel if the Auto-Collapse Icon Panels preference is enabled (which it is by default).

- ✔ **Selection — Shift Select:** This option is enabled by default. It means that you have to press Shift to select more than one object (by clicking). If you don't press Shift, the first object is deselected. Clearing this option means that you can click as many objects as you want to select them. This method is an efficient way to work, but most people aren't familiar with it. If you select something by accident, press Shift and click the object to deselect it.

- ✔ **Selection — Show Tooltips:** By default, this option shows short explanations of Flash interface features (such as toolbars and buttons) when you hover your cursor over them. You can make these tooltips go away by deselcting this check box.

- ✔ **Selection — Contact-Sensitive Selection and Lasso Tools:** By default, you need to completely surround objects with the selection or lasso tools to select them. Select this check box to select any object that is just partly within the selection or lasso selection border.

✓ **Timeline — Span Based Selection:** Lets you click between two keyframes to select the entire section between them, à la Flash 5.

✓ **Timeline — Named Anchor on Scene:** Automatically creates a named anchor at the beginning of each scene. (Named anchors enable viewers to use the Web browser's Back button effectively while navigating within a Flash movie. This would be a great feature if it worked, but many browsers don't support it.)

✓ **Highlight Color:** Lets you specify the color of the box around selected symbols and groups. You can select Use Layer Color to use the layer's outline color. Or click the color swatch to display all the available colors and choose a different color, for each kind of element listed (drawing objects, drawing primitives, groups, symbols, and other elements).

✓ **Project — Close Files with Project:** If this option is selected, Flash closes all the files in a project when you close a project. (Flash *project* files are used to group files and to manage complex applications.)

✓ **Project — Save Files on Test or Publish Project:** If this option is selected, Flash saves all the files in a project each time you test or publish a project.

✓ **Version Cue — Enable Version Cue:** Select this option to use Adobe Version Cue in Flash CS3. Version Cue is a version control and file-sharing utility that lets you track and manage different versions of your files.

✓ **Printing — Disable PostScript:** (For Windows only.) Selecting this check box disables PostScript output when you print to a PostScript printer. Select this check box only if you have trouble printing to a PostScript printer.

ActionScript category

The ActionScript category offers settings relating to the ActionScript Editor so that you can customize how ActionScript looks and functions on the Action panel:

✓ **Editing:** By default, any ActionScript that you type is automatically indented. The tab size (amount of indentation) is four spaces. You can remove the automatic indentation or change the tab size. Code hints help you complete your code by providing pop-up text in the Actions panel. You can remove these hints by deselecting the Code Hints check box.

✓ **Delay:** You can drag the slider to set a delay before code hints are displayed.

✓ **Font:** You can set the font type and size in the ActionScript Editor. For Windows only: Select the Use Dynamic Font Mapping check box to have

Flash substitute a font if the selected font family doesn't have the required glyphs (character shapes). Dynamic font mapping is generally useful if you're working with multilingual text.

✓ **Open/Import:** This specifies the encoding used for fonts when opening or importing ActionScript (.as) files. The default, UTF-8, provides Unicode encoding that supports multiple languages.

✓ **Save/Export:** This specifies the encoding used for fonts when saving or exporting ActionScript (.as) files. The default, UTF-8, provides Unicode encoding that supports multiple languages.

✓ **Reload Modified Files:** You can have Flash prompt you to reload modified ActionScript files or choose Never or Always options. Reloading files keeps your ActionScript up to date.

✓ **Syntax Colors:** By default, ActionScript code is colored based on its syntax. For example, comments are displayed in grey. You can remove coloring or change the colors for each syntax type.

✓ **Language:** You can put ActionScript in frames and in multiple separate ActionScript text files, and you can also put ActionScript 2.0 in buttons and movie clips. If you click the ActionScript 3.0 (or 2.0) Settings button here, you can modify the places that Flash searches when your ActionScript 3.0 (or 2.0) in one place references certain kinds of ActionScript (called *classes*), which might be elsewhere. If you're just starting out with Flash, you almost certainly are not defining new class definition files in ActionScript, in which case you don't have to worry about this.

Click the Reset to Defaults button to return all the settings in this category to their defaults.

Auto Format category

This category offers specific options for formatting ActionScript. Programmers are picky about how their code looks, and this category lets you format your code the way you like. Select the various check boxes; the preview pane shows the result.

Clipboard category

The Clipboard category enables you to set preferences for displaying, exporting, and importing certain objects. Here are your choices:

✓ **Bitmaps — Color Depth:** (For Windows only.) Specifies the color depth for bitmaps copied to the Clipboard. You can choose to match the screen or set a color depth from 4-bit to 32-bit with Alpha. You can use this setting to reduce the size of bitmaps that you paste into Flash from the Windows Clipboard.

- **Bitmaps — Resolution:** (For Windows only.) Sets the resolution of bitmaps copied to the Clipboard. Select Screen to match your screen resolution or select 72, 150, or 300. You can use this setting to reduce the size of bitmaps you paste into Flash from the Windows Clipboard.

- **Bitmaps — Size Limit:** (For Windows only.) Lets you specify a size limit in kilobytes for the amount of RAM (memory) used for a bitmap on the Windows Clipboard. If you have large images, you might need to increase this number, which is set to 250K by default.

- **Gradient Quality:** (For Windows only.) Lets you specify the quality of gradients that you copy to the Clipboard for use in other applications. Your options range from None to Best.

- **PICT Settings:** (For Mac only.) Lets you specify the method and resolution used to copy art to the Clipboard. From the Type menu, select Objects to copy art as vector graphics, or select one of the bitmap settings to copy art as a bitmap. In the Resolution input box, type the resolution you want in dots per inch. If you want to include PostScript data, select the Include PostScript check box. In the Gradients menu, select the Gradient quality you want when you paste the Clipboard into a document outside Flash. (When pasting within Flash, this setting is ignored, and you always get the full gradient quality.)

- **FreeHand Text:** By default, the Maintain Text as Blocks check box is selected so that text pasted from FreeHand can be edited in Flash.

Drawing category

Click the Drawing category to set the following items:

- **Pen Tool — Show Pen Preview:** Displays a preview of the line or curve segment before you click the next point. Recommended!

- **Pen Tool — Show Solid Points:** When marked, shows filled points at vertices.

- **Pen Tool — Show Precise Cursors:** Displays a small crosshair rather than the pen-shaped cursor, for more precise placement of points.

We cover the rest of the drawing settings in this category in Chapter 3.

Text category

The Text category allows you to specify your text preferences, as follows:

- **Font Mapping Default:** This is the default that Flash uses when you open a movie that contains a font that you don't have on your computer. Select an option from the drop-down list.

- **Vertical Text — Default Text Orientation:** Sets vertical text as the default. Use this option for some Asian fonts.

- **Right to Left Text Flow:** Sets text lines to flow from right to left by default. This option is usually used for Arabic and Hebrew.

- **No Kerning:** Removes kerning from vertical text.

- **Input Method:** (Windows only.) If you're working in Japanese, Chinese, or Korean, select the appropriate language.

Warnings category

The Warnings category lists 16 situations in which Flash displays a warning message. All are enabled by default, so you're safe. If you find these warnings annoying or unnecessary, deselect the appropriate check boxes.

PSD File Importer category

In the PSD File Importer category, you can set preferences for the default settings for importing Photoshop documents:

- **Import Image Layers:** You can choose to import image layers as bitmaps with editable layer styles or as flattened bitmaps. You can also choose whether to create movie clips to contain each imported image layer.

- **Import Text Layers:** You can import text layers as editable text, vector outlines, or flattened bitmaps. And you can choose whether to create movie clips to contain each imported text layer.

- **Import Shape Layers:** You can choose to import shape layers with editable paths and layer styles, or as flattened bitmaps. And again you can choose whether to create movie clips to contain each imported shape layer.

- **Layer Groups:** You can choose whether to create movie clips to contain each layer group.

- **Merged bitmaps:** You can choose whether to create movie clips to contain each merged bitmap.

- **Import Image Layers:** You can choose to import layers with editable layer styles or as flattened bitmaps. You can also choose whether to create movie clips to contain each imported layer.

- **Movie Clip Registration:** Click one of the nine dots that form the small rectangle to specify the location of the registration point of any movie clips that you create when importing the Photoshop document.

✔ **Publish Settings — Compression:** You can specify whether to use lossy or lossless compression (for potentially smaller file size or better image quality, respectively) for the default Publish setting in the Photoshop document importer. This Publish setting controls how the layers in the Photoshop file are compressed when you publish your Flash file. (See Chapter 13 for more on publishing your Flash files.)

✔ **Publish Settings — Quality:** If you choose Lossy as the Compression preference, you can specify the default quality of that compression in this setting. If you choose Use Publish Setting, Flash uses the level of JPEG quality specified in the Flash tab of the dialog box that appears when you choose File⇨Publish Settings. If you instead choose Custom, you can specify a custom setting of JPEG quality, from 0 to 100.

AI File Importer category

Your choices for the defaults for the Adobe Illustrator (AI) file importer are similar to the choices you have for the defaults for the Photoshop file importer, described in the preceding section. In addition, you can choose whether to show the Import dialog box before importing the Illustrator file, whether to exclude objects outside the crop area of the Illustrator file, and whether to import hidden layers that are in the Illustrator file.

Customizing Keyboard Shortcuts

You can create a shortcut for any menu item and change existing shortcuts. (See the Cheat Sheet at the front of this book for commonly used keyboard shortcuts.) Besides the standard set of shortcuts, Flash CS3 comes with some built-in shortcuts based on other programs, including FreeHand, Illustrator, and Photoshopso that you can use those same familiar shortcuts in Flash CS3.

To create shortcuts, choose Edit⇨Keyboard Shortcuts (Windows) or Adobe Flash CS3⇨Keyboard Shortcuts (Mac) to open the Keyboard Shortcuts dialog box. In Figure A-2 the dialog box is displayed with the Drawing Menu Commands option displayed in the Commands drop-down list.

You can't change the original set of shortcuts. Instead, create a duplicate set of shortcuts and modify the duplicate. Give the duplicate a new name, such as *MyWay,* and then use these shortcuts:

 To duplicate a shortcut set, click the Duplicate Set button at the top of the Keyboard Shortcuts dialog box.

 To rename a set of shortcuts, click the Rename Set button at the top of the Keyboard Shortcuts dialog box. (This option is not available until you duplicate a shortcut set.)

To export a set of shortcuts as a Web page, click the Export Set as HTML button at the top of the Keyboard Shortcuts dialog box. Then you can use the Web page as a reference, to view your list of keyboard shortcuts.

To delete a set of shortcuts, click the Delete Set button at the top of the Keyboard Shortcuts dialog box.

Figure A-2:
The
Keyboard
Shortcuts
dialog box
enables you
to use your
fingers the
way *you*
want.

When you have a new set of shortcuts, select from the Commands drop-down list the types of commands that you want to change. You can change all six (Windows) or eight (Mac) types of commands, but only one at a time:

- ✔ **Actions Panel Commands:** Changes shortcuts for working in the Actions panel.

- ✔ **Debug Movie Commands:** Changes shortcuts for commands from the menus that appear when you are in a debugging session.

- ✔ **Drawing Menu Commands:** Changes shortcuts for commands from the default menus (the menus that appear when you are drawing, working in the Timeline, and so on.)

- ✔ **Script Edit Commands:** Changes shortcuts for commands from the menu that appears when you are using the Script window. This is the editor window that appears when you choose File⇨New (or File⇨Open) and then choose a script file to edit, such as an ActionScript (.as) file or a Flash JavaScript (.jsfl) file.

- ✔ **Test Movie Menu Commands:** Changes shortcuts for commands from the menu that appears when you choose Control⇨Test Movie.

✔ **Timeline Commands:** Changes shortcuts for commands that move and select frames on the Timeline.

✔ **Tools Panel:** Changes shortcuts for the tools in the Tools panel.

✔ **Workspace Accessibility Commands:** Changes shortcuts for commands that change the focus to the Stage or the Timeline, select panels, and select objects within a panel.

For each type of command set, click the plus sign (+) in Windows or the right-pointing arrow on the Mac on the list to display all the commands and their current shortcuts. Here's how to create a new shortcut:

1. **Select the command that you want to customize.**

2. **Click the Add Shortcut button.**

   Flash adds a new shortcut, named `empty`.

3. **Press the keyboard combination that you want to use.**

   You must include Ctrl (Windows)/⌘ (Mac), Alt (Windows)/Option (Mac), or Shift before the second key. Flash tells you whether that combination is already assigned to another shortcut.

   • If you want to use that shortcut, click Change. Flash alerts you if the shortcut is already taken and lets you reassign the shortcut.

   • If you don't want to use that shortcut, select the `empty` shortcut from the Shortcuts list and click the Remove Shortcut button.

4. **Repeat Steps 2 and 3 to change as many shortcuts as you want.**

5. **Click OK when you have finished changing shortcuts.**

Until you get accustomed to your new shortcuts, create a list by clicking the Extract Set as HTML button, at the top of the Keyboard Shortcuts dialog box, to save the list of new shortcuts in a Web page. Then print the Web page listing your shortcuts, and tape it to the side of your monitor or place it nearby for easy reference.

Appendix B

The Property Inspector and the Panels

· ·

Several panels have been changed in Flash CS3. The panels often have unlabeled buttons and flyout menus that hold hidden treasures — or at least hidden features — if you know where to look. In this appendix, we help you discover these features.

The Tools Panel

The Tools panel contains all the drawing tools as well as many editing tools. You'll use this panel a lot! Most drawing tools have their own *modifiers* that control how the drawing tool works. In Figure B-1, you see only one set of modifiers — the ones for the Brush tool. Other tools offer different modifiers, so the options section of the Tools panel will look different depending on the tool you're using.

Several buttons have *flyouts*, which are like submenus for toolbars. You click a tiny arrow at the lower-right corner of the button to display additional tools. For example, the Rectangle flyout reveals the Oval tool, the Rectangle Primitive tool, the Oval Primitive tool, and the PolyStar tool. Check out Chapter 3 for the full scoop on the Tools panel and all its helpful tools.

Figure B-1:
The Tools
panel.

The Property Inspector Gadget

The Property inspector is *context sensitive,* which means that it displays information that's useful to what you're doing at the time. In this section, you see some variations on this theme.

Property inspector with no selection

When no object is selected and the cursor is on the Stage, you see the document properties, as shown in Figure B-2.

Figure B-2:
Property
inspector
when an
object is not
selected.

Property inspector with a shape selected

When you select a shape, the Property inspector displays properties of the shape so that you can edit them, as you see in Figure B-3.

Stroke color   Stroke height   Custom stroke style   Cap type

Figure B-3: Property inspector when a shape is selected.

Fill color   Stroke style   Join type

Property inspector with keyframe selected

When you click a keyframe on the Timeline, the Property inspector displays properties of the frame, as you see in Figure B-4.

Frame label   Tween type   Sound name

Figure B-4: Property inspector when a keyframe is selected.

Sync mode   Number of times to loop

Property inspector with a symbol instance selected

When you select an instance of a symbol, in this case a movie clip, the Property inspector displays properties of the instance so that you can edit them. See Figure B-5.

Figure B-5:
Property
inspector
when a
symbol
instance is
selected.

Instance behavior   Color style

Instance name   Swap symbol   Blend

The Align Panel

The Align Panel (see Figure B-6) gets your objects in line, where they ought to be. For more information, flip to Chapter 4.

Align objects
horizontally

Align/distribute
relative to
entire Stage

Align objects
vertically

Figure B-6:
The Align
panel.

Match
by width,
by height,
or both

Space objects
evenly
horizontally
or vertically

Distribute objects evenly

The Color Panel

The Color panel is similar to an artist's palette. See Figure B-7. You can create your own colors for both strokes (lines) and fills.

Swap Colors

Stroke Color

Fill Color

Black and White

No Color

Fill Style

Color Space

Brightness

Transparency
(Alpha) value

Hexidecimal
value

Figure B-7:
The Color
panel.

Color Specifications

The Swatches Panel

You can use the Swatches panel to manage your colors. See Figure B-8. New colors and fills that you create appear in this panel for easy access. (See Chapter 3 for more information.)

Figure B-8:
The
Swatches
panel.

The Info Panel

The Info panel lets you control the precise size and location of objects. (Check out Chapter 4 for more information on using this panel.) The X and Y measurements are relative to the upper-left corner of the Stage. See Figure B-9. The lower-right corner shows the current position of the mouse cursor. Depending on the object, you may also see color and Alpha information.

Width   X Location

Figure B-9:
The Info
panel.

Height   Y Location

The Scene Panel

The Scene panel is quite simple, as shown in Figure B-10. You can use it to move from one scene to another, change the order of scenes, and rename, add, or delete scenes. Choose Window➪Other Panels➪Scene.

Figure B-10:
The Scene
panel.

Duplicate Scene   Delete Scene

Add Scene

The Transform Panel

Use the Transform panel to scale, rotate, and skew objects with precision. You scale by percentage, and you rotate and skew by degrees (increasing degrees going clockwise). See Figure B-11. To use the Copy and Apply Transform button, the first button in the lower-right corner, select an object and specify the transform settings you want. Then click Copy and Apply Transform. Flash creates a new object with the new settings on top of the old object. You can leave the new object there to create a composite object or immediately move it to a new location. Use the Reset button, the second button in the lower-right corner, to return a transformed object to its original properties. Chapter 4 gives you more information about this panel.

Height

Width   Rotation

Figure B-11:
The
Transform
panel.

Skew Vertically

Reset

Skew Horizontally   Copy and Apply Transform

The Actions Panel

The Actions panel is where all the action is — the ActionScript, that is. On this panel, you write or insert code that makes your movies interactive. See Figure B-12. Chapter 10 offers more information on this panel.

Actions Toolbox   Insert Target Path

Add New Item to Script   Autoformat   Script Assist

Figure B-12:
The Actions
panel.

Find   Show Code Hint

Check Syntax   Script Pane

The Movie Explorer Panel

Explore the depths of your movie with the Movie Explorer panel, shown in Figure B-13. Refer to Chapter 12 for details.

Show Text

Show ActionScript

Show Frames and Layers

Customize which items to show

Figure B-13: The Movie Explorer panel.

Show Video, Sounds, and Bitmaps

Show Buttons, Movie Clips, and Graphics

The Output Panel

Use the Output panel as a way to test the ActionScript code in your movie. Choose Control⇨Test Movie and then choose Window⇨Output. The Output panel opens automatically if you test a movie with errors, and you can also choose List Objects or List Variables from the Debug menu in the Player window to view a list of objects and variables.

On Windows, the Output panel is by default a tab of the Property inspector. See Figure B-14. On Mac, you have a stand-alone Output panel by default — although, like any other panel, you can add it to the Property inspector or any other panel group.

Figure B-14: The Output panel.

```
Level #0: Frame=4
  Shape:
  Button: Target="_level0.instance959"
    Shape:
```

The Accessibility Panel

Accessibility features make your movies more accessible to people with certain disabilities or limitations, such as limited or no sight. You can display or hide objects, depending on the needs of your viewers. These features make some of the nongraphical objects in your movie available to screen readers, which read parts of the screen out loud. Choose Window⇨Other Panels⇨ Accessibility to display the Accessibility panel, shown in Figure B-15.

Figure B-15:
The Accessibility panel.

The Components Panel

Components are prebuilt movie clips that come with predefined parameters that you can set to alter their appearance and behavior. They allow you to build complex Flash applications even if you don't have an advanced understanding of ActionScript. Some components are nonvisual and allow you to do such things as manipulate information from data sources (for a Flash movie with a news ticker, for instance). Other components are interface elements, such as check boxes, radio buttons, and drop-down lists (combo boxes), which you can add to your movies to create interactivity. For more information, see Chapter 12. The Components panel is shown in Figure B-16.

Figure B-16:
The Components panel.

The Component Inspector Panel

Use the Component Inspector panel to assign labels and parameters to components, such as check boxes, lists, and other interface elements. See Figure B-17.

Figure B-17:
The
Component
Inspector
panel.

The History Panel

The History panel stores all your commands. See Figure B-18. You can review them, repeat them, or save them to use again later. Choose Window⇨ Other Panels⇨History. See Chapter 4 for details.

Figure B-18:
The History
panel.

The Strings Panel

Use the Strings panel, shown in Figure B-19, to create strings of text in various languages. You can use these for Web sites in multiple languages. Choose Window⇨Other Panels⇨Strings. Then click the Settings button to set up the languages.

Figure B-19:
The Strings
panel.

Appendix C

What's on the Companion Web Site

• •

*H*ere's some of the cool stuff that you can find on the *Adobe Flash CS3 For Dummies* companion Web site, at www.dummies.com/go/flashcs3:

✔ A library of geometric, fanciful, and artistic vector graphics ready to be instantly opened in any Flash movie. We've added new shapes for this edition.

✔ Flash movies that you can dissect.

Your Own Personal Library of Vector Graphics

We've created more than 50 vector graphics that you can use in your Flash movies. Some are geometric shapes that are hard to create in Flash. We added fun shapes . . . some practical and others whimsical, such as our thought bubble and explosion. Finally, we included some art drawings of everyday objects. We hope you like them! (Please keep in mind that these files are provided for your personal use and are not to be sold or redistributed.)

To download the library of graphics, point your Web browser to www.dummies.com/go/flashcs3 and click the download link to download the zip file for this book. When you unzip the file, you'll see a file named Flash CS3 For Dummies Library.fla. All that you see when you open this file in Flash is a blank screen. To see the graphics, choose Window➪Library. To use these shapes in another Flash file, choose File➪Import to Library and choose the file named Flash CS3 For Dummies Library.fla from the location where you saved it on your computer.

An even better idea is to copy the `.fla` file from wherever it is on your computer to the Libraries subfolder of your Flash CS3 folder. (In Windows, you find this at `Program Files\Adobe\Adobe Flash CS3\en\Configuration\Libraries` on your hard drive. On the Mac, you find it in `Applications/Adobe Flash CS3/Configuration/Libraries` on your hard drive.) Then you can access this file at any time by choosing Window ➪ Common Libraries.

Flash Movies Galore

Throughout this book, we refer you to the companion Web site to look at Flash movies as examples of the features we are explaining. These movies are organized by chapter. They help you understand some of the more complex capabilities of Flash that are hard to explain or show in a figure. Some of these movies are real-world Flash movies that come from active Web sites. Others are examples we created for you to isolate a Flash feature. Either way, we hope that you can use them to further your understanding of Flash.

To examine and use these movie files, you need to first download them to your hard drive. Point your Web browser to `www.dummies.com/go/flashcs3` and download the zipped file. When you unzip it, you can open the file you want. Here are a few troubleshooting tips to keep in mind when you use the Flash movie files provided on the Web site:

- **The Flash movie doesn't play.** Sometimes when you open a Flash movie, nothing happens when you try to play the animation. Choose Control➪ Test Movie to see the animation.

- **The fonts look different.** If some of the fonts required by the Flash files aren't available on your system, you might see less-than-satisfactory substitutions when you play the Flash Player files. You might also see a message asking you to substitute fonts. You can click Default or choose any fonts you want.

Bonus Chapter

Also on the Web site's download, you'll find a bonus chapter titled "What Those Obscure Terms Really Mean." It's a glossary of need-to-know terms for Flash designers. Be sure to check it out.

Index

• *G* •

• *H* •

BUSINESS, CAREERS & PERSONAL FINANCE

0-7645-9847-3

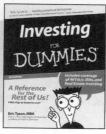

0-7645-2431-3

Also available:
- Business Plans Kit For Dummies
  0-7645-9794-9
- Economics For Dummies
  0-7645-5726-2
- Grant Writing For Dummies
  0-7645-8416-2
- Home Buying For Dummies
  0-7645-5331-3
- Managing For Dummies
  0-7645-1771-6
- Marketing For Dummies
  0-7645-5600-2

- Personal Finance For Dummies
  0-7645-2590-5*
- Resumes For Dummies
  0-7645-5471-9
- Selling For Dummies
  0-7645-5363-1
- Six Sigma For Dummies
  0-7645-6798-5
- Small Business Kit For Dummies
  0-7645-5984-2
- Starting an eBay Business For Dummies
  0-7645-6924-4
- Your Dream Career For Dummies
  0-7645-9795-7

HOME & BUSINESS COMPUTER BASICS

0-470-05432-8

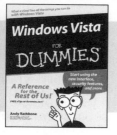

0-471-75421-8

Also available:
- Cleaning Windows Vista For Dummies
  0-471-78293-9
- Excel 2007 For Dummies
  0-470-03737-7
- Mac OS X Tiger For Dummies
  0-7645-7675-5
- MacBook For Dummies
  0-470-04859-X
- Macs For Dummies
  0-470-04849-2
- Office 2007 For Dummies
  0-470-00923-3

- Outlook 2007 For Dummies
  0-470-03830-6
- PCs For Dummies
  0-7645-8958-X
- Salesforce.com For Dummies
  0-470-04893-X
- Upgrading & Fixing Laptops For Dummies
  0-7645-8959-8
- Word 2007 For Dummies
  0-470-03658-3
- Quicken 2007 For Dummies
  0-470-04600-7

FOOD, HOME, GARDEN, HOBBIES, MUSIC & PETS

0-7645-8404-9

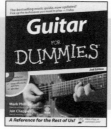

0-7645-9904-6

Also available:
- Candy Making For Dummies
  0-7645-9734-5
- Card Games For Dummies
  0-7645-9910-0
- Crocheting For Dummies
  0-7645-4151-X
- Dog Training For Dummies
  0-7645-8418-9
- Healthy Carb Cookbook For Dummies
  0-7645-8476-6
- Home Maintenance For Dummies
  0-7645-5215-5

- Horses For Dummies
  0-7645-9797-3
- Jewelry Making & Beading For Dummies
  0-7645-2571-9
- Orchids For Dummies
  0-7645-6759-4
- Puppies For Dummies
  0-7645-5255-4
- Rock Guitar For Dummies
  0-7645-5356-9
- Sewing For Dummies
  0-7645-6847-7
- Singing For Dummies
  0-7645-2475-5

INTERNET & DIGITAL MEDIA

0-470-04529-9

0-470-04894-8

Also available:
- Blogging For Dummies
  0-471-77084-1
- Digital Photography For Dummies
  0-7645-9802-3
- Digital Photography All-in-One Desk Reference For Dummies
  0-470-03743-1
- Digital SLR Cameras and Photography For Dummies
  0-7645-9803-1
- eBay Business All-in-One Desk Reference For Dummies
  0-7645-8438-3
- HDTV For Dummies
  0-470-09673-X

- Home Entertainment PCs For Dummies
  0-470-05523-5
- MySpace For Dummies
  0-470-09529-6
- Search Engine Optimization For Dummies
  0-471-97998-8
- Skype For Dummies
  0-470-04891-3
- The Internet For Dummies
  0-7645-8996-2
- Wiring Your Digital Home For Dummies
  0-471-91830-X

* Separate Canadian edition also available
† Separate U.K. edition also available

Available wherever books are sold. For more information or to order direct: U.S. customers visit www.dummies.com or call 1-877-762-2974.
U.K. customers visit www.wileyeurope.com or call 0800 243407. Canadian customers visit www.wiley.ca or call 1-800-567-4797.

SPORTS, FITNESS, PARENTING, RELIGION & SPIRITUALITY

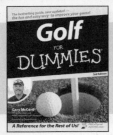

0-471-76871-5

0-7645-7841-3

Also available:
- Catholicism For Dummies
  0-7645-5391-7
- Exercise Balls For Dummies
  0-7645-5623-1
- Fitness For Dummies
  0-7645-7851-0
- Football For Dummies
  0-7645-3936-1
- Judaism For Dummies
  0-7645-5299-6
- Potty Training For Dummies
  0-7645-5417-4
- Buddhism For Dummies
  0-7645-5359-3

- Pregnancy For Dummies
  0-7645-4483-7 †
- Ten Minute Tone-Ups For Dummies
  0-7645-7207-5
- NASCAR For Dummies
  0-7645-7681-X
- Religion For Dummies
  0-7645-5264-3
- Soccer For Dummies
  0-7645-5229-5
- Women in the Bible For Dummies
  0-7645-8475-8

TRAVEL

0-7645-7749-2

0-7645-6945-7

Also available:
- Alaska For Dummies
  0-7645-7746-8
- Cruise Vacations For Dummies
  0-7645-6941-4
- England For Dummies
  0-7645-4276-1
- Europe For Dummies
  0-7645-7529-5
- Germany For Dummies
  0-7645-7823-5
- Hawaii For Dummies
  0-7645-7402-7

- Italy For Dummies
  0-7645-7386-1
- Las Vegas For Dummies
  0-7645-7382-9
- London For Dummies
  0-7645-4277-X
- Paris For Dummies
  0-7645-7630-5
- RV Vacations For Dummies
  0-7645-4442-X
- Walt Disney World & Orlando
  For Dummies
  0-7645-9660-8

GRAPHICS, DESIGN & WEB DEVELOPMENT

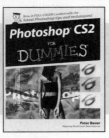

0-7645-8815-X

0-7645-9571-7

Also available:
- 3D Game Animation For Dummies
  0-7645-8789-7
- AutoCAD 2006 For Dummies
  0-7645-8925-3
- Building a Web Site For Dummies
  0-7645-7144-3
- Creating Web Pages For Dummies
  0-470-08030-2
- Creating Web Pages All-in-One Desk
  Reference For Dummies
  0-7645-4345-8
- Dreamweaver 8 For Dummies
  0-7645-9649-7

- InDesign CS2 For Dummies
  0-7645-9572-5
- Macromedia Flash 8 For Dummies
  0-7645-9691-8
- Photoshop CS2 and Digital
  Photography For Dummies
  0-7645-9580-6
- Photoshop Elements 4 For Dummies
  0-471-77483-9
- Syndicating Web Sites with RSS Feeds
  For Dummies
  0-7645-8848-6
- Yahoo! SiteBuilder For Dummies
  0-7645-9800-7

NETWORKING, SECURITY, PROGRAMMING & DATABASES

0-7645-7728-X

0-471-74940-0

Also available:
- Access 2007 For Dummies
  0-470-04612-0
- ASP.NET 2 For Dummies
  0-7645-7907-X
- C# 2005 For Dummies
  0-7645-9704-3
- Hacking For Dummies
  0-470-05235-X
- Hacking Wireless Networks
  For Dummies
  0-7645-9730-2
- Java For Dummies
  0-470-08716-1

- Microsoft SQL Server 2005 For Dummies
  0-7645-7755-7
- Networking All-in-One Desk Reference
  For Dummies
  0-7645-9939-9
- Preventing Identity Theft For Dummies
  0-7645-7336-5
- Telecom For Dummies
  0-471-77085-X
- Visual Studio 2005 All-in-One Desk
  Reference For Dummies
  0-7645-9775-2
- XML For Dummies
  0-7645-8845-1

HEALTH & SELF-HELP

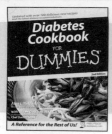

0-7645-8450-2

0-7645-4149-8

Also available:
- Bipolar Disorder For Dummies
  0-7645-8451-0
- Chemotherapy and Radiation
  For Dummies
  0-7645-7832-4
- Controlling Cholesterol For Dummies
  0-7645-5440-9
- Diabetes For Dummies
  0-7645-6820-5* †
- Divorce For Dummies
  0-7645-8417-0 †

- Fibromyalgia For Dummies
  0-7645-5441-7
- Low-Calorie Dieting For Dummies
  0-7645-9905-4
- Meditation For Dummies
  0-471-77774-9
- Osteoporosis For Dummies
  0-7645-7621-6
- Overcoming Anxiety For Dummies
  0-7645-5447-6
- Reiki For Dummies
  0-7645-9907-0
- Stress Management For Dummies
  0-7645-5144-2

EDUCATION, HISTORY, REFERENCE & TEST PREPARATION

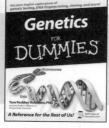

0-7645-8381-6

0-7645-9554-7

Also available:
- The ACT For Dummies
  0-7645-9652-7
- Algebra For Dummies
  0-7645-5325-9
- Algebra Workbook For Dummies
  0-7645-8467-7
- Astronomy For Dummies
  0-7645-8465-0
- Calculus For Dummies
  0-7645-2498-4
- Chemistry For Dummies
  0-7645-5430-1
- Forensics For Dummies
  0-7645-5580-4

- Freemasons For Dummies
  0-7645-9796-5
- French For Dummies
  0-7645-5193-0
- Geometry For Dummies
  0-7645-5324-0
- Organic Chemistry I For Dummies
  0-7645-6902-3
- The SAT I For Dummies
  0-7645-7193-1
- Spanish For Dummies
  0-7645-5194-9
- Statistics For Dummies
  0-7645-5423-9

Get smart @ dummies.com®

- **Find a full list of Dummies titles**
- **Look into loads of FREE on-site articles**
- **Sign up for FREE eTips e-mailed to you weekly**
- **See what other products carry the Dummies name**
- **Shop directly from the Dummies bookstore**
- **Enter to win new prizes every month!**

* Separate Canadian edition also available
† Separate U.K. edition also available

Available wherever books are sold. For more information or to order direct: U.S. customers visit www.dummies.com or call 1-877-762-2974.
U.K. customers visit www.wileyeurope.com or call 0800 243407. Canadian customers visit www.wiley.ca or call 1-800-567-4797.